MOON

- BEST OF -

YELLOWSTONE & GRAND TETON

BECKY LOMAX

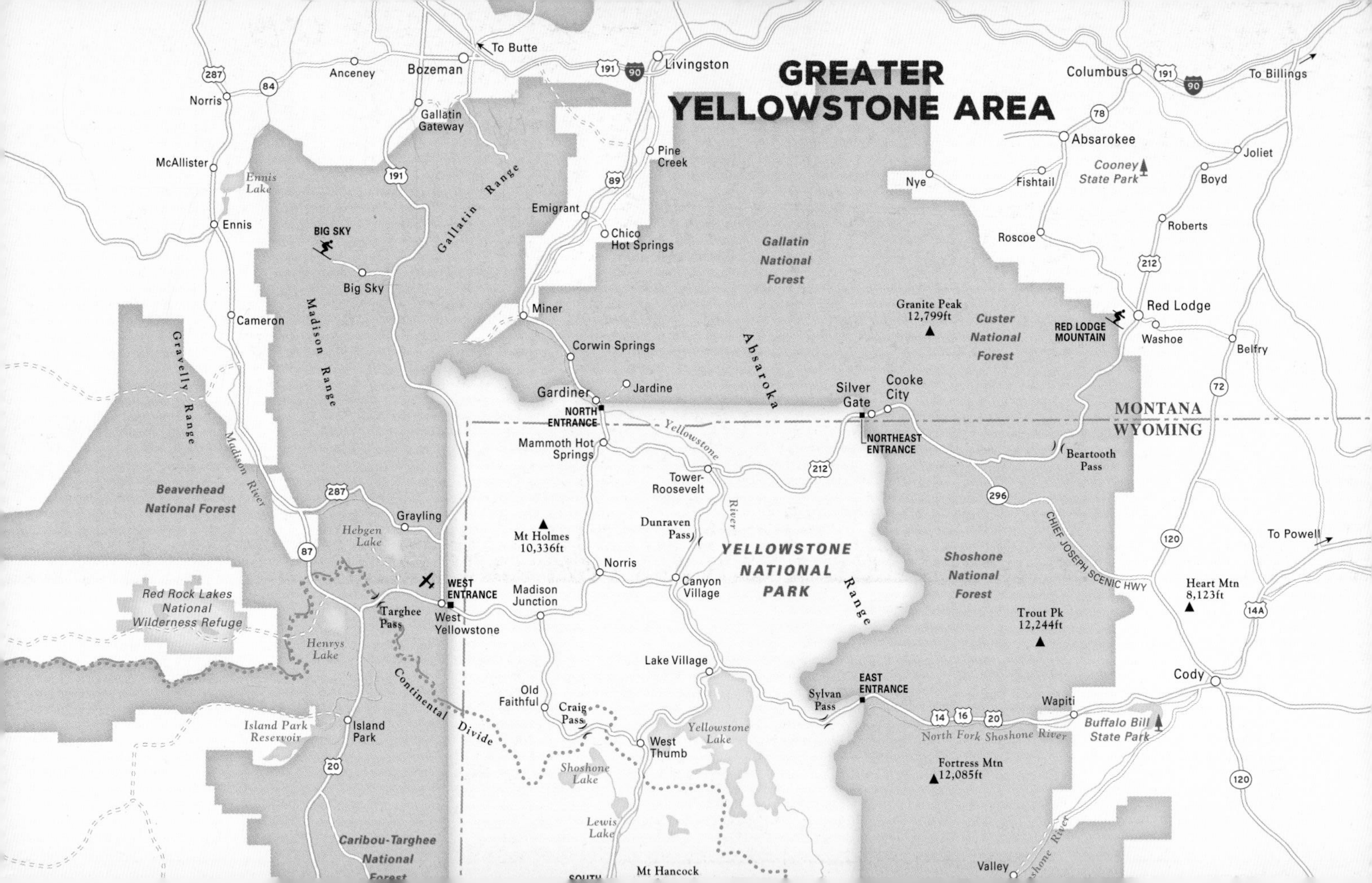
GREATER YELLOWSTONE AREA
To Butte
Bozeman
Anceney
Norris
McAllister
Ennis Lake
Ennis
Cameron
Gallatin Gateway
Gallatin Range
BIG SKY
Big Sky
Madison Range
Gravelly Range
Madison River
Beaverhead National Forest
Livingston
Pine Creek
Emigrant
Chico Hot Springs
Miner
Corwin Springs
Gardiner
Jardine
NORTH ENTRANCE
Mammoth Hot Springs
Gallatin National Forest
Absaroka Range
Granite Peak 12,799ft
Custer National Forest
Silver Gate
Cooke City
NORTHEAST ENTRANCE
Yellowstone River
Tower-Roosevelt
Dunraven Pass
YELLOWSTONE NATIONAL PARK
Canyon Village
Norris
Mt Holmes 10,336ft
Madison Junction
Grayling
Hebgen Lake
WEST ENTRANCE
West Yellowstone
Targhee Pass
Henrys Lake
Red Rock Lakes National Wilderness Refuge
Island Park Reservoir
Island Park
Continental Divide
Old Faithful
Craig Pass
West Thumb
Shoshone Lake
Lewis Lake
Yellowstone Lake
Lake Village
Mt Hancock
Caribou-Targhee National Forest
Sylvan Pass
EAST ENTRANCE
North Fork Shoshone River
Fortress Mtn 12,085ft
Shoshone National Forest
Trout Pk 12,244ft
Wapiti
Buffalo Bill State Park
Cody
Valley
Shoshone River
Heart Mtn 8,123ft
To Powell
CHIEF JOSEPH SCENIC HWY
Beartooth Pass
MONTANA
WYOMING
Columbus
To Billings
Absarokee
Cooney State Park
Joliet
Boyd
Nye
Fishtail
Roberts
Roscoe
Red Lodge
RED LODGE MOUNTAIN
Washoe
Belfry
287
84
191
90
89
87
20
212
296
14
16
72
120
14A
78

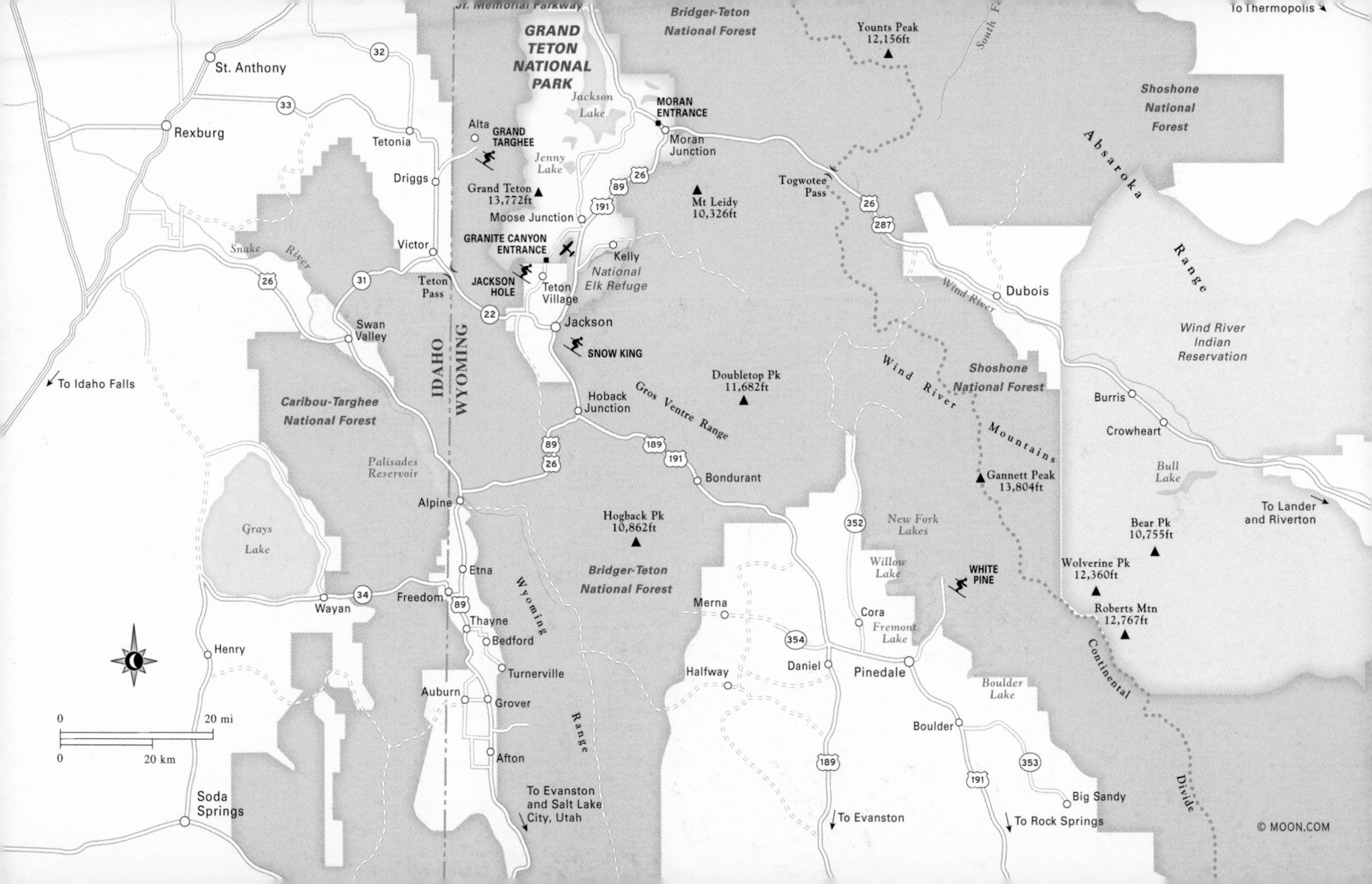

GRAND TETON NATIONAL PARK
Bridger-Teton National Forest
Shoshone National Forest
Absaroka Range
Wind River Indian Reservation
Younts Peak 12,156ft
To Thermopolis
Jackson Lake
MORAN ENTRANCE
Moran Junction
St. Anthony
Rexburg
Tetonia
Alta
GRAND TARGHEE
Jenny Lake
Driggs
Grand Teton 13,772ft
Mt Leidy 10,326ft
Togwotee Pass
Moose Junction
GRANITE CANYON ENTRANCE
Kelly
National Elk Refuge
Victor
Snake River
Teton Pass
JACKSON HOLE
Teton Village
Dubois
Wind River
Jackson
SNOW KING
Swan Valley
To Idaho Falls
IDAHO
WYOMING
Caribou-Targhee National Forest
Hoback Junction
Gros Ventre Range
Doubletop Pk 11,682ft
Wind River Mountains
Burris
Crowheart
Palisades Reservoir
Bondurant
Gannett Peak 13,804ft
Bull Lake
Alpine
Hogback Pk 10,862ft
New Fork Lakes
To Lander and Riverton
Bear Pk 10,755ft
Grays Lake
Etna
Wyoming Range
Bridger-Teton National Forest
Willow Lake
WHITE PINE
Wolverine Pk 12,360ft
Wayan
Freedom
Merna
Cora
Roberts Mtn 12,767ft
Thayne
Fremont Lake
Bedford
Henry
Halfway
Daniel
Pinedale
Continental Divide
Turnerville
Boulder Lake
Auburn
Grover
0
20 mi
0
20 km
Boulder
Afton
Soda Springs
To Evanston and Salt Lake City, Utah
To Evanston
To Rock Springs
Big Sandy
© MOON.COM

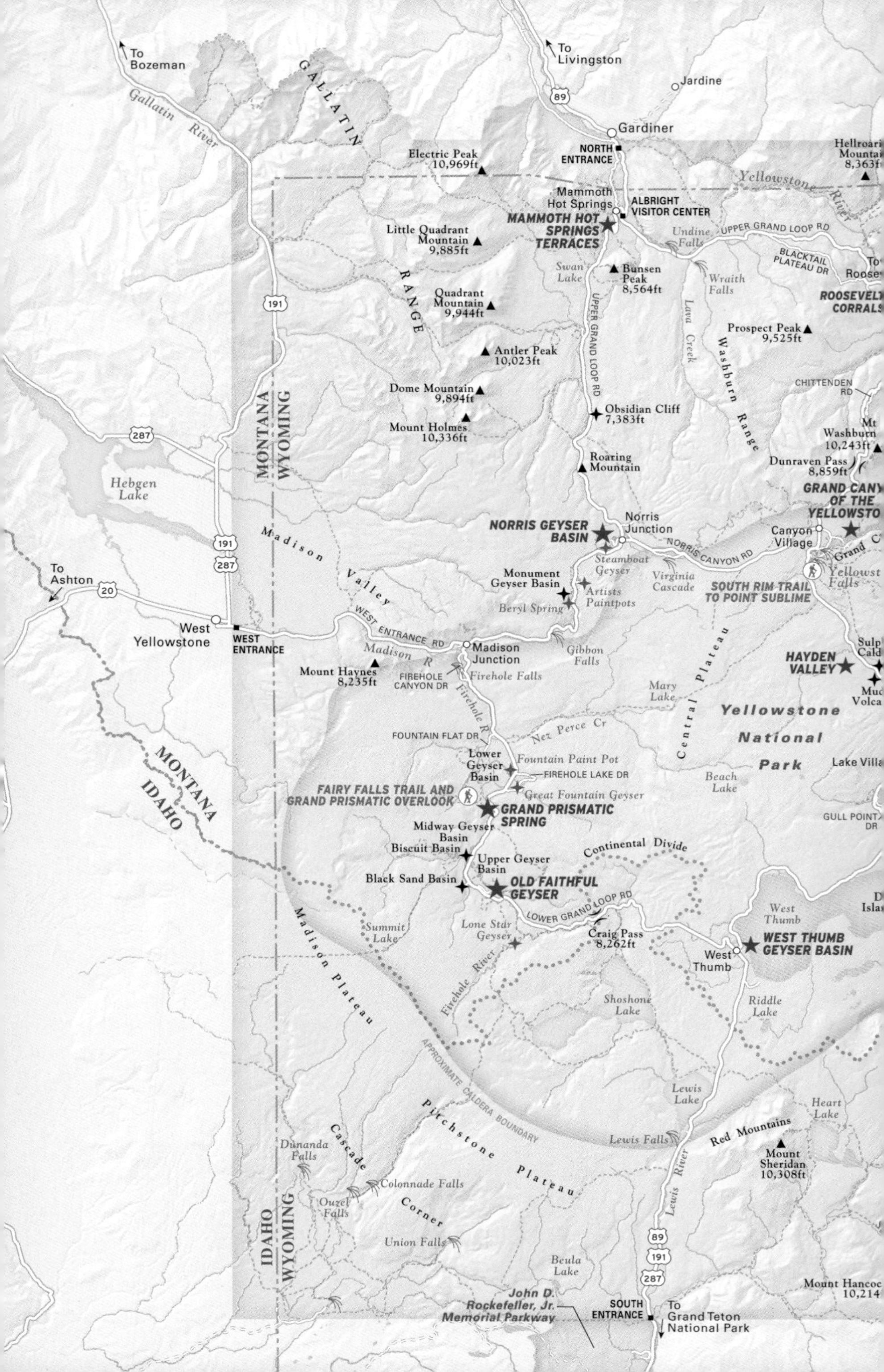

To Bozeman
To Livingston
Jardine
Gardiner
GALLATIN RANGE
Gallatin River
NORTH ENTRANCE
Electric Peak 10,969ft
Hellroaring Mountain 8,363ft
Yellowstone River
Mammoth Hot Springs
ALBRIGHT VISITOR CENTER
MAMMOTH HOT SPRINGS TERRACES
Undine Falls
UPPER GRAND LOOP RD
Little Quadrant Mountain 9,885ft
BLACKTAIL PLATEAU DR
Swan Lake
Bunsen Peak 8,564ft
Wraith Falls
ROOSEVELT CORRALS
Quadrant Mountain 9,944ft
Prospect Peak 9,525ft
Lava Creek
Washburn Range
Antler Peak 10,023ft
UPPER GRAND LOOP RD
CHITTENDEN RD
Dome Mountain 9,894ft
Obsidian Cliff 7,383ft
Mount Holmes 10,336ft
Mt Washburn 10,243ft
MONTANA
WYOMING
Roaring Mountain
Dunraven Pass 8,859ft
Hebgen Lake
GRAND CANYON OF THE YELLOWSTONE
NORRIS GEYSER BASIN
Norris Junction
Canyon Village
NORRIS CANYON RD
Madison Valley
Steamboat Geyser
Grand Canyon
To Ashton
Monument Geyser Basin
Artists Paintpots
Virginia Cascade
SOUTH RIM TRAIL TO POINT SUBLIME
Yellowstone Falls
Beryl Spring
West Yellowstone
WEST ENTRANCE
WEST ENTRANCE RD
Madison Junction
Madison R
Gibbon Falls
Mount Haynes 8,235ft
FIREHOLE CANYON DR
Firehole Falls
HAYDEN VALLEY
Central Plateau
Mary Lake
Yellowstone National Park
Firehole R
FOUNTAIN FLAT DR
Nez Perce Cr
MONTANA
IDAHO
Lower Geyser Basin
Fountain Paint Pot
FIREHOLE LAKE DR
Beach Lake
Lake Village
FAIRY FALLS TRAIL AND GRAND PRISMATIC OVERLOOK
Great Fountain Geyser
GRAND PRISMATIC SPRING
GULL POINT DR
Midway Geyser Basin
Continental Divide
Biscuit Basin
Upper Geyser Basin
Black Sand Basin
OLD FAITHFUL GEYSER
LOWER GRAND LOOP RD
West Thumb
Summit Lake
Lone Star Geyser
Craig Pass 8,262ft
WEST THUMB GEYSER BASIN
West Thumb
Madison Plateau
Firehole River
Shoshone Lake
Riddle Lake
APPROXIMATE CALDERA BOUNDARY
Lewis Lake
Heart Lake
Pitchstone Plateau
Cascade Corner
Dunanda Falls
Lewis Falls
Red Mountains
Mount Sheridan 10,308ft
Colonnade Falls
Lewis River
Ouzel Falls
IDAHO
WYOMING
Union Falls
Beula Lake
Mount Hancock 10,214ft
John D. Rockefeller, Jr. Memorial Parkway
SOUTH ENTRANCE
To Grand Teton National Park

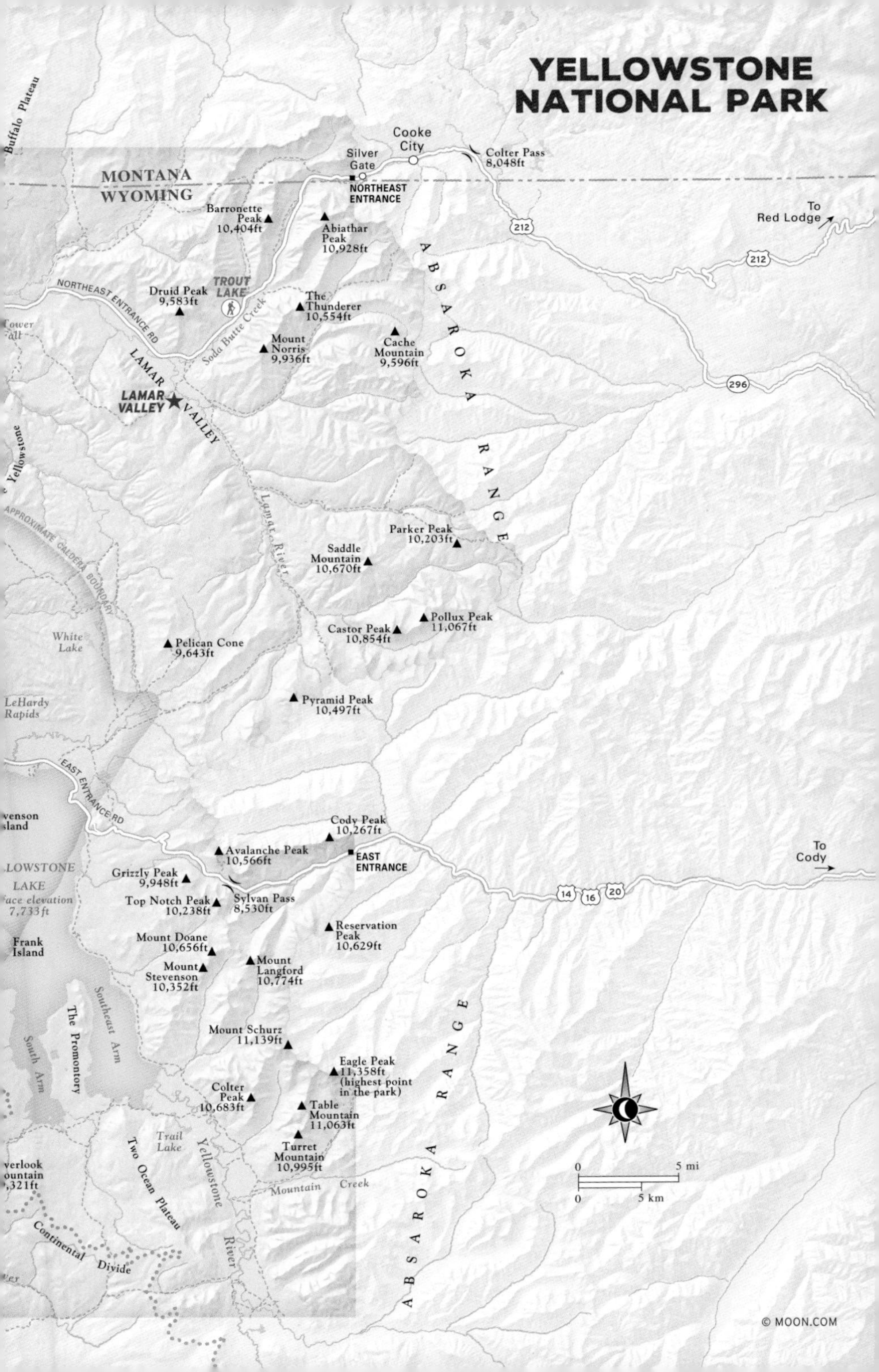

YELLOWSTONE NATIONAL PARK

Buffalo Plateau
MONTANA
WYOMING
Cooke City
Silver Gate
NORTHEAST ENTRANCE
Colter Pass 8,048ft
To Red Lodge
212
Barronette Peak 10,404ft
Abiathar Peak 10,928ft
ABSAROKA RANGE
NORTHEAST ENTRANCE RD
Druid Peak 9,583ft
TROUT LAKE
Soda Butte Creek
The Thunderer 10,554ft
Mount Norris 9,936ft
Cache Mountain 9,596ft
296
LAMAR VALLEY
Yellowstone
APPROXIMATE CALDERA BOUNDARY
Lamar River
Parker Peak 10,203ft
Saddle Mountain 10,670ft
Castor Peak 10,854ft
Pollux Peak 11,067ft
White Lake
Pelican Cone 9,643ft
Pyramid Peak 10,497ft
LeHardy Rapids
EAST ENTRANCE RD
Cody Peak 10,267ft
Avalanche Peak 10,566ft
EAST ENTRANCE
To Cody
14 16 20
Grizzly Peak 9,948ft
Top Notch Peak 10,238ft
Sylvan Pass 8,530ft
Reservation Peak 10,629ft
Mount Doane 10,656ft
Mount Stevenson 10,352ft
Mount Langford 10,774ft
Frank Island
Southeast Arm
The Promontory
South Arm
Mount Schurz 11,139ft
Eagle Peak 11,358ft (highest point in the park)
Colter Peak 10,683ft
Table Mountain 11,063ft
Turret Mountain 10,995ft
ABSAROKA RANGE
Trail Lake
Two Ocean Plateau
Yellowstone River
Mountain Creek
Continental Divide
0 5 mi
0 5 km

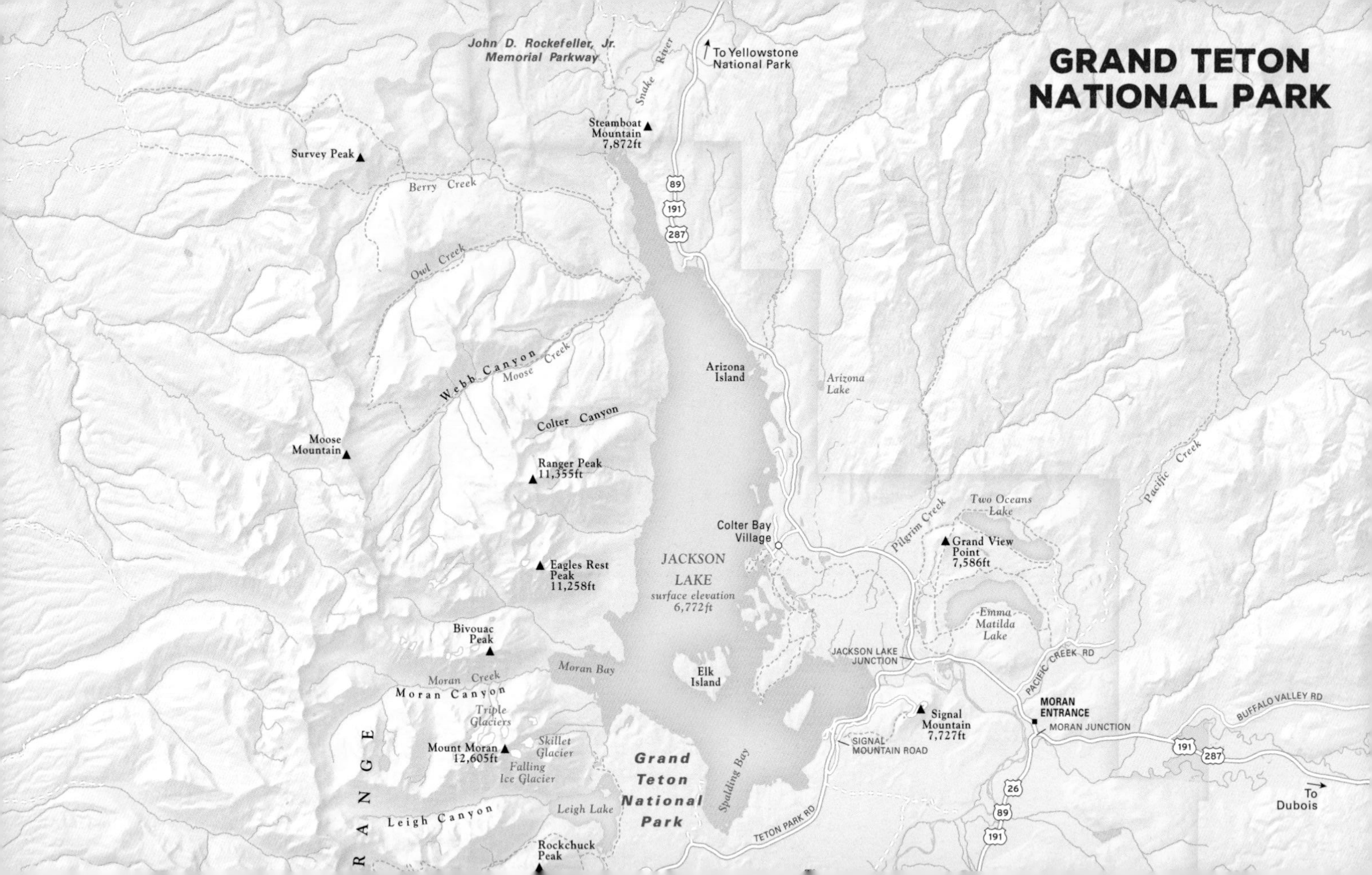
GRAND TETON NATIONAL PARK
John D. Rockefeller, Jr. Memorial Parkway
To Yellowstone National Park
Snake River
Steamboat Mountain 7,872ft
Survey Peak
Berry Creek
89
191
287
Owl Creek
Webb Canyon
Moose Creek
Arizona Island
Arizona Lake
Colter Canyon
Moose Mountain
Ranger Peak 11,355ft
Pacific Creek
Two Oceans Lake
Pilgrim Creek
Grand View Point 7,586ft
Colter Bay Village
JACKSON LAKE
surface elevation 6,772ft
Eagles Rest Peak 11,258ft
Emma Matilda Lake
Bivouac Peak
Moran Bay
Elk Island
JACKSON LAKE JUNCTION
PACIFIC CREEK RD
Moran Creek
Moran Canyon
MORAN ENTRANCE
BUFFALO VALLEY RD
Triple Glaciers
Signal Mountain 7,727ft
MORAN JUNCTION
SIGNAL MOUNTAIN ROAD
Mount Moran 12,605ft
Skillet Glacier
Falling Ice Glacier
Grand Teton National Park
Spalding Bay
Leigh Lake
Leigh Canyon
26
To Dubois
RANGE
TETON PARK RD
Rockchuck Peak

LAKE
Shuttle
Cascade Creek
Cascade Canyon
HIDDEN FALLS AND INSPIRATION POINT
Mount Owen 12,928ft
Grand Teton 13,770ft
Teewinot Mountain 12,325ft
Teton Glacier
TETON PARK ROAD
Teton Creek
TETON
Middle Teton 12,804ft
South Teton 12,514ft
Nez Perce
Bradley Lake
Taggart Lake
Mount Wister
Buck Mountain 11,938ft
Static Peak
Darby Creek
Teton Crest Trail
Prospectors Mountain
Phelps Lake
Mount Hunt
Fox Creek
RIVER RD
Snake River
Antelope Flats
Shadow Mountain
Ditch Creek
MORMON ROW
ANTELOPE FLATS RD
MOOSE ENTRANCE
PARK HEADQUARTERS
MOOSE JUNCTION
MORMON ROW
GROS VENTRE RD
Lower Slide Lake
Kelly
JACKSON HOLE AIRPORT
Rendezvous Mountain 10,450ft
GRANITE CANYON ENTRANCE
Aerial Tramway
Teton Village
JACKSON HOLE
Gros Ventre River
National Elk Refuge
GROS VENTRE JUNCTION
26
89
191
Rendezvous Peak
Moose Creek
MOOSE-WILSON RD
To Driggs
22
Phillips Ridge
FISH CREEK ROAD
Teton Pass 8,431ft
Wilson
22
Jackson
© MOON.COM
0
5 mi
0
5 km

CONTENTS

Although every effort was made to make sure the information in this book was accurate when going to press, research was impacted by the COVID-19 pandemic and things may have changed since the time of writing. Be sure to confirm specific details, like opening hours, closures, and travel guidelines and restrictions, when making your travel plans. For more detailed information, see page 274.

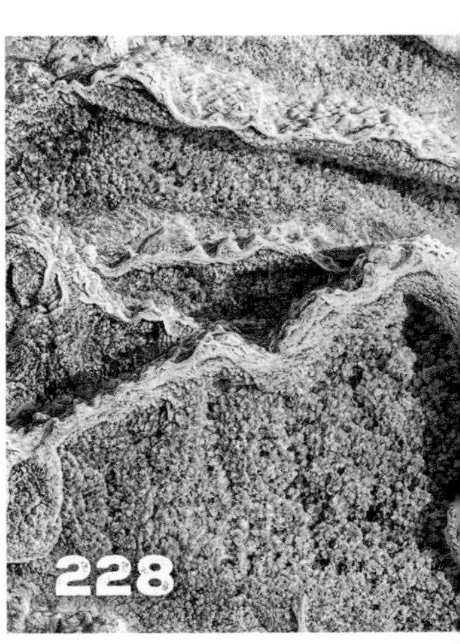

Wall Pool at Biscuit Basin

WELCOME TO YELLOWSTONE & GRAND TETON

The earth's tremendous forces have made Yellowstone and Grand Teton National Parks a land of fire and ice. The parks bear the marks of ancient seas, volcanic heat, tectonic upthrusting, and ice scouring. Even today, they shake and roar.

In Yellowstone National Park, rumblings of a supervolcano boil to the surface—spewing, spitting, oozing, and bubbling. Steam rolls from vividly colored pools, muddy cauldrons burp smelly gases, and blasts of hot water shoot high into the air. The cantankerous landscape gushes with spouters like iconic Old Faithful. In Grand Teton National Park, toothy spires claw the sky in one of the newest mountain ranges in the Rockies. Glaciers have chewed the terrain, leaving lakes, bowls, and canyons in their wake. Mountains tower thousands of feet high, culminating in the Grand Teton.

Throughout the Greater Yellowstone area, sagebrush prairies make wildlife easy to spot. Bison, elk, antelope, wolves, and even grizzly bears enchant visitors. Hiking trails, alpine lakes, bicycle paths, rivers, and ski trails in winter all create a four-season recreation paradise to explore.

Grand Prismatic Spring in Midway Geyser Basin

BEST DAY IN YELLOWSTONE

Morning

1 Head to Upper Geyser Basin early in the morning to avoid the crowded part of the day. Plan to arrive by 8am if possible (page 95).

2 **Check the time listed at the visitor center for Old Faithful Geyser to erupt, and aim to be at the arena for about 30 minutes in advance to claim a seat (page 95).**

3. Tour **Old Faithful Visitor Education Center** to learn about Yellowstone's volcanic activity, especially the difference between geysers, hot springs, mud pots, and fumaroles (page 123).

4. Saunter the boardwalk around **Geyser Hill** in the Upper Geyser Basin to see blue Heart Spring and the Lion Group of small geysers (page 96).

5 **Circle the Firehole River Loop, if time permits, to see Castle Geyser, Grand Geyser, Grotto Geyser, and Morning Glory Pool (page 98).**

6 **Stop in Old Faithful Inn to explore the National Historic Landmark (page 120).**

7 **Drive north to Midway Geyser Basin to walk the boardwalk to admire the radiant orange arms of Grand Prismatic Spring (page 95).**

Afternoon

8 **Picnic for lunch at the Nez Perce Picnic Area on the Firehole River (page 118).**

9 **Drive to Norris Geyser Basin to walk by Black Growler and the colorful Porcelain Basin (page 101).**

10 **Pop eastward in the car to the Grand Canyon of the Yellowstone to admire the Lower Fall from Red Rock Point on the North Rim, then the Upper Fall and Artist Point on the South Rim** **(page 135).**

11 Continue south into Hayden Valley to spot wildlife such as bison, elk, and trumpeter swans from pullouts (page 139).

Evening

12 Finish the adventure at the historic Lake Yellowstone Hotel, with dinner and a walk along the lake at sunset before spending the night (page 164).

ITINERARY DETAILS

- This itinerary works best **mid-May–early October,** when most of Yellowstone is open.
- Avoid the largest crowds by traveling **outside the July–August window.**
- Make **reservations** for lodging and dining at Lake Yellowstone Hotel 12–18 months in advance after May 1 (307/344-7311; www.yellowstonenationalparklodges).
- Download the **NPS Yellowstone National Park app** before you leave home due to limited cell service. Use it for traveling and checking eruption time predictions for six geysers, including Old Faithful Geyser.
- **Pack a cooler** with a picnic lunch, water, and snacks.
- **Parking** may be full, especially in summer, at Midway Geyser Basin and some overlooks at Grand Canyon of the Yellowstone. You may have to be flexible with the schedule.
- Stop to use the vault toilets at picnic areas along Lower Grand Loop Road rather than waiting in long lines at geyser basins and visitors centers.

Old Faithful

SEASONS OF YELLOWSTONE & GRAND TETON

SPRING
(APR.-MAY, OFF-SEASON)

Mid-April offers **car-free park roads** to cyclists before roads open to vehicles in late April or May. As the snow melts, flowers like yellow bells emerge. Come in **May** for bison calving season, or **June** to spot bighorn sheep ewes with newborn lambs and grizzly bears foraging along Yellowstone Lake. In May, many **visitor services return.** Days may be rainy and cold, and some trails remain snow-covered into June. Snow can fall up to a foot (30.5 cm).

Temperatures

Day: 30 to 60°F (0 to 16°C)
Night: -4 to 23°F (-20 to -5°C)

Road and Trail Access

In Yellowstone, not all roads open at one point in spring. In **mid-April,** roads open between Mammoth Hot Springs and Madison Junction, West Yellowstone, and Old Faithful. After that, other roads open in early May.

yellow bells

Last to open in late May are the high-elevation roads over **Dunraven Pass** between Tower Junction and Canyon Junction and **Sylvan Pass** on the East Entrance Road. In Grand Teton, **Teton Park Road** remains closed through April 30 from Taggart Lake Trailhead to Signal Mountain Lodge.

Hiking trails are often snow-covered, especially those at higher elevations. Some lower elevation trails can be snow-free by mid-May.

SUMMER
(JUNE-AUG., HIGH SEASON)

Summer sees the most visitors, with **July** and **August** luring the biggest crowds. All park **lodges, campgrounds,** and **visitors centers** are open. **June** through **early July** buzzes with mosquitoes, while July through early August brings on rampant wildflowers. **August** also yields the best high-elevation hiking in the Tetons, and warmer days produce less steam for better hot spring viewing in Yellowstone.

Temperatures

Day: 70 to 80°F (25 to 30°C)
Night: 35 to 45°F (1.6 to 7°C)

Road and Trail Access

Most **park roads are open**, with the exception of those that may be closed for construction. Most trails are snow-free, except for high elevations. Teton Crest Trail often has snow into mid-July.

FALL
(SEPT.-NOV., OFF-SEASON)

Cooler, bug-free days yield pleasant hiking with **thinner crowds.** Come in late **September** for the elk rut, when bulls gather harems to prove their dominance and their bugles break the nighttime quiet. Sporadic snowstorms depositing up to a foot (30.5cm) can **close park roads.** Some services close in fall.

Temperatures

Day: 30 to 60°F (0 to 16°C)
Night: -4 to 23°F (-20 to -5°C)

Road and Trail Access

In Yellowstone, **roads close in early November** for the season. Snowstorms may temporarily close roads earlier. The only road remaining open goes from the North Entrance at Gardiner to Mammoth Hot Springs and the Northeast Entrance. In Grand Teton, **Teton Park Road** closes November 1 for the winter; the closure goes from the Taggart Lake Trailhead to Signal Mountain Lodge. Snow buries high-elevation trails starting in October. Many low-elevation trails remain snow-free until November.

WINTER
(DEC.-MAR., HIGH SEASON)

In winter, deep snows bury the parks. Cross-country skiers tackle groomed and untracked trails in both parks. Touring in Yellowstone is via guided **snowcoach** or **snowmobile,** while lodging is available at **Mammoth Hot Springs, Old Faithful,** and towns surrounding the parks.

Temperatures

Day: 0 to 28°F (-20 to -2°C)
Night: -5 to 5°F (-20 to -15°C)

Road and Trail Access

Most **roads are closed in both parks** (Nov.-late Apr.), with the exception of the park road between Yellowstone's North and Northeast Entrances, plus the road in Grand Teton between Yellowstone's South Entrance and Jackson. Trails are buried in snow. Cross-country skis or snowshoes are needed for exploring on foot.

Mammoth Hot Springs in winter (left); bull elk bugling in fall (right)

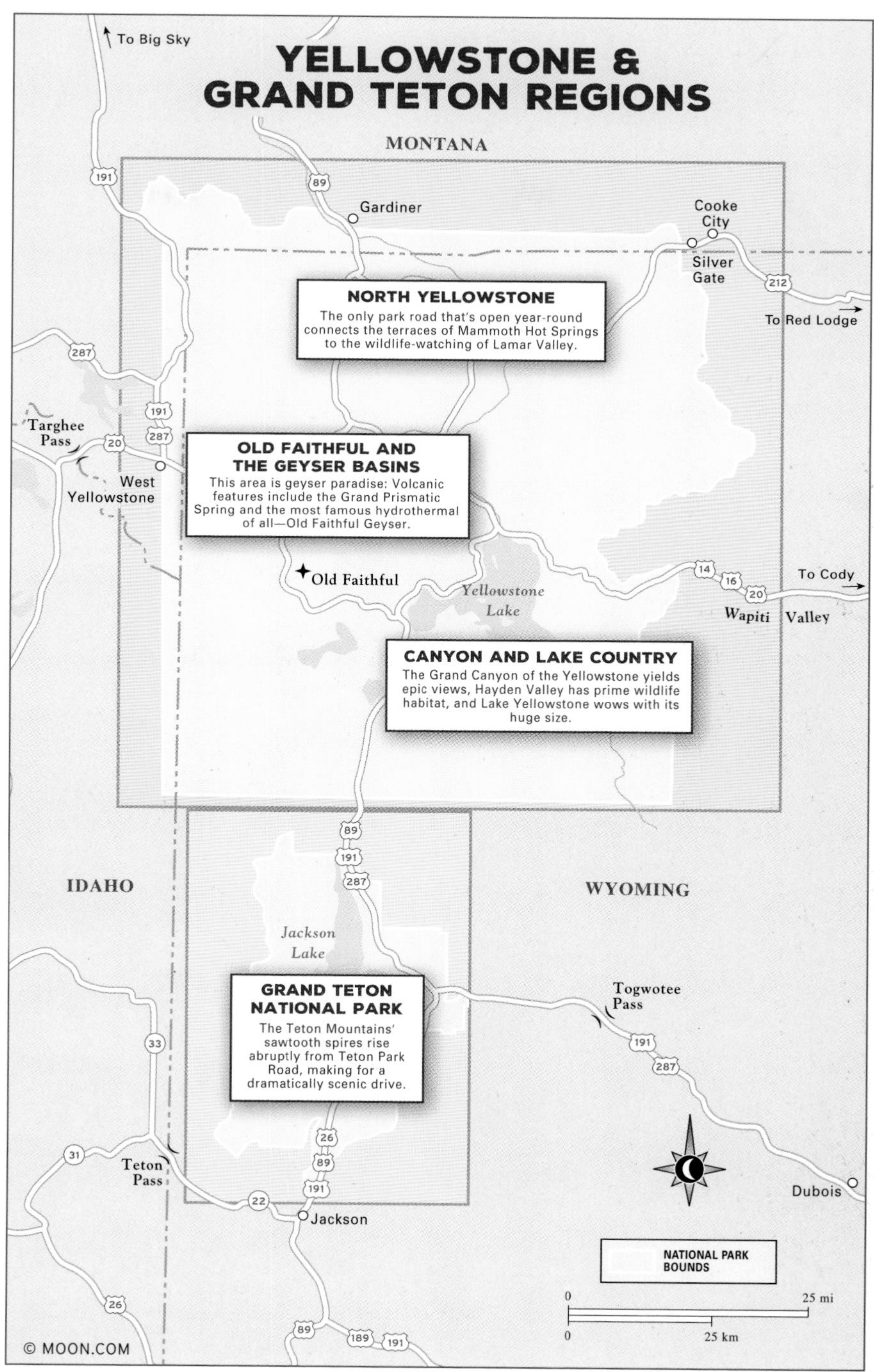

To Big Sky
YELLOWSTONE & GRAND TETON REGIONS
MONTANA
Gardiner
Cooke City
Silver Gate
To Red Lodge
NORTH YELLOWSTONE
The only park road that's open year-round connects the terraces of Mammoth Hot Springs to the wildlife-watching of Lamar Valley.
Targhee Pass
West Yellowstone
OLD FAITHFUL AND THE GEYSER BASINS
This area is geyser paradise: Volcanic features include the Grand Prismatic Spring and the most famous hydrothermal of all—Old Faithful Geyser.
Old Faithful
Yellowstone Lake
To Cody
Wapiti Valley
CANYON AND LAKE COUNTRY
The Grand Canyon of the Yellowstone yields epic views, Hayden Valley has prime wildlife habitat, and Lake Yellowstone wows with its huge size.
IDAHO
WYOMING
Jackson Lake
GRAND TETON NATIONAL PARK
The Teton Mountains' sawtooth spires rise abruptly from Teton Park Road, making for a dramatically scenic drive.
Togwotee Pass
Teton Pass
Jackson
Dubois
NATIONAL PARK BOUNDS
0
25 mi
0
25 km
© MOON.COM

view of Jackson Lake from Signal Mountain

BEST OF THE BEST YELLOWSTONE & GRAND TETON

BEST HIKES

TROUT LAKE

North Yellowstone
EASY

A short, steep 1.2-mi (1.9-km) round-trip trail leads to idyllic Trout Lake, rimmed with wildflower meadows, and a shoreline loop in the Absaroka Mountains.

trail circling Trout Lake (top); bighorn sheep along a Mt. Washburn trail (bottom)

★ FAIRY FALLS AND GRAND PRISMATIC OVERLOOK

Old Faithful and the Geyser Basins
EASY TO MODERATE

If you only do one hike in Yellowstone, this is the one to do. Traipse 6.8 mi (10.9 km) round-trip through a young lodgepole forest to reach the 197-ft (60-m) Fairy Falls. From a narrow slot, the falls plunge into a deep pool. In winter, the falls are draped with icicles. En route, add on a side loop to an overlook of radiant Grand Prismatic Spring.

OBSERVATION POINT

Old Faithful and the Geyser Basins
MODERATE

Climb 2.1 mi (3.4 km) round-trip up a couple of switchbacks to a point where you can peer down on Old Faithful Geyser. Crowds below look tiny, and the viewpoint gives a different angle on the erupting geyser. Descend via a different route to complete the loop.

MT. WASHBURN

Canyon and Lake Country
STRENUOUS

A 6.4-mi (10.3-km) round-trip climb leads to the 10,243-ft (3,122-m) summit of Mt. Washburn for 360-degree panoramic views. It's a grunt, but the lookout provides huge rewards.

Fairy Falls

trail to Inspiration Point (left); Taggart Lake Trail (right)

HIDDEN FALLS AND INSPIRATION POINT

Grand Teton National Park
MODERATE

The most popular hike in Grand Teton National Park is a 2-mi (3.2-km) round-trip that starts with a boat shuttle across Jenny Lake and takes in Hidden Falls before summiting Inspiration Point, a rocky outcrop with impressive views of Jackson Hole. If you want a longer hike, instead of taking the boat shuttle, you can hike the Jenny Lake Loop, a gentle 7.3-mi (11.7-km) round-trip circle around the lake, before climbing to Hidden Falls and Inspiration Point.

TAGGART AND BRADLEY LAKES

Grand Teton National Park
EASY TO MODERATE

This 5.9-mi (9.5-km) loop takes you to two lakes at the base of Avalanche and Garnet Canyons. At Bradley lake, you can stare straight up at the Grand Teton.

NEED TO KNOW: YELLOWSTONE

- **Park Website:** www.nps.gov/yell
- **Entrance Fee:** $35 per vehicle
- **Main Entrances:** **North Entrance** (US 89, near Gardiner; open year-round), **West Entrance** (US 20, West Yellowstone; open mid-Apr.-early Nov.), and **South Entrance** (US 89/191/287; open early May-early Nov.)
- **Main Visitors Centers:** **Albright Visitor Center** (Mammoth Hot Springs), **Old Faithful Visitor Education Center** (Old Faithful Village) and **Canyon Visitor Education Center** (Canyon Village)
- **Hotel and park activity reservations:** www.yellowstonenationalparklodges.com
- **Campsite reservations:** www.yellowstonenationalparklodges.com
- **Gas in the park:** Mammoth, Tower Junction, Old Faithful, Canyon Village, Fishing Bridge, Grant Village
- **High season:** June-Aug.

NEED TO KNOW: GRAND TETON

- **Park Website:** www.nps.gov/grte
- **Entrance Fee:** $35 per vehicle
- **Main Entrances:** **Moose Entrance** (Teton Park Road; open year-round), **Moran Entrance** (US 89/191/287; open year-round)
- **Main Visitors Centers:** **Craig Thomas Discovery & Visitor Center** (Moose), **Colter Bay Visitor Center** (Colter Bay)
- **Hotel and park activity reservations:** www.gtlc.com, www.signalmountainlodge.com
- **Campsite reservations:** www.gtlc.com
- **Gas in the park:** Flagg Ranch, Colter Bay, Jackson Lake Lodge, Signal Mountain Lodge, Moose
- **High season:** June-Aug.

BEST VIEWS

PORCELAIN SPRINGS

Old Faithful and the Geyser Basins, Norris Geyser Basin

This sprawling collection of springs varies in color from brilliant white to splotches of orange, offset by green and blue pools.

Porcelain Springs (top); view of the Tetons from Signal Mountain (bottom)

ARTIST POINT

Canyon and Lake Country, Grand Canyon of the Yellowstone

At Artist Point, you'll get classic views of the canyon and of Lower Falls, the tallest and most famous waterfall in the park.

LAKE BUTTE OVERLOOK

Canyon and Lake Country, Yellowstone Lake

Take in big views of the Absaroka Mountains, Lake Yellowstone, sunsets, and the Teton Mountains in the distance on clear days.

MORMON ROW

Grand Teton National Park

This cluster of buildings from an 1890s Mormon ranch settlement with the spectacular backdrop of the Teton Mountains makes for an impressive image, even for amateur photographers.

SIGNAL MOUNTAIN

Grand Teton National Park

Its position as the lone peak above the valley of Jackson Hole makes for big views of islands in Jackson Lake and the Teton Mountains.

view from Artist Point

Mormon Row

BEST GEOLOGIC HOTSPOTS

MAMMOTH HOT SPRINGS

North Yellowstone

Seen nowhere else in Yellowstone, springs at Mammoth create **travertine terraces,** which vary seasonally with the amount of water that flows down the stairstep hillsides.

ROARING MOUNTAIN

North Yellowstone

Roaring Mountain is a mountainside collection of **fumaroles** that earned its name from its constant hissing.

OLD FAITHFUL GEYSER

Old Faithful and the Geyser Basins, Upper Geyser Basin

The most famous geyser anywhere, Old Faithful acquired its name thanks to its regular eruptions—an average of one every 88 minutes since 2013 (eruption intervals can vary 45-120 minutes). The area around Old Faithful, Upper Geyser Basin, has 410 geysers, the most in the park.

FOUNTAIN PAINT POT

Old Faithful and the Geyser Basins, Lower Geyser Basin

Iron oxides tint the Fountain Paint Pot pink, beige, and gray—a prime example of **mud pots.**

GRAND PRISMATIC SPRING

Old Faithful and the Geyser Basins, Midway Geyser Basin

Grand Prismatic Spring is Yellowstone's largest **hot spring** at 370 ft (113 m) in diameter and 121 ft (37 m) deep. It radiates stunning colors from its blue center to orange and brown rays.

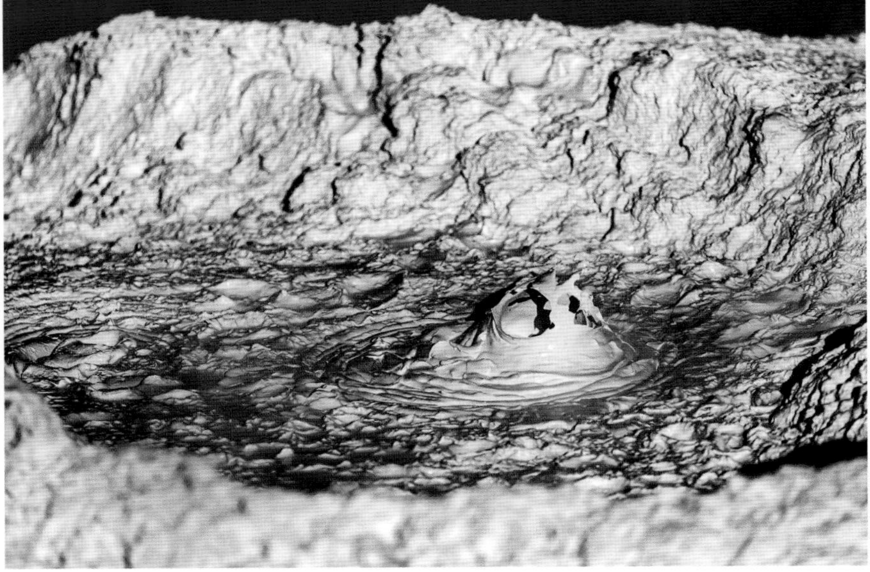

bubbling Fountain Paint Pot (top); Old Faithful against the Milky Way (bottom left); Canary Spring at Mammoth Hot Springs (bottom right)

INDIGENOUS PEOPLES OF YELLOWSTONE & GRAND TETON

HISTORY

Archaeological evidence in Yellowstone and Grand Teton National Parks shows that Indigenous people appeared around 11,000 years ago after the Yellowstone Ice Cap melted. A few stone tools indicate their presence, including an obsidian Clovis point. Other points and projectiles were found around Yellowstone Lake in what was probably a summer camp.

Increased use of what became the Yellowstone and Grand Teton area spiked about 3,000 years ago as many Indigenous people found hospitable summer environments, wildlife for hunting, fish, and edible or usable vegetation. Harsh winters made them move to warmer and more protected locations. The **Northern Cheyenne, Northern Arapahoe, Shoshone, Bannock, Crow, Gros Ventre, Kiowa, Blackfeet, Flathead,** and **Nez Perce** are some of the Indigenous people to use these lands. Some groups used geothermal areas for sacred ceremonies and medicine rites. Shortly after Yellowstone became a national park, it served as a temporary haven for the Nez Perce in 1877 on their 1,170-mi (1,880-km) flight toward Canada to escape the U.S. Army.

The **Tukudeka,** or Sheep Eaters, members of the Mountain Shoshone, were assumed to be permanent residents of the high plateaus that became Yellowstone. They relied on bighorn sheep for survival. While structures including conical timber lodges, called wickiups, are attributed to the Tukudeka, more than 1,900 archeological sites in Yellowstone are attributed to several groups of Indigenous people.

By the time Yellowstone became a national park in 1872, the Tukudeka had mysteriously disappeared. Other Indigenous people were removed from the park under the auspices of making it safe for tourists. Park superintendents and politicians who had never visited Yellowstone further justified the forced displacement of Indigenous people by spreading rumors that the Indigenous people were afraid of the evil spirits in geysers.

As Yellowstone and Grand Teton were mapped by white explorers, they named places for expedition members, friends, and the people who funded their work. But the land had Indigenous names for millennia prior to mapping; only a tiny handful are still in use today. For instance, the Shoshone called the Teton Mountains **"Teewinot,"** which referred to the series of pinnacles. Today, only one peak in the Tetons bears that name.

TODAY

Yellowstone has 26 associated tribes with historical connections to the land. Four of those tribes have

Teewinot Mountain (left peak) above String Lake

treaty rights to hunt Yellowstone bison. Since Yellowstone began its ethnographic program in 2000, the National Park Service and several sovereign Indigenous nations have consulted together on mutual issues, including concerns about bison that leave the park and wickiup preservation. Their collaborative work also developed interpretation on the Yellowstone portion of the Nez Perce National Historic Trail. The National Park Service of both parks inventories culturally important and sacred sites.

Three of the tribes that hunted, camped, fished, and held ceremonies in Yellowstone and Grand Teton National Parks have reservations nearby, but not bordering the parks. Some members still visit for religious, ceremonial, or medicinal purposes, and each reservation celebrates its culture every summer with a powwow and rodeo. Most are open to non-tribal members, but check current details online. Southeastern Montana is home to the **Crow Nation** (www.crownsn.gov) that celebrates the heritage of the Apsáalooke, or "Children of the Large-Beaked Bird" in June. Adjacent to the Crow, the **Northern Cheyenne Nation** (www.cheyennenation.com) combines two merged groups known as the Tsitsistas and the Só'taeo'o, who celebrate in early July with additional events throughout the summer. Flanking the Wind River Mountains of Wyoming, the **Eastern Shoshone** (http://easternshoshone.org) and the **Northern Arapaho** (www.northernarapahoe.com) host one of the largest powwows in the region during **Eastern Shoshone Indian Days** in late June, followed by smaller weekly events and the Arapaho powwow in late summer. The Arapaho also convene a powwow in late

The Madison River runs alongside part of the Nez Perce National Historic Trail.

August or early September. Smaller powwows happen weekly in summer (http://windriver.org).

EXPERIENCES

Obsidian Cliff

Yellowstone: North Yellowstone, Grand Loop Road between Mammoth Hot Springs and Norris Junction

The 0.5-mi-long (0.8-km-long) Obsidian Cliff, a National Historic Landmark and archaeological site, resulted from a 180,000-year-old rhyolite lava flow that crystallized. Look closely to see the shiny black bits of obsidian in the layers, but do so with binoculars or from a car as the site is closed to exploring. Early Indigenous people in the area quarried the sharp obsidian for making knives, arrowheads, and other tools. North of the cliff on the west side of the road, the **Obsidian Cliff interpretive kiosk** is one of the first interpretive exhibits created by the National Park Service. It contains an obsidian sample you can touch.

Nez Perce National Historic Trail

Yellowstone: Old Faithful and the Geyser Basins, North Yellowstone, Grand Loop Road from West Yellowstone to Yellowstone Lake and north to the Northeast Entrance

In 1877 on their flight toward Canada to escape the U.S. Army, the Nez Perce, or Nee-Me-Poo, spent two weeks crossing Yellowstone, bumping into a few visitors. The 1,170-mile (1,880-km) Nez Perce National Historic Trail (www.fs.usda.gov/main/npnht) that commemorates their flight traverses the central part of Yellowstone. You can follow portions of their route on a driving tour. A few locations on the route bear the Nez Perce name (a creek, two picnic areas, and a trail).

David T. Vernon Collection of Indigenous Artifacts

Grand Teton: Colter Bay Indian Arts Museum, Craig Thomas Discovery & Visitor Center, Jackson Lake Lodge

Grand Teton National Park owns an extensive collection of crafts and arts from the Indigenous people of the region. Ten thousand artifacts were originally collected by David T. Vernon and later purchased by Laurance S. Rockefeller, who donated a portion of the collection to the park. Artifacts include intricate beadwork, clothing, moccasins, jewelry, tools, cradleboards, toys, saddles, pottery, and weapons.

You can see selections of these artifacts in three locations. **Jackson Lake Lodge** (101 Jackson Lake Lodge Rd.; mid-May-early Oct.) exhibits a few pieces in the entry and upstairs lobby, and the **Craig Thomas Discovery & Visitor Center** (Moose; 8am-7pm daily Apr.-Oct., shorter hours spring and fall) includes artifacts in its historical exhibits. The largest portion of the collection is on display at the **Colter Bay Indian Arts Museum** (Colter Bay Visitor Center; 8am-7pm daily mid-May-early Oct., 8am-5pm daily spring and fall). You can also see samples online (https:artsandculture.google.com, search "David T. Vernon Collection").

BEST SCENIC DRIVE

LOWER GRAND LOOP ROAD, YELLOWSTONE

PARK AREA: Old Faithful and the Geyser Basins
SEASON: mid-May-early Nov.
DRIVING DISTANCE: 96 mi (154 km) round-trip
DRIVING TIME: 4 hours round-trip (without stops)

If you only do one drive in Yellowstone and Grand Teton, make it Lower Grand Loop Road. This route links the major areas of the park and takes in loads of wildlife-watching, plus Norris Geyser Basin, Grand Canyon of the Yellowstone, Hayden Valley, Yellowstone Lake, West Thumb Geyser Basin, and the Old Faithful complex.

Follow the West Entrance Road from **Madison Junction** to **Norris Junction.** From Norris, zip east over the forested road to **Canyon Village,** where the road heads south through bison jams in **Hayden Valley** along the **Yellowstone River** and around the shores of **Yellowstone Lake** to **West Thumb.** From West Thumb, head west to **Old Faithful,** crossing the **Continental Divide** twice, and from there, complete the loop north to **Madison.**

A portion of the **Nez Perce National Historic Trail** follows Lower Grand Loop Road. To follow that route instead, start on the West Entrance Road, turn right at Madison Junction (instead of north as described above), and go around Old Faithful and Yellowstone Lake to Canyon Village.

bison jam in Hayden Valley (left); Sand Point on Yellowstone Lake (right)

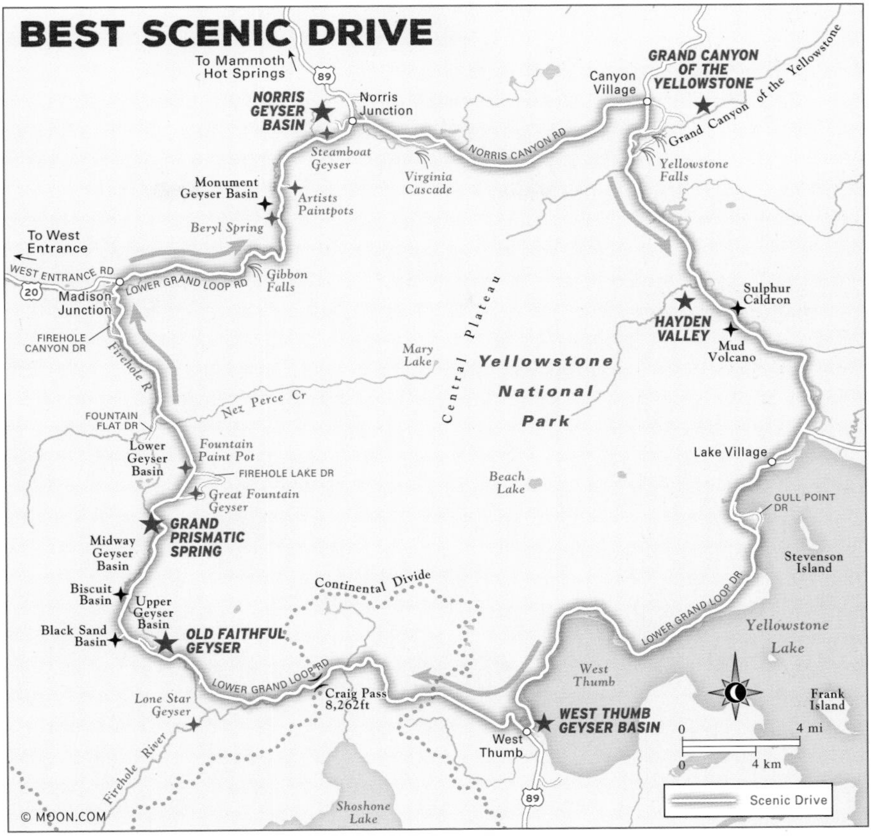
BEST SCENIC DRIVE
To Mammoth Hot Springs
89
NORRIS GEYSER BASIN
Norris Junction
Steamboat Geyser
Virginia Cascade
NORRIS CANYON RD
Canyon Village
GRAND CANYON OF THE YELLOWSTONE
Grand Canyon of the Yellowstone
Yellowstone Falls
Monument Geyser Basin
Artists Paintpots
Beryl Spring
To West Entrance
WEST ENTRANCE RD
20
Madison Junction
LOWER GRAND LOOP RD
Gibbon Falls
FIREHOLE CANYON DR
Firehole R
Central Plateau
Mary Lake
Yellowstone National Park
HAYDEN VALLEY
Sulphur Caldron
Mud Volcano
Nez Perce Cr
FOUNTAIN FLAT DR
Lower Geyser Basin
Fountain Paint Pot
FIREHOLE LAKE DR
Great Fountain Geyser
Beach Lake
Lake Village
GULL POINT DR
GRAND PRISMATIC SPRING
Midway Geyser Basin
Stevenson Island
Continental Divide
Biscuit Basin
Upper Geyser Basin
Black Sand Basin
OLD FAITHFUL GEYSER
LOWER GRAND LOOP RD
Yellowstone Lake
West Thumb
LOWER GRAND LOOP RD
Craig Pass 8,262ft
Lone Star Geyser
Frank Island
WEST THUMB GEYSER BASIN
West Thumb
0 4 mi
0 4 km
Firehole River
89
Scenic Drive
Shoshone Lake
© MOON.COM

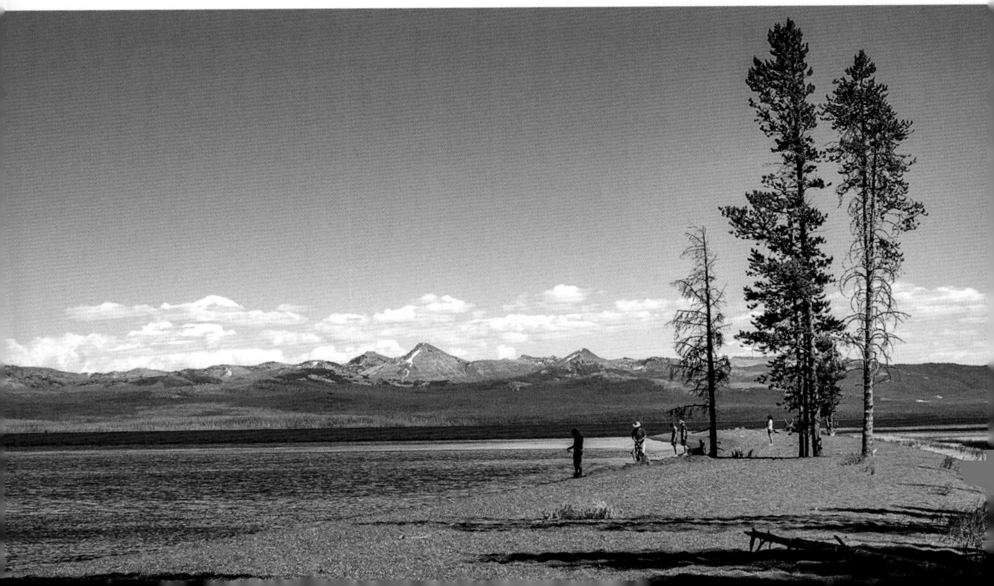

Bicycle the Multi-Use Pathway in Grand Teton to enjoy the peaks rather than driving the road.

PRACTICE SUSTAINABLE TRAVEL IN YELLOWSTONE & GRAND TETON

- Bring a refillable water bottle instead of disposable plastic bottles.
- Buy locally made products.
- Go with local park-approved guide companies.
- Bring binoculars to watch wildlife while maintaining a safe distance for you and the animals.
- Minimize driving by hiking, biking, paddling, and skiing to experience the parks.
- Turn off the car engine rather than idling when you use pullouts to watch wildlife.
- Use established paved or gravel pullouts for wildlife-watching and photography rather than pulling over onto meadow edges.
- Be a conscientious park visitor by following Leave No Trace at all times.
- Adjust your schedule to visit crowded sites at less popular times or seasons.
- Always have a Plan B in case crowds preclude your Plan A.

Binoculars are useful for viewing wildlife in Yellowstone..

morning at Trout Lake

NORTH YELLOWSTONE

BALANCING VOLCANIC FEATURES AND SOARING MOUNTAINS, North Yellowstone clings to the park's Montana-Wyoming border.

Slicing across North Yellowstone between the high Gallatin and Absaroka Mountains, sagebrush plateaus proliferate with wildlife. Elk hang out on the lawns in Mammoth Hot Springs. Bears and wolves hunt at Swan Lake Flat in Gardner's Hole. Vast herds of bison congregate in Lamar Valley. Pronghorn race through sagebrush, bighorn sheep feed on steep slopes, and, higher yet, mountain goats walk the cliffs. Bring binoculars and spotting scopes for watching the action.

Beneath the landscape, hot water boils to the earth's surface. It spews out steaming in Mammoth Hot Springs, creating otherworldly sculptures of ever-changing colorful travertine. Soak up the smells, sounds, and sights on its boardwalks.

Between wildlife and hot springs, the Yellowstone River plunges through the narrow canyons, alternating with pools in the flats. As the longest free-flowing river in the Lower 48, it provides clean passage for native trout to lure anglers to its waters.

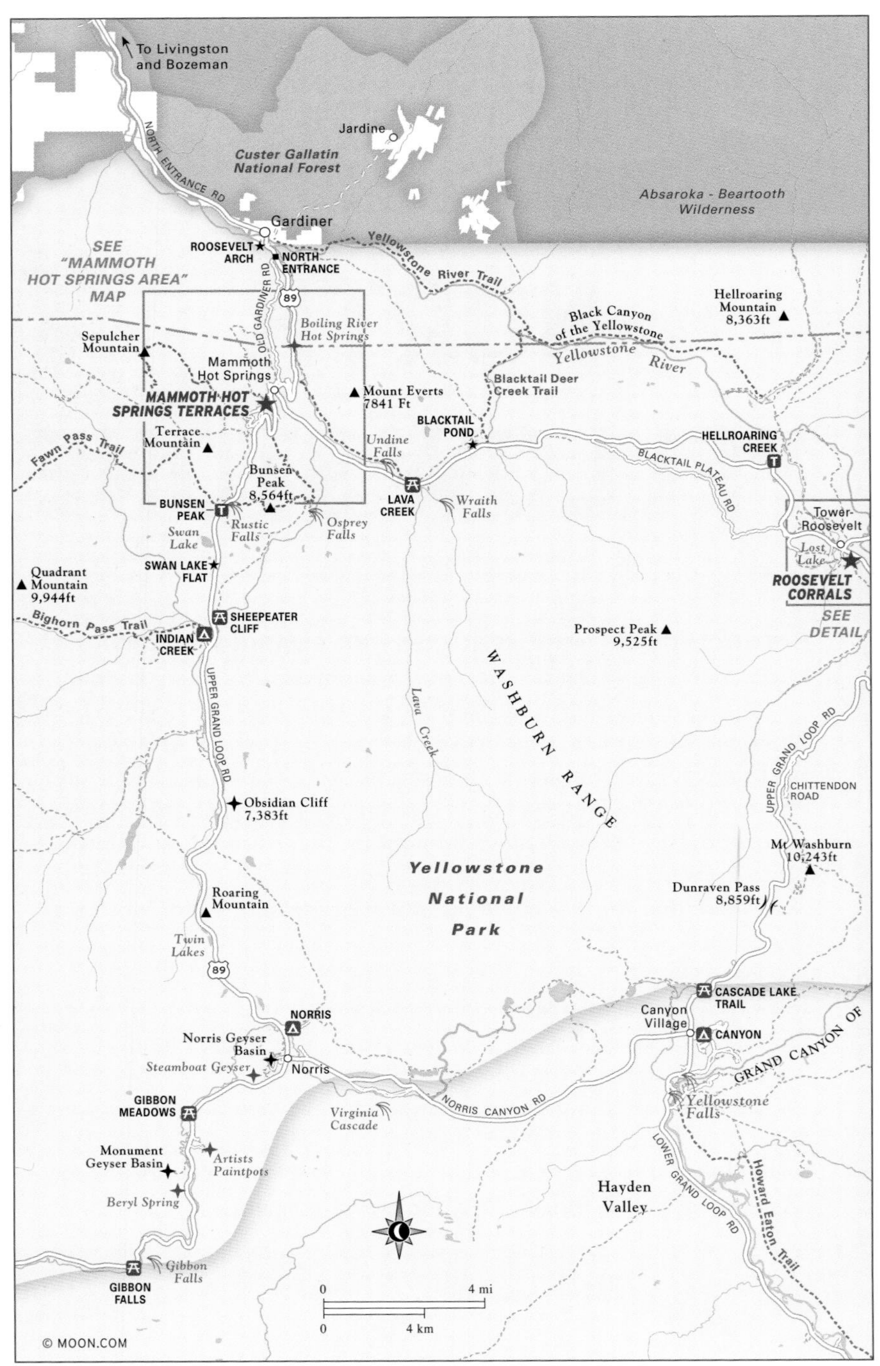
To Livingston and Bozeman
Jardine
Custer Gallatin National Forest
Absaroka - Beartooth Wilderness
NORTH ENTRANCE RD
Gardiner
ROOSEVELT ARCH
NORTH ENTRANCE
Yellowstone River Trail
SEE "MAMMOTH HOT SPRINGS AREA" MAP
OLD GARDINER RD
89
Boiling River Hot Springs
Hellroaring Mountain 8,363ft
Black Canyon of the Yellowstone
Yellowstone River
Sepulcher Mountain
Mammoth Hot Springs
MAMMOTH HOT SPRINGS TERRACES
Mount Everts 7841 Ft
Blacktail Deer Creek Trail
BLACKTAIL POND
HELLROARING CREEK
BLACKTAIL PLATEAU RD
Terrace Mountain
Fawn Pass Trail
Undine Falls
Bunsen Peak 8,564ft
BUNSEN PEAK
LAVA CREEK
Wraith Falls
Rustic Falls
Osprey Falls
Swan Lake
Tower-Roosevelt
Lost Lake
ROOSEVELT CORRALS
SEE DETAIL
SWAN LAKE FLAT
Quadrant Mountain 9,944ft
Bighorn Pass Trail
SHEEPEATER CLIFF
INDIAN CREEK
Prospect Peak 9,525ft
WASHBURN RANGE
UPPER GRAND LOOP RD
Lava Creek
UPPER GRAND LOOP RD
CHITTENDON ROAD
Obsidian Cliff 7,383ft
Mt Washburn 10,243ft
Yellowstone National Park
Dunraven Pass 8,859ft
Roaring Mountain
Twin Lakes
89
NORRIS
CASCADE LAKE TRAIL
Canyon Village
CANYON
Norris Geyser Basin
Steamboat Geyser
Norris
GRAND CANYON OF
GIBBON MEADOWS
NORRIS CANYON RD
Virginia Cascade
Yellowstone Falls
Monument Geyser Basin
Artists Paintpots
Beryl Spring
LOWER GRAND LOOP RD
Howard Eaton Trail
Hayden Valley
Gibbon Falls
GIBBON FALLS
0
4 mi
0
4 km

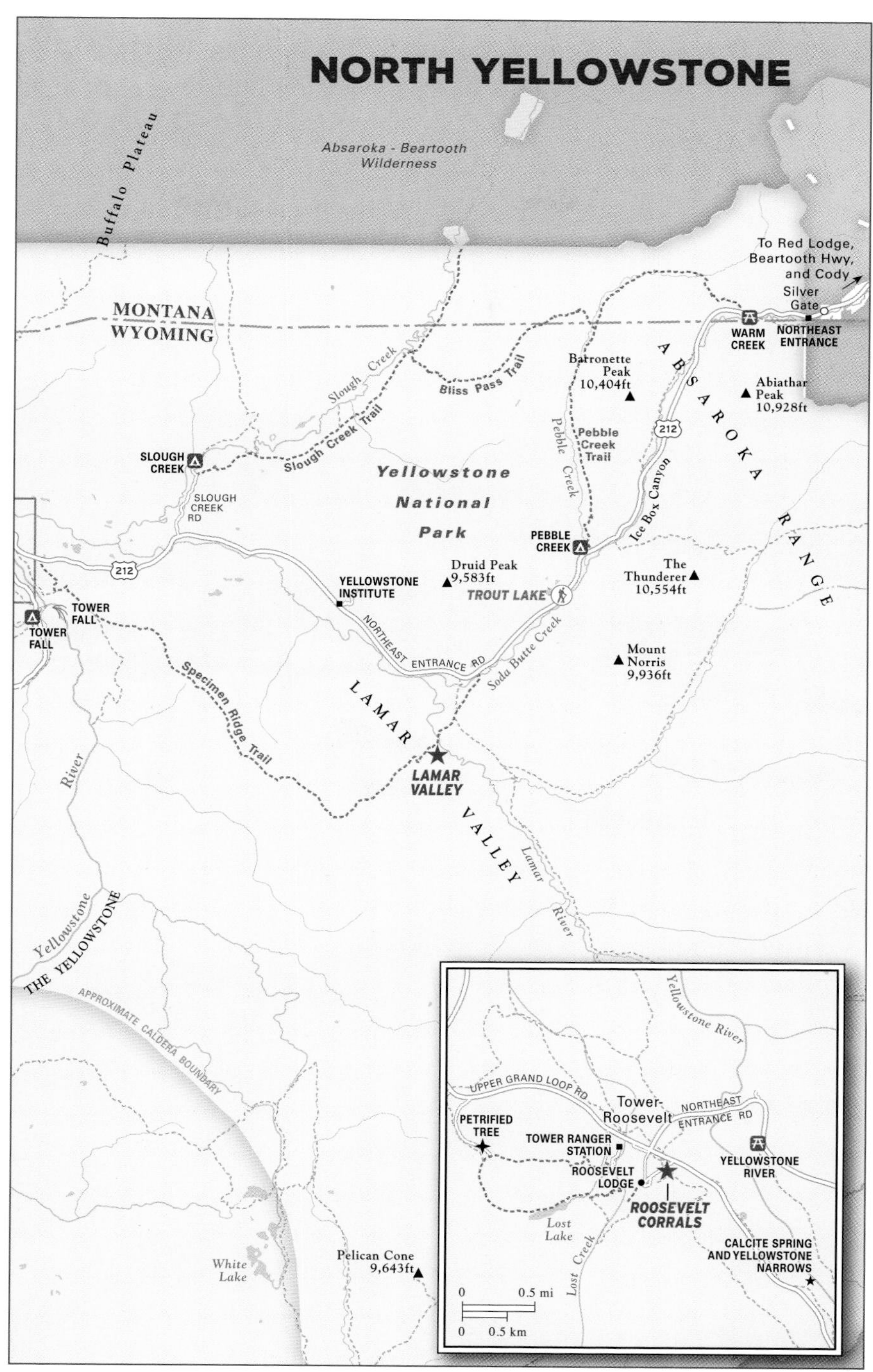
NORTH YELLOWSTONE
Absaroka - Beartooth Wilderness
Buffalo Plateau
MONTANA
WYOMING
To Red Lodge, Beartooth Hwy, and Cody
Silver Gate
WARM CREEK
NORTHEAST ENTRANCE
Slough Creek
Bliss Pass Trail
Slough Creek Trail
SLOUGH CREEK
SLOUGH CREEK RD
Barronette Peak 10,404ft
Abiathar Peak 10,928ft
ABSAROKA RANGE
Pebble Creek
Pebble Creek Trail
Ice Box Canyon
212
Yellowstone National Park
PEBBLE CREEK
Druid Peak 9,583ft
YELLOWSTONE INSTITUTE
TROUT LAKE
The Thunderer 10,554ft
TOWER FALL
NORTHEAST ENTRANCE RD
Soda Butte Creek
Mount Norris 9,936ft
Specimen Ridge Trail
LAMAR VALLEY
River
Lamar River
Yellowstone
THE YELLOWSTONE
APPROXIMATE CALDERA BOUNDARY
White Lake
Pelican Cone 9,643ft
Yellowstone River
UPPER GRAND LOOP RD
Tower-Roosevelt
NORTHEAST ENTRANCE RD
PETRIFIED TREE
TOWER RANGER STATION
YELLOWSTONE RIVER
ROOSEVELT LODGE
ROOSEVELT CORRALS
Lost Lake
Lost Creek
CALCITE SPRING AND YELLOWSTONE NARROWS
0 0.5 mi
0 0.5 km

1

TOP 3

★ **1. MAMMOTH HOT SPRINGS TERRACES:** Stroll the lower formations of these otherworldly travertine terraces and drive through the dormant upper terraces (page 59).

★ **2. ROOSEVELT CORRALS:** Experience the Old West on horseback or in a stagecoach from Roosevelt Corrals (page 62).

★ **3. WILDLIFE IN LAMAR VALLEY:** Huge bison herds, elk, pronghorn antelope, bears, wolves, bighorn sheep, and raptors range across the valley known as "America's Serengeti" (page 63).

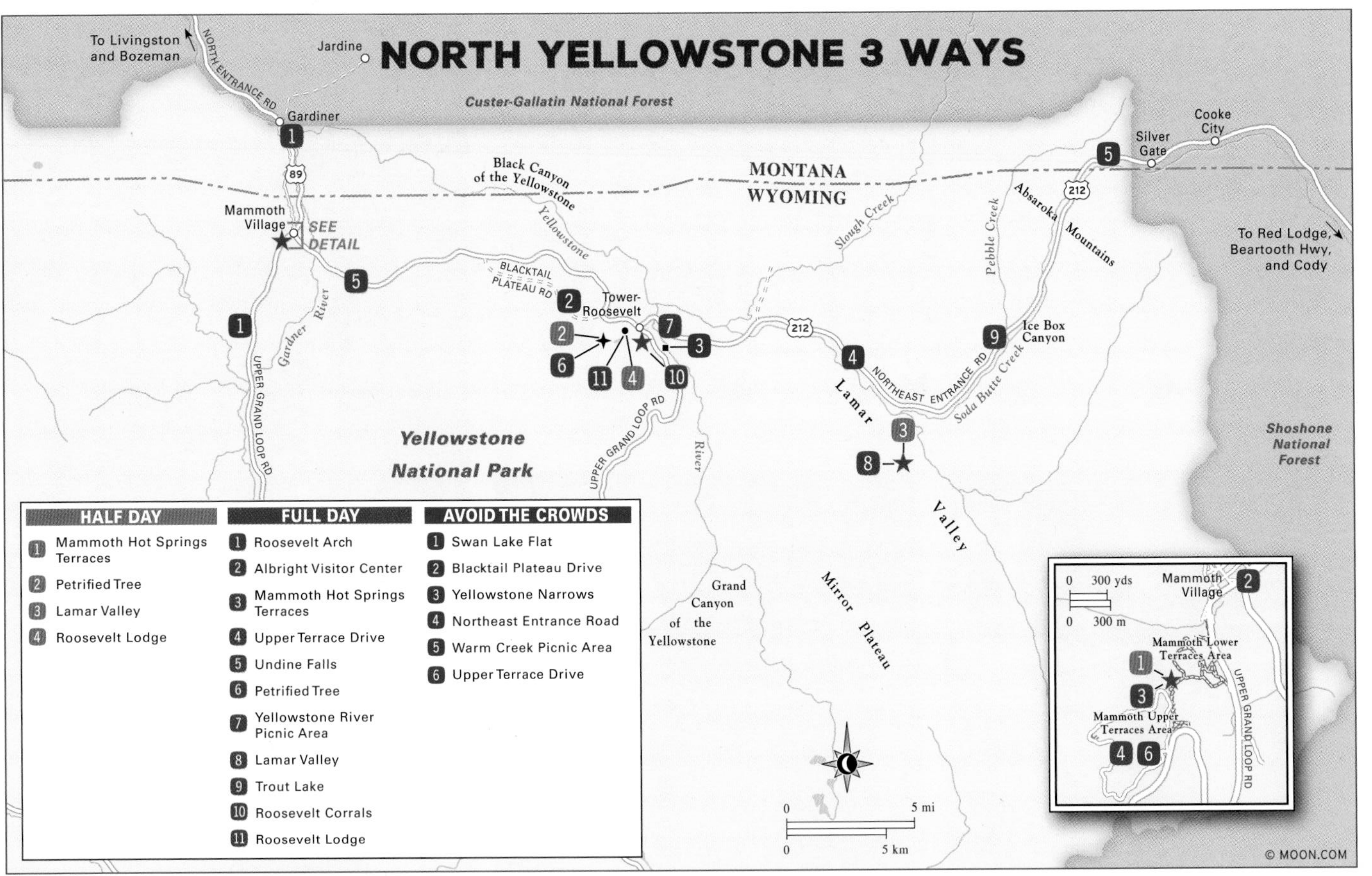

NORTH YELLOWSTONE 3 WAYS
To Livingston and Bozeman
NORTH ENTRANCE RD
Jardine
Gardiner
Custer-Gallatin National Forest
89
Mammoth Village
SEE DETAIL
Black Canyon of the Yellowstone
Yellowstone
MONTANA
WYOMING
Slough Creek
BLACKTAIL PLATEAU RD
Tower-Roosevelt
Gardner River
UPPER GRAND LOOP RD
212
NORTHEAST ENTRANCE RD
Lamar
Valley
Pebble Creek
Absaroka Mountains
Soda Butte Creek
Ice Box Canyon
Silver Gate
Cooke City
To Red Lodge, Beartooth Hwy, and Cody
Shoshone National Forest
Yellowstone National Park
River
Grand Canyon of the Yellowstone
Mirror Plateau
0 5 mi
0 5 km
0 300 yds
0 300 m
Mammoth Lower Terraces Area
Mammoth Upper Terraces Area
HALF DAY
1 Mammoth Hot Springs Terraces
2 Petrified Tree
3 Lamar Valley
4 Roosevelt Lodge
FULL DAY
1 Roosevelt Arch
2 Albright Visitor Center
3 Mammoth Hot Springs Terraces
4 Upper Terrace Drive
5 Undine Falls
6 Petrified Tree
7 Yellowstone River Picnic Area
8 Lamar Valley
9 Trout Lake
10 Roosevelt Corrals
11 Roosevelt Lodge
AVOID THE CROWDS
1 Swan Lake Flat
2 Blacktail Plateau Drive
3 Yellowstone Narrows
4 Northeast Entrance Road
5 Warm Creek Picnic Area
6 Upper Terrace Drive
© MOON.COM

NORTH YELLOWSTONE 3 WAYS

HALF DAY

With only a few hours, focus your time on experiencing volcanic activity and wildlife from Mammoth Hot Springs to Lamar Valley. An early start will help you fit it all in.

1 Tour the boardwalks through the **terraces** at **Mammoth Hot Springs,** including Palette Spring and Minerva Terrace. You can also continue climbing boardwalks to Canary Spring, or look up at the orange spring from the road below as you depart.

2 From there, head east to **Petrified Tree.** Walk the short path to see this relic of a wetter climate before Yellowstone's supervolcanic eruption.

3 Continue on to **Lamar Valley.** Plan to spend an hour at pullouts in this valley sprawling with bison herds. Look on the surrounding slopes for bears and wolves.

4 Stop for a meal in the historic **Roosevelt Lodge** before returning to Mammoth Hot Springs.

3

1

FULL DAY

Take a full day to explore the sights and experience northern Yellowstone from Gardiner, Montana. A pair of binoculars will be especially helpful for wildlife-watching in Lamar Valley.

1 Drive through the historic **Roosevelt Arch,** built in 1903, which marks the North Entrance to Yellowstone.

2 Orient yourself by touring exhibits in the **Albright Visitor Center,** located in the Bachelor Officers' Quarters building left over from when the U.S. Army managed the park.

3 Head to **Mammoth Hot Springs** and walk the accessible boardwalk past Liberty Cap to see Palette Spring at the base of the Lower Terraces. Climb the boardwalk and stairs to loop around Minerva Terrace.

4 After touring the Lower Terraces, circle the one-way loop of **Upper Terrace Drive** through older features such as Orange Spring Mound. Park to descend the staired boardwalk to Canary Spring.

5 Back in your car, head onto Upper Grand Loop Road. Pull over at **Undine Falls** on the north segment of the road to marvel at the three-tiered waterfall.

6 Farther along, stop at the **Petrified Tree** to see a petrified specimen of the ancient redwood trees that used to populate these slopes.

7 Cross the Yellowstone River on the Northeast Entrance Road for lunch at **Yellowstone River Picnic Area.**

8 After lunch, drive through **Lamar Valley** on Northeast Entrance Road, stopping at pullouts to look for bison, bears, wolves, sandhill cranes, pronghorn, and bighorn sheep.

9 Stretch your legs with a hike to idyllic **Trout Lake,** where you may see spawning fish in the inlet stream and the lake rimmed with wildflowers.

10 After the hike, head back toward Upper Grand Loop Road. Hop on a horseback, wagon, or authentic stagecoach ride at **Roosevelt Corrals.** Or you can combine a ride with the Old West Dinner Cookout.

11 Dine in the historic **Roosevelt Lodge** before calling it a day.

2

5

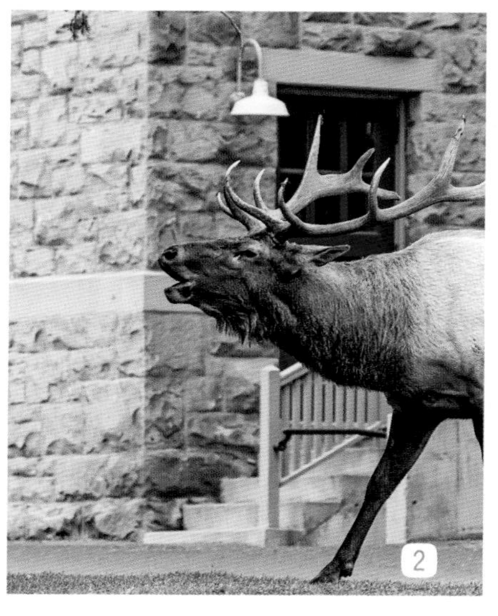

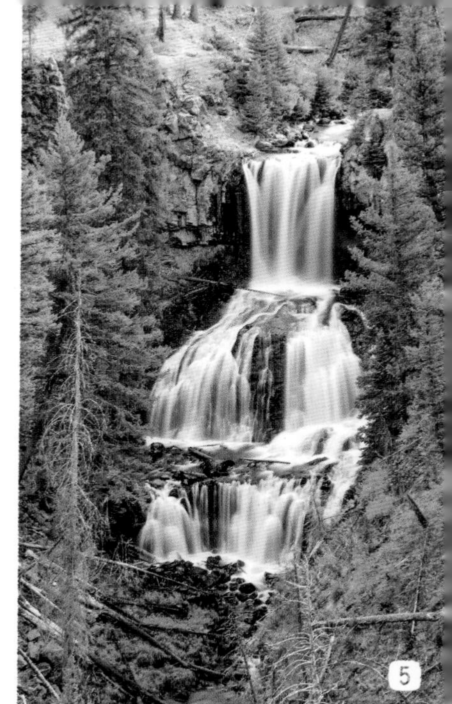

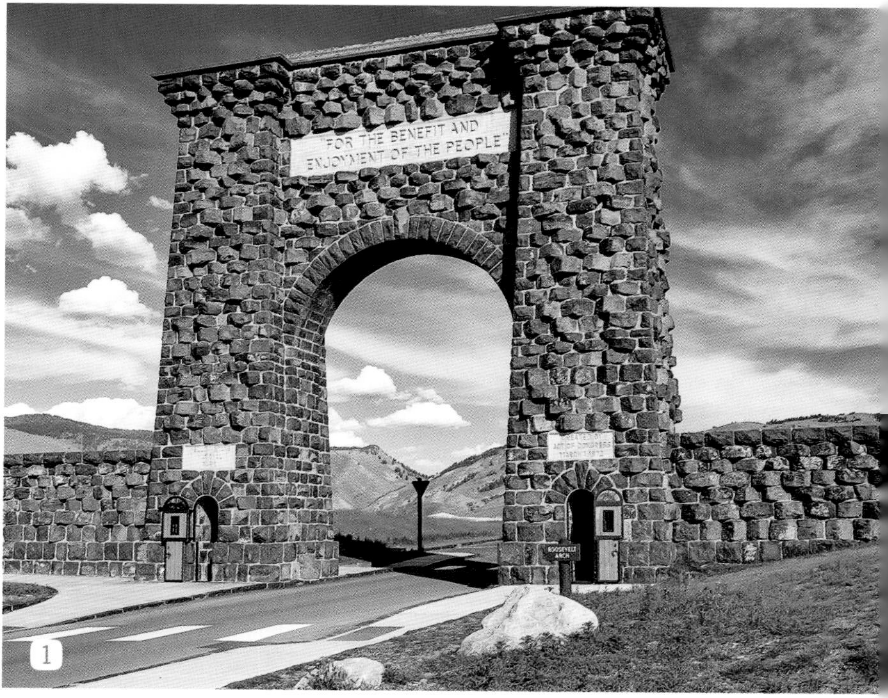
"FOR THE BENEFIT AND
ENJOYMENT OF THE PEOPLE"
ROOSEVELT ARCH
1

AVOID THE CROWDS

Crowded boardwalks and bison jams are part of the summer experience in Yellowstone. Visit the northern corridor, with roads open year-round, in the fall for quieter trails and fun wildlife-watching.

1 Drive south to **Swan Lake Flat** at sunrise from Mammoth Hot Springs on Grand Loop Road. Park and scan the scenery with binoculars for elk. You may hear the bull elk bugling before you spot them rounding up their harems. Watch also for wolves and trumpeter swans.

2 Head west onto Grand Loop Road, detouring onto the one-way, rough dirt **Blacktail Plateau Drive** for more wildlife-watching. Look here for bears, bison, and fall colors.

3 Back on Grand Loop Road, head to the Yellowstone River Picnic Area trailhead, where you can hike the **Yellowstone Narrows** to peer down on Calcite Springs and the Yellowstone River.

4 Tour the **Northeast Entrance Road** as it squeezes through the Absaroka Mountains. You may see bighorn sheep or mountain goats on steep mountain slopes.

5 Enjoy a picnic at **Warm Creek Picnic Area** before heading back to Mammoth Hot Springs. (If temperatures preclude picnicking, Cooke City is just outside the Northeast Entrance.)

6 Take an early evening drive on the one-way loop of **Upper Terrace Drive.** Park to overlook the Lower Terraces and walk to Canary Spring.

More Activities with Fewer Crowds

- Sepulcher Mountain hike
- Cross-country skiing and snowshoeing

2

4

HIGHLIGHTS

ROOSEVELT ARCH

North Entrance

Located at Yellowstone's North Entrance, Roosevelt Arch may be one of the best human-built park entrances in the country. The original entrance road crosses under the stone-and-mortar arch dedicated to President Theodore Roosevelt, who laid the cornerstone in 1903. Reconstruction of Park Street, the viewing park and amphitheater, and the arch area for the 2016 anniversary of the National Park Service has improved access for photographing the arch. The reconstruction also reopened walkway doors. A signed shortcut road lets large RVs bypass the narrow entrance through the arch, but cars can still drive through it. To walk around the arch and **Arch Park,** park on Park Street.

HISTORIC FORT YELLOWSTONE

In the pre-National Park Service decades, the village of Mammoth was Fort Yellowstone when the U.S. Cavalry managed the park. A self-guided walking tour visits the streets of stone buildings erected by the army between 1891 and 1916. Start at **Albright Visitor Center** (tel. 307/344-2263; 8am-6pm daily summer, 9am-5pm daily fall, winter, spring), once the Bachelor Officers' Quarters, where you can pick up an interpretive brochure ($1). Across from the visitors center, the **parade grounds** (sometimes called the drill field) are covered with sagebrush and wandering bison or elk. Walk down the row of houses to see the **Captain's Quarters, Field Officer's Quarters,** and **Officers' Quarters.** Today, most of the buildings house park service personnel and their families or serve as supply depots and offices; as such, they are not open to the public. Additional sights include the **granary, chapel, hospital, blacksmith,** and **stables.**

★ MAMMOTH HOT SPRINGS TERRACES

Lower Terrace

Raised boardwalks and stairways loop 1.8 mi (2.9 km) through the Lower Terrace of Mammoth Hot Springs, where limestone creates travertine terraces. The boardwalks offer an opportunity to view the changing calcium carbonate sculptures, and sulfur fills the air. From the parking lot, be ready to climb 300 ft (90 m) in elevation to reach the Upper Terrace.

Access the boardwalk at one of three lower parking lots on the park road south of Mammoth Village, or walk there from the Albright Visitor

Historic Fort Yellowstone

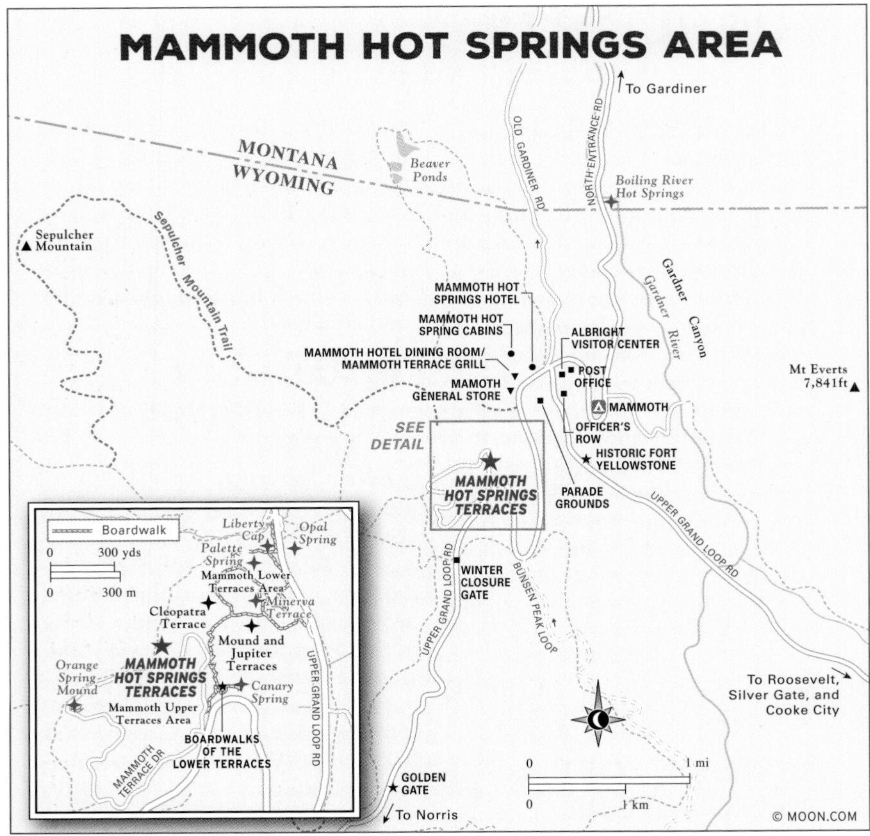

Center. To start, follow the northwest boardwalk to see **Liberty Cap,** a 37-ft-tall dormant hot springs cone. Across the street from Liberty Cap is **Opal Spring,** which amasses a new foot of travertine every year. Past Liberty Cap, a spur on the right leads to the colorful **Palette Spring,** where thermophiles create orange and brown colors spilling down the stairstep terraces. Continue on the main boardwalk to circle the loop around **Minerva Terrace,** known for its striking travertine sculptures that alternate between watery and dry. **Cleopatra, Mound,** and **Jupiter Terraces** flank the stair climbs to the overlook at the Upper Terrace Drive parking lot. A spur boardwalk with steps heads left to the striking orange and brilliant white sinter **Canary Spring.**

Upper Terrace

At Mammoth Hot Springs, the 0.75-mi (1.2-km), one-way, single-lane Upper Terrace Drive (mid-May-early Nov., groomed for cross-country skiing in winter) snakes through unique limestone features created from once-active hydrothermals. From several locations, walk to overlooks for views of the Gallatin Mountains, the village below, the Lower Terraces, and **Canary Spring.** Drive by the striking **Orange Spring**

BEST PLACE TO WATCH THE SUNSET

Head to **Lamar Valley** for wildlife-watching at dusk, one of the best times to watch animals. Then, stick around for the sunset.

Mound. The narrow, curvy loop drive squeezes between firs and junipers; trailers or RVs over 25 ft (8 m) are prohibited. Locate the entrance to the Upper Terrace about 2 mi (3.2 km) south of Mammoth Village on the road toward Norris.

GOLDEN GATE

Driving south from Mammoth, the curvy road climbs 1,500 ft (460 m) in 3 mi (4.8 km) on a cliff-clinging viaduct to reach Kingman Pass. The passage through Glen Creek Canyon is known as the Golden Gate, named for the vivid color of yellow lichens on the rhyolite cliffs. While the road has been rebuilt several times, its first incarnation in 1884 was a rickety wooden trestle bridge. A unique rock pillar, which was moved with each reconstruction of the road, sits at the bottom of the climb, while at the top, **Rustic Falls** sprays down 47 ft (14 m) of natural stair-step stones. Bunsen Peak, a cone volcano, looms above. An overlook on the east side of the road between the rock pillar and falls offers a viewing location.

SWAN LAKE FLAT

Wildlife frequents Swan Lake Flat, and so do wildlife-watchers. Bring the binoculars, cameras, and telephoto lenses. Located on the Grand Loop Road about 5 mi (8 km) south of Mammoth (look for a small parking lot on the west side), the sagebrush prairie of Swan Lake Flat in Gardner's Hole offers a great chance to see gray wolves, grizzly bears, and elk. Tiny Swan Lake, which once filled

Canary Spring

the entire flat, often houses trumpeter swans in summer, along with other waterfowl. The vast, open, high-elevation valley makes for a broad arena, where almost any movement is visible. In winter, look for bison.

OBSIDIAN CLIFF

Located between Mammoth and Norris on the east side of Grand Loop Road, the 0.5-mi-long (0.8-km-long) Obsidian Cliff, a National Historic Landmark and archaeological site, resulted from a 180,000-year-old rhyolite lava flow that crystallized. Look closely to see the shiny black volcanic glass bits of obsidian in the layers, but do so with binoculars or from a car as the site is closed to exploring. Early native peoples in the area quarried the sharp obsidian for making knives, arrowheads, and other tools. North of the cliff on the west side of the road, the **Obsidian Cliff interpretive kiosk,** an early National Park Service exhibit, shows an obsidian sample you can touch.

ROARING MOUNTAIN

Five mi (8 km) north of Norris Geyser Basin, the seemingly barren hillside of Roaring Mountain is riddled with fumaroles. Steam billows from multiple vents across the hillside. While the roar has lessened considerably in the past century, you can still hear the hissing when you get out of your vehicle at the interpretive site. Excessive tree-killing heat, gases, and billowing steam make the hillside look like the aftermath of a fire. Some thermophiles survive in this toxic environment. Steam is more visible in early morning, evening, or winter.

Roaring Mountain

PETRIFIED TREE

Tucked off a side road about 0.8 mi (1.3 km) west of Tower Junction, a lone Petrified Tree trunk stands on a steep hillside. Once a giant ancient redwood, the now-petrified tree is a testament to ancient redwoods that once populated Yellowstone in a wetter climate, prior to a supervolcano eruption. A 0.3-mi (0.5-km) path leads to the solidified tree. Ravaged by souvenir seekers, this specimen is now fenced off for protection.

★ ROOSEVELT CORRALS

Adjacent to Roosevelt Lodge, the Roosevelt Corrals is the place for all things horse and Western related: stagecoach rides, horseback rides, and a wagon or horseback ride to an outdoor western cookout.

Stagecoach Adventure

tel. 307/344-7311; www.yellowstonenationalparklodges.com; daily June-early Sept.; $16 adults, $9 children 3-11

For a taste of early Western travel, take a stagecoach tour on the Stagecoach Adventure. Setting off from the Roosevelt Corrals, the half-hour ride in a replica stagecoach gives a glimpse into the park's history, and authenticity comes from the dust. The brave can ride up top.

Horseback Rides

SADDLE UP TOURS

tel. 307/344-7311; www.yellowstonenationalparklodges.com; daily early June-early Sept.

The one-hour wrangler-led horseback tour (departures noon-1:30pm; $55) goes around sagebrush flats, while the two-hour ride (9:15am; $75) makes Lost Lake a destination.

For saddling up in Western tradition for trail rides, you don't need cowboy gear. But do wear long pants, sturdy shoes (no sandals), and a hat for sun or wind protection. Children must be at least 5-8 years old (exact minimum age varies). Make reservations in advance and tip your wrangler 15 percent for day trips, 20 percent for overnights.

Old West Dinner Cookout

tel. 307/344-7311; www.yellowstonenationalparklodges.com; rides start at dusk daily early June-mid-Sept.; $66-102 adults, $53-92 children ages 8-11

The Old West Dinner Cookout is adventure dining. Guests saddle up or ride a wagon from the Roosevelt Corrals to Yancy's Hole. At the cookout, wranglers grill up steaks to order and serve up traditional cookout sides along with coffee cooked on a fire. (With advance notice, vegetarian options can replace the steak.) Check-in times at the Roosevelt Corral range 2:30pm-4:45pm (hours vary seasonally). Horseback rides take 1-2 hours to reach the site; the wagon ride takes 30-45 minutes. All return rides take 30 minutes. Reservations are required.

CALCITE SPRING AND YELLOWSTONE NARROWS

The Calcite Spring boardwalk loop (0.2 mi/0.3 km) takes in several

Roosevelt Corrals

interpretive overlooks. One peers down on steaming Calcite Spring, a white hillside with multiple vents spilling into the Yellowstone River. The other overlooks give a bit of vertigo, looking into the Narrows where the Yellowstone River squeezes into a gorge of frothing water. Views also take in a layer of columnar basalt on the opposite side of the Narrows and scads of eroded pinnacles.

TOWER FALL

Tower Fall plunges 132 ft (40 m) from its brink between rhyolite spires, dropping from a hanging valley into a ribbon that spews in a long freefall. An overlook 0.1 mi (0.2 km) from the Tower Fall parking lot offers the best view. Due to a washout in 2004, the viewing platform and trail to the base of the falls are closed. Find the site 2.3 mi (3.7 km) south of Tower Junction.

★ LAMAR VALLEY

Park guides often refer to the massive Lamar Valley as "America's Serengeti" due to its hefty numbers of **wildlife.** The Lamar River flows through the sagebrush valley, where immense herds of bison feed. Between herds, look for pronghorn, bighorn sheep, elk, bears, coyote, and wolves. The valley also provides rich hunting grounds for predators. In fall, listen for bighorn sheep butting horns or elk bugling as displays of dominance.

From Tower Junction, follow the Northeast Entrance Road east past the turnoff for Slough Creek. Multiple pullouts along the road allow for observation. Wildlife is most active at dawn and dusk; bring spotting scopes, cameras, and binoculars.

SCENIC DRIVES

NORTH ENTRANCE TO NORTHEAST ENTRANCE

DRIVING DISTANCE:
52 mi (84 km) one-way
DRIVING TIME: approx. 2 hours one-way
START: Roosevelt Arch, US-89
END: Northeast Entrance Station

The road between the **North Entrance Station** at Gardiner and the **Northeast Entrance Station** at Silver Gate and Cooke City is the only road in Yellowstone **open year-round** to private cars and RVs. The road is plowed in winter, but snowstorms can cause temporary closures in the fall, winter, and spring. For current road conditions, call 307/344-2117. Plan about two hours one-way for this tour. Add on more time for stops.

The two-lane road starts as US-89 in Gardiner, Montana, on Park Street. Drive under the **Roosevelt Arch** (RVs take the signed shortcut) to reach the entrance station. The road then climbs south through ancient mudflows, crossing the **45th Parallel** at the bridge over the Gardner River, then hitting the Montana/Wyoming state line before reaching Mammoth Hot Springs in 5 mi (8 km). Watch for

Blacktail Plateau Drive

elk, pronghorn, and bighorn sheep in the **Gardner Canyon**.

From **Mammoth Hot Springs to Tower Junction** (18 mi/29 km; 45 min) the route follows **Grand Loop Road.** Stop to see **Undine Falls** and the **Petrified Tree**. Between the two sights, **Blacktail Plateau Drive** (6 mi/9.5 km; 30 min; July-early Nov.; no RVs or trailers) offers a scenic detour on a curvy, one-way dirt road, while Grand Loop Road swings by **Blacktail Pond**, which attracts wildlife like pronghorn, coyote, and bald eagles. The route gains territorial views, goes through fire successions, and is good habitat for elk, bears, and bison. Also, to learn about this northern high plateau, tour the **Forces of the Range** (0.5 mi/0.8km) interpretive boardwalk loop.

From **Tower Junction to the Northeast Entrance** (29 mi/47 km; 60 min), the route crosses the **Yellowstone River** into **Lamar Valley** and swings northeast along **Soda Butte Creek** into the **Absaroka Mountains** (pronounced ab-ZOR-ka) that stretch into rugged peaks more than 12,000 ft (3,700 m) high. After Pebble Creek, the road climbs into the narrow passageway of **Ice Box Canyon,** flanked by frozen waterfalls in winter and early spring. The road continues to climb into a high-elevation, forested valley tucked below **Barronette Peak,** which spouts with waterfalls in May. Scan its cliffs for mountain goats before reaching the Northeast Entrance.

UPPER GRAND LOOP ROAD

DRIVING DISTANCE: 70 mi (113 km) round-trip
DRIVING TIME: approx. 3 hours round-trip
START/END: Mammoth Hot Springs

Absaroka Mountains above Soda Butte Creek

Upper Grand Loop Road links **Mammoth Hot Springs** with **Norris Geyser Basin, Canyon Village,** and **Tower-Roosevelt.** The road east from **Mammoth to Tower Junction** (18 mi/29 km; 45 min) is open year-round; all other segments of the Upper Grand Loop Road are closed in winter. You can drive the entire loop (late May-early Nov.) in three hours; stops and side trips add time.

From **Mammoth Hot Springs to Norris Junction** (21 mi/34 km; 45 min; late Apr.-early Nov.), the road climbs south through the hoodoos, monster travertine boulders formed by a landslide on Terrace Mountain. It then crawls along the cliffs of **Golden Gate** before topping out at **Swan Lake Flat,** where you can often spot wolves and bison. Continuing south, you'll pass **Obsidian Cliff,** a site of geological, Native American, and historical significance. Stop again at **Roaring Mountain** to listen to the thermal activity and look for trumpeter swans in nearby **Twin Lakes.** Your first leg ends at the **Norris Geyser Basin,** a hotbed of geothermal activity.

From the Norris Junction, go east toward **Canyon Village** (12 mi/19.5 km; 30 min; late Apr.-early Nov.). Continue the loop north from Canyon Village to reach **Tower Junction** (19 mi/31 km; 45 min; late May-early Nov.). The road climbs over Dunraven Pass before descending to Tower Fall and the Tower-Roosevelt area before completing the loop by heading west to Mammoth. Note that in 2021, the road on the north side between Dunraven Pass and Tower Fall will be closed for construction.

BEST HIKES

BUNSEN PEAK AND OSPREY FALLS

DISTANCE: 4.2 mi (6.8 km) round-trip or a 6.6- to 11.6-mi (10.6- to 18.7-km) loop
DURATION: 3-7 hours round-trip
ELEVATION CHANGE: 1,278-2,058 ft (390-627 m)
EFFORT: Strenuous
TRAILHEAD: Old Bunsen Peak Road Trailhead, 4.8 mi (7.7 km) south of Mammoth on the east side of Grand Loop Road

The peak, a volcanic cone named for Robert Bunsen, who invented the Bunsen burner, contains a summit weather station. The building and connecting power lines pose a minor disruption to the wilderness feel. In summer, go early to nab a parking spot at the popular trailhead.

Starting in a sagebrush meadow, the trail climbs through steep forests, meadows, and 1988 burns to the 8,564-ft (2,610-m) summit. Shortly after starting the climb, spot the Golden Gate from above along with Glen Creek Canyon hoodoos. The trail winds back and forth around the mountain, passing **Cathedral Rock** at 1.4 mi (2.3 km), where views

Sepulcher Mountain

plunge to Mammoth Hot Springs. Steep switchbacks then lead across talus slopes to the summit. The reward is the view of Electric Peak in the Gallatin Range and Gardner's Hole. For the shortest hike, retrace your route back down. Or, for an alternative, drop eastward 1.4 steep mi (2.3 km) through a burn zone to the **Old Bunsen Peak Road,** turning right to circle 3 gentle mi (4.8 km) (shared by bikers) around the south of **Bunsen Peak** (6.6 mi/10.6 km total).

Strong hikers can lengthen the loop with a descent and return climb to see 150-ft (46-m) **Osprey Falls** on the Gardner River. Descend eastward from the peak to the Old Bunsen Peak Road, then turn left to find the Osprey Falls Trailhead. From the trailhead, a 1.4-mi (2.6-km) trail traverses the edge of Sheepeater Canyon, with the basalt-columned Sheepeater Cliffs visible on the opposite side. Drop down steep, narrow, sunny switchbacks into the ravine below the falls. After climbing the 780 ft (238 m) back up, follow the old road south around Bunsen Peak to return to your vehicle. Those wanting to avoid the Bunsen Peak climb can hike out and back on the old road to see Osprey Falls (8.8 mi/14.2 km; 780 ft/237 m elevation gain).

SEPULCHER MOUNTAIN

DISTANCE: 12.5 mi (20.1 km) round-trip
DURATION: 7 hours round-trip
ELEVATION CHANGE: 2,366 ft (721 m)
EFFORT: Strenuous
TRAILHEAD: Glen Creek Trailhead opposite Old Bunsen Peak Road Trailhead, 4.8 mi (7.7 km) south of Mammoth

Lost Lake on Lost Lake Loop (top); basalt columns in Yellowstone Narrows (middle); bridge over Hellroaring Creek (bottom)

Distance: 1.2 mi (1.9 km) round-trip
Duration: 1 hour round-trip
Elevation change: 220 ft (67 m)
Effort: Easy
Trailhead: a small pullout with limited parking on the Northeast Entrance Road, 3 mi (4.8 km) north of Soda Butte Trailhead and 1.5 mi (2.4 km) south of Pebble Creek Campground

An idyllic little lake sitting at about 7,000 ft (2,100 m) in elevation, **Trout Lake** is actually the largest of three small lakes tucked near the Northeast Entrance Road in the **Absaroka Mountains.** From the trailhead, the path catapults vertically through a Douglas fir forest to the lake. About 0.3 mi (0.5 km) up the trail, the **route splits** to circle the lake. Go either way. The trail circles the shoreline, which is semi-forested on the east shore and open meadows on the west shore. In early summer, phlox blankets the hillsides, cutthroat trout spawn in the inlet stream, and ospreys hang around to fish.

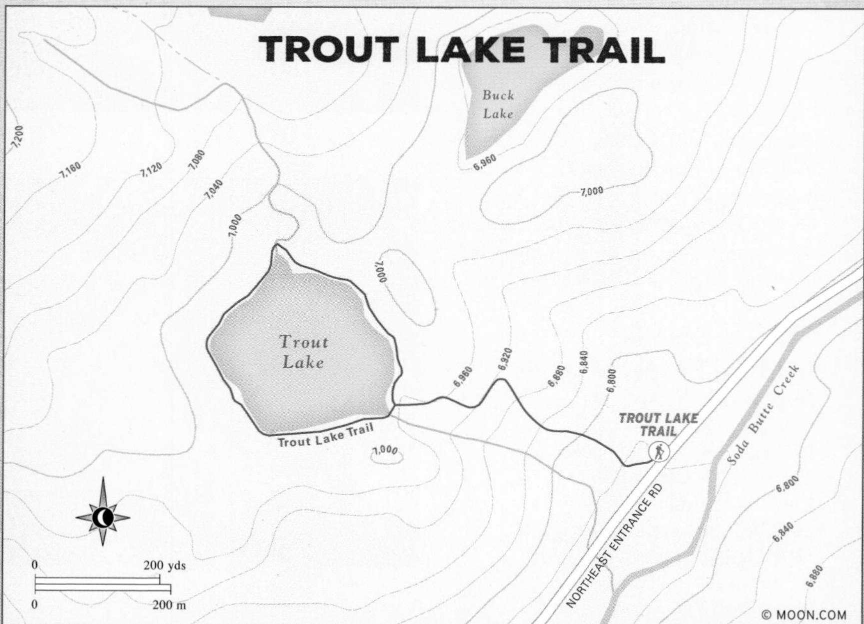

TROUT LAKE TRAIL

Buck Lake
Trout Lake
Trout Lake Trail
TROUT LAKE TRAIL
NORTHEAST ENTRANCE RD
Soda Butte Creek
7,200
7,160
7,120
7,080
7,040
7,000
6,960
7,000
7,000
6,960
6,920
6,880
6,840
6,800
7,000
6,800
6,840
6,880
0 200 yds
0 200 m
© MOON.COM

Bunsen Peak

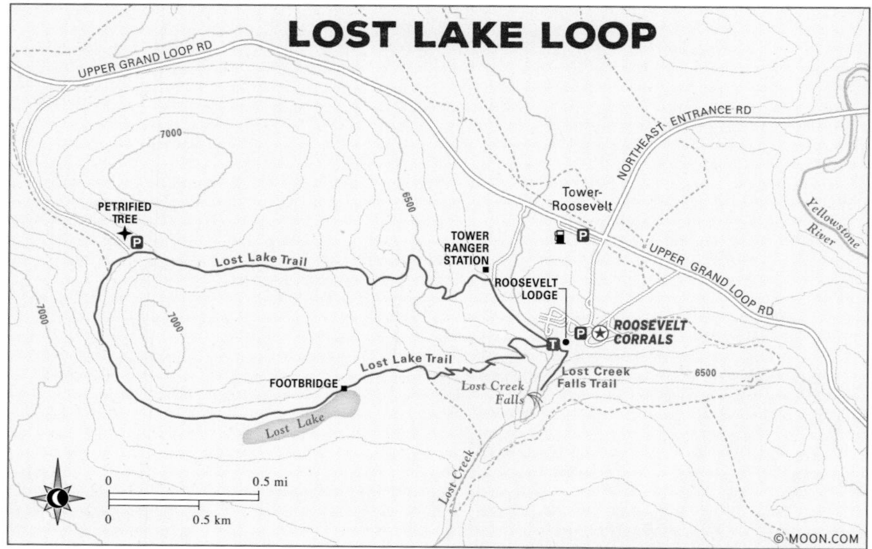

Sepulcher Mountain attracts hikers out for big views without the crowds of Bunsen Peak. But since the trail uses the same crowded parking lot at Bunsen Peak, you'll need to get an early start. The trail begins with a gentle 1.8-mi (2.9-km) walk through sagebrush meadows below **Terrace Mountain,** home to bighorn sheep. Continue through several junctions where trails turn off to Fawn Pass, Snow Pass, and Sportsman Lake Trail. After the third turnoff, begin climbing the switchbacks up an open mountainside with views of Electric Peak. With less than 0.5 mi (0.8 km) to go, the trail enters a forest before popping out on the summit for views of the Absaroka Mountains. A jaunt along the 9,652-ft (2,942-m) **summit** yields more views, including the Yellowstone River and Gardiner far below.

Continue the loop by following the cliff edge and then descending through pines and meadows overlooking Mammoth Hot Springs. At the junction with the Clagett Butte Trail, turn right to climb uphill to the **Snow Pass Trail.** Turn right again for 1 mi (2 km) to cross Snow Pass. Turn left to return to Glen Creek Trailhead.

LOST LAKE LOOP

DISTANCE: 4 mi (6.4 km) round-trip
DURATION: 2.5 hours round-trip
ELEVATION CHANGE: 608 ft (185 m)
EFFORT: Moderate
TRAILHEAD: Behind Roosevelt Lodge, the Petrified Tree parking lot, or Tower Fall Campground

Hikers can start this trail from a variety of trailheads, and it has plenty of things to see: a waterfall, the small lake, Petrified Tree, and views of the Absaroka Mountains. The trail is also used by horses.

From behind Roosevelt Lodge, take the left spur to the **Lost Creek Falls Trail,** which climbs up a pine-shaded ravine to the 40-ft (12-m) falls. Return to the junction to continue up the **Lost Lake Trail.** Switchbacks head up the steep hill to reach the small bridge at the lake's outlet. The trail rims the lake until it heads west through another ravine to **Petrified Tree.** From the Petrified Tree parking lot, the trail mounts a hill east to a sagebrush meadow before dropping to swing behind **Tower Ranger Station** and then around to Roosevelt Lodge.

NARROWS OF THE YELLOWSTONE RIVER

DISTANCE: 4 mi (6.4 km) round-trip
DURATION: 2.5 hours round-trip
ELEVATION CHANGE: 393 ft (120 m)
EFFORT: Easy
TRAILHEAD: Yellowstone River Picnic Area Trailhead, 1.2 mi (1.9 km) east of Tower Junction on the Northeast Entrance Road

A steep grunt uphill through sagebrush meadows with pink sticky geraniums and arrowleaf balsamroot leads to the east rim of the Narrows of the Yellowstone River. The trail saunters along the rim above the deep canyon and has several viewpoints. In 1 mi (1.6 km), the trail overlooks **Calcite Springs.** As it traverses a ridge 500 ft (150 m) above the Yellowstone River, the route affords spectacular views of the narrows, sculpted minarets, and columnar basalt. It's also a good place to spot bighorn sheep, ospreys, and peregrine falcons. Pronghorn cross the ridge, and marmots live in the rocks. In 2 mi (3.2 km), you'll reach a **four-way trail junction**, which is where most hikers turn around. Those with gumption add on a 0.8-mi (1.3-km) drop to the Yellowstone River and back on the spur trail that plunges steeply 0.4 mi (0.6 km) to the historic **Bannock Indian Ford.**

BACKPACKING

In North Yellowstone, the top spots for backpacking are in Absaroka Mountains and along the Yellowstone River.

BLISS PASS

19-21 mi (31-34 km)

In the Absaroka Mountains, the grassy Bliss Pass trek yields rugged mountain views and walking through a combo of river valleys, subalpine meadows, and forest. The pass connects Pebble Creek with Slough Creek on a point-to-point hike. The three trailheads of Slough Creek, Pebble Creek, and Warm Creek access the route, but the eastern trailheads make for 1,000 ft (300 m) less of elevation climbing. Challenges with this trip include fords and setting up a car shuttle. No backcountry campsites are on the central cross over Bliss Pass. Bliss Pass is snow-free by mid-July or so; fording the creeks is easier in August.

YELLOWSTONE RIVER

16.5-20 mi (26.5-32 km)

The Yellowstone River slices between the Buffalo and Blacktail Deer Plateaus, before plunging through the Black Canyon of the Yellowstone. Since the closure of the west end of the Black Canyon of the Yellowstone Trail at Gardiner, point-to-point backpacking trips in the canyon go from **Hellroaring Creek Trailhead to Blacktail Creek Trailhead.** Plan three days for the trip, and mentally prepare for the ascent on the last day. Watch for ticks. Due to the short mileage on the middle day, explore the Yellowstone River Trail running west downstream through the Black

Canyon, but note that it is only maintained for about 2 mi (3.2 km). With lower elevation, this backpack trip is usually viable in early May, but hikers must use the longer Hellroaring Bridge route (20 mi/32 km) rather than the shortcut ford that isn't safe until August.

PERMITS

Backpackers must obtain permits ($3/person, children 8 and younger free) for assigned backcountry campsites. Permits are available in person 48 hours in advance from the backcountry offices. For more information, see the *Essentials* chapter.

BIKING

Biking is not permitted on trails inside the park, but paved and dirt roads offer places to ride.

ROAD BIKING

Late March to mid-April, roads open to bicyclists but remain closed to vehicles, offering car-free riding from Mammoth to Norris and from Tower Junction to Tower Fall. Bring your own bike; rentals are not available. Road bikers can ride any paved roads, but be aware of narrow shoulders and curvy roads with large RVs on them.

MOUNTAIN BIKING

Three popular mountain bike routes are in the park's north end.

Old Gardiner Road

5 mi (8 km) one-way; late Apr.-early Nov.

For 1,500 ft (460 m) of climbing or descending, the Old Gardiner Road connects Gardiner with Mammoth Hot Springs. While cars can only go downhill from Mammoth, bikers can go both directions. Road access is behind Mammoth Hot Springs Hotel or at the North Entrance Station.

Bunsen Peak Loop

6 mi (9.7 km) one-way; May-early Nov.

South of Mammoth, Bunsen Peak Loop starts from Bunsen Peak Trailhead to circle Bunsen Peak's east side. The trail drops through employee housing before joining the Grand Loop Road between the Upper and Lower Terraces.

Blacktail Plateau Drive

6 mi (9.7 km) one-way; mid-July-early Nov.

On the Grand Loop Road 9.5 mi (15.3 km) east of Mammoth, Blacktail Plateau Drive rolls through higher-elevation terrain with wildlife. Vehicles can only go eastbound, but bicyclists can travel in both directions.

WINTER SPORTS

CROSS-COUNTRY SKIING AND SNOWSHOEING

Winter transforms Yellowstone into a prime cross-country ski and snowshoe locale. All unplowed roads become trails, which allows for experiencing them differently than in summer. With the exception of the plowed road

biking around Bunsen Peak (left); cross-country skiers on Snow Pass Trail (right)

between Gardiner, Mammoth, and Cooke City, all other roads closed to wheeled vehicles are open for skiing. Some have snowcoach and snowmobile traffic. Winter trail maps are located online (www.nps.gov/yell) and at Albright Visitor Center.

Around Mammoth Hot Springs, **Upper Terrace Loop, Bunsen Peak Trail,** and **Blacktail Plateau Trail** are groomed for cross-country skiing. Other trails for skiers are the **Snow Pass, Sheepeater,** and **Indian Creek-Bighorn Loop** trails. Warming huts sit at the Indian Creek and Upper Terrace Trailheads. Parking to access all trails is at Upper Terrace Loop and the lower Bunsen Peak Trailhead. The **Old Gardiner Road Trail,** located behind the hotel, and **Upper Terrace Loop** provide good snowshoeing.

Rentals and Guides

BEAR DEN SKI SHOP

tel. 307/344-7311; www.yellowstonenationalparklodges.com; 7:30am-5pm daily mid-Dec.-Feb.

In Mammoth Hot Springs, the Bear Den Ski Shop rents gear for a half or full day for $3-15 per item: snowshoes, gaiters, cross-country skis, poles, ski boots, and Yaktrax. A full-day ski package costs $27, and discounts are given for three days or more. The shop also offers repairs, wax, lessons, and guided tours to Tower Fall. By reservation, **ski shuttles** (Sat.-Sun., Tues., and Thurs. mid-Dec.-Feb.; $24 each way, kids half price) go to **Indian Creek.** Catch the snowcoach both directions for self-guided skiing on Indian Creek Trails or one-way for skiing back to Mammoth.

GUIDED SNOWSHOE TOURS

2pm Fri.-Sun. and Wed. late Dec.-Feb.; free

Park naturalists guide free two-hour snowshoe tours around Upper Terrace Drive in winter. Bring snowshoes, winter layers, and a pack to meet at Upper Terrace Drive parking lot.

NORTH YELLOWSTONE FOOD OPTIONS

NAME	LOCATION	TYPE
Mammoth Hotel Dining Room	Mammoth Hot Springs	sit-down restaurant
Mammoth Terrace Grill	Mammoth Hot Springs	sit-down restaurant
Mammoth General Store	Mammoth Hot Springs	take-out
★ **Roosevelt Lodge Dining Room**	Roosevelt Lodge	sit-down restaurant
Roosevelt Store	Roosevelt Lodge	convenience groceries
Tower Fall General Store	Tower Fall	convenience groceries and snack bar

YELLOWSTONE FOREVER INSTITUTE

tel. 406/848-2400; www.yellowstone.org

Yellowstone Forever Institute offers expert-led educational ski and snowshoe trips starting from Gardiner, Mammoth, or Lamar Valley. Private tours, one-day, and multiday programs are available with varied rates.

Snowcoach Tours

From Mammoth Hot Springs Hotel, **Xanterra** (tel. 307/344-7311; www.yellowstonenationalparklodges.com; 12:30pm-5:30pm, Tues., Thurs., Sat., and Sun.; $89) runs snowcoach tours to Norris Geyser Basin to walk to Porcelain Basin's steamy landscape.

FOOD

Xanterra (tel. 307/344-7311; www.yellowstonenationalparklodges.com) operates the park lodge restaurants, grills, and cookouts. All restaurants are first-come, first-seated, except that **reservations** are mandatory in winter for dinner at **Mammoth Hotel Dining Room.** In all park restaurants, casual dress is common; no dresses, heels, or ties needed. For traveling, all lodges sell deli lunches to go or items to create your own lunch.

FOOD	PRICE	HOURS
contemporary American	moderate	6:30am-10am, 11:30am-2:30pm, 5pm-10pm daily late Apr.-early Nov. and mid-Dec.-early Mar. (till 9pm mid-Sept.-early Nov.)
fast food	budget	7am-9pm daily late Apr.-mid-Oct.; hours vary seasonally
fast food	budget	7:30am-9:30pm daily in summer; shorter winter hours
Western American	moderate	7am-10am, 11:30am-9:30pm daily June-Sept.
general goods	budget	7:30am-9:30pm daily early June-Aug.
general goods and snacks	budget	7:30am-9:30pm daily mid-May-mid-Sept.

STANDOUTS

Roosevelt Lodge Dining Room

tel. 307/344-7311; www.yellowstonenationalparklodges.com; 7am-10am and 11:30am-9:30pm daily June-Sept.; $8-30

With a cowboy-friendly menu and a lobby bar, dining at Roosevelt Lodge just feels Western. Lauded by many locals as the best food in the park, Roosevelt Lodge Dining Room designs menu items for flexibility with plenty of size, topping, side, and gluten-free choices. Breakfast skillets, Tex-Mex, bison, and smoked barbecue ribs are house specialties. At 4:30pm, the menu expands with additional Western-style dinner options. A kiddie menu is available. You can also order to-go items.

BEST PICNIC SPOTS

Sheepeater Cliff

On Upper Grand Loop Road between Mammoth Hot Springs and Norris Junction, across from Indian Creek Campground

This small, sunny picnic area accessed via a dirt road sits at the base of Sheepeater Cliff. Lava cooling 500,000 years ago formed columnar basalt, creating a vertical wall of pillars. It is named for the Shoshone Indians, the Tukadika, who lived and hunted bighorn sheep in Yellowstone. The picnic area includes a few tables and an accessible vault toilet. It also has a short trail to the left that goes to the top of the cliffs.

Lava Creek

On Upper Grand Loop Road between Mammoth Hot Springs and Tower Junction, near Lava Creek Trailhead

NORTH YELLOWSTONE CAMPGROUNDS

NAME	LOCATION	SEASON
Mammoth	Mammoth Hot Springs	year-round
Indian Creek	Between Mammoth Hot Springs and Norris Junction	mid-June–mid-Sept.
Tower Fall	South of Tower Junction	late May–late Sept.
★ **Slough Creek**	Northeast Entrance Road	mid-June–mid-Oct.
★ **Pebble Creek**	Northeast Entrance Road	mid-June–late Sept.

A few picnic tables and an accessible vault toilet sit on Lava Creek, a tributary of the Gardner River. You can tack on a walk to see nearby Undine Falls on the Lava Creek Trail, a different perspective than from the usual viewpoint on the road.

Warm Creek Picnic Area

Yellowstone River

On the Northeast Entrance Road between Tower Junction and Lamar Valley, east of Yellowstone River Bridge

The trailhead for the Narrows of the Yellowstone River Trail also departs from here, making it a good place for lunch and a hike. It has picnic tables, a few grills (bring your own firewood), and an accessible vault toilet.

Warm Creek

On the Northeast Entrance Road between Lamar Valley and the

SITES AND AMENITIES	RV LIMIT	PRICE	RESERVATIONS
85 sites; most can accommodate RVs; tent pads at 51 sites; flush toilets and water faucets; accessible sites available	up to 75 ft/23 m (30 ft/9 m in winter)	$20	no
70 sites; vault toilets and potable water; 1 accessible site available	35 ft/11 m	$15	no
31 sites; vault toilets and hand water pump	30 ft/9 m	$15	no
23 sites; vault toilets and hand water pumps	30 ft/9 m	$15	no
27 sites; only a few fit large RVs; vault toilets and hand water pump; 1 accessible site available	55 ft/17 m	$15	no

Northeast Entrance Station, in the Absaroka Mountains
With tables and an accessible vault toilet, this shady picnic area sits on Soda Butte Creek, which offers good fishing for Yellowstone cutthroat trout. It is often less crowded because of its remote location.

CAMPING

This region of Yellowstone has smaller campgrounds than elsewhere in the park. With the exception of Mammoth Campground, each offers a quiet place to get away from crowds, although you must claim a campsite early, often before 8am July-early August. Amenities include potable water, picnic tables, bear boxes for food storage, fire rings with grills, and flush or vault toilets, but no showers. Accessible sites are available at Mammoth and Indian Creek Campgrounds.

Reservations

Reservations are not accepted; all campgrounds are **first-come, first-served.**

Tips

Check online (www.nps.gov/yell) to see what time the campgrounds filled on the previous day and then

NORTH YELLOWSTONE LODGING

NAME	LOCATION	SEASON
★ Mammoth Hot Springs Hotel	Mammoth Hot Springs	late Apr.-early Nov. and mid-Dec.-early Mar.
Roosevelt Lodge and Cabins	Tower-Roosevelt	June-early Sept.

aim to grab a campsite before then. In midsummer, campgrounds can fill before 8am. Due to the time-consuming task of moving camps and finding another campsite, you are better off staying for several days at these campgrounds to explore other portions of the park on day trips.

STANDOUTS

Slough Creek Campground

mid-June-mid-Oct.; $15

Often filling up by 8am midsummer, Slough Creek Campground is prized for its remoteness, solitude, wildlife-watching, and fishing. Lined up along Slough Creek at 6,250 ft (1,900 m) in elevation, the 23 campsites vary from open sagebrush meadows to shady conifers. Prime campsites include creek frontage within earshot of the water. All sites have less than 30-ft (9-m) parking pads; amenities include hand pumps for water and vault toilets. This primitive campground is accessed via the dirt Slough Creek Road, 5 mi (8 km) east of Tower Junction on the Northeast Entrance Road.

Pebble Creek Campground

mid-June-late Sept.; $15

North of Lamar Valley at 6,900 ft (2,100 m) elevation, Pebble Creek Campground loops through forest-flanked wildflower meadows. It often fills up by 8am midsummer. Some of the 27 campsites are open with views of the surrounding Absaroka Mountains, and a few are walk-in tent-only sites. Facilities include a hand pump for water and vault toilets. Nearby, you can access the trailhead to Trout Lake, fishing in Soda Butte Creek, wildlife-watching in Lamar Valley, or Silver Gate and Cooke City. The campground is along the Northeast Entrance Road, 13 mi (21 km) past Slough Creek Road.

LODGING

Reservations

In-park lodging fills up first and fast. **Xanterra** (tel. 307/344-7311; www.yellowstonenationalparklodges.com) runs all the lodges inside Yellowstone. Reservations are recommended 12-18 months in advance for summer starting May 1. Winter reservations open March 15. Cancellations may free up last-minute bookings, but with limited choices.

Tips

In keeping with the historical ambience, most in-park rooms and cabins lack televisions, radios, telephones, and air-conditioning, so expect

OPTIONS	PRICE
hotel rooms, suites, and cabins	hotel rooms and cabins starting at $118
cabins	cabins starting at $110

rustic experiences. If you are a light sleeper, bring earplugs; if you are traveling during midsummer heat, you may want to bring a small fan with an extension cord (very few are available from the front desk). ADA rooms are available.

STANDOUTS

Mammoth Hot Springs Hotel

1 Grand Loop Rd.; late Apr.-early Nov. and mid-Dec.-early Mar.; $118-330 rooms and cabins, $503-602 suites

In a busy tourist center, Mammoth Hot Springs Hotel is a large complex with 79 hotel rooms and 125 cabins. The U.S. Cavalry built the north wing of the four-story hotel in 1911; the main lobby and remainder of the hotel were erected in 1936. A $30 million renovation was completed in 2019, and private bathrooms were added to all hotel guest rooms. The historic attraction off the lobby is the **Map Room,** containing a new bar and a large wooden U.S. map constructed in 1937. The hotel is within walking distance from the Albright Visitor Center, travertine terrace boardwalks, trailheads, and two restaurants. Free Internet access for guests is available in public spaces. In winter, Mammoth is the only hotel in the park accessible by private vehicles on plowed roads, although rooms are limited.

The lodge has several types of accommodations, including guest rooms and two-room suites, both with private bathrooms. Cabin styles include one- or two-room rustic cabins with no bathrooms, cabins with baths, and hot tub cabins. Cabins without baths can use shared community facilities. An elevator accesses the upper floors of the hotel. Four cabins have the added perk of fenced private hot tubs.

INFORMATION AND SERVICES

The main hubs for services in North Yellowstone are Mammoth Village and Tower-Roosevelt. Open year-round, **Mammoth Village,** near Mammoth Hot Springs, is home to the Albright Visitor Center, Mammoth Hot Springs Hotel, historic Fort Yellowstone, a campground, a picnic area, and other services. **Tower-Roosevelt,** at Tower Junction where Upper Grand Loop Road and Northeast Entrance Road meet, is smaller, with Roosevelt Lodge, Roosevelt Corrals, a general store, and a ranger station.

Entrance Stations

$35 vehicle, $30 motorcycles, $20 hike-in/bike-in; annual Yellowstone pass $70

Two entrance stations provide access to North Yellowstone. The two entrances are connected by a 52-mi (84-km) road that is open year-round (except for temporary winter storm closures).

North Entrance

The North Entrance (open year-round) sits on US-89 on the edge of Gardiner, Montana. Smaller vehicles can enter the park through the Roosevelt Arch; RVs and trailers should take the signed shortcut from Park Street to the entrance station. After you pass the pay station, the park hub of Mammoth Hot Springs is 5 mi (8 km) south.

Northeast Entrance

On US-212, the remote Northeast Entrance is west of Silver Gate and Cooke City, Montana. Snow closes the roads east of Cooke City (mid-Oct.-late May), effectively making the Northeast Entrance a dead end in winter.

Visitors Centers

Albright Visitor Center

tel. 307/344-7381; 8am-6pm daily summer, 9am-5pm daily fall, winter, spring

The renovated Albright Visitor Center is located in Mammoth Hot Springs. One of the historic buildings from the days when the U.S. Cavalry ran the park, the red-tiled roof, brick structure, and large-columned veranda retain the look of Fort Yellowstone when it served as quarters for bachelor officers. The visitors center has park maps, trail information, brochures, updates, and a **backcountry office** (8am-4:30pm daily June-Aug.) with permits for backcountry camping, boating, and fishing. Exhibits cover cultural history, wildlife, and the northern area of the park. There's also a small bookstore inside.

TRANSPORTATION

Getting There

The road between the North Entrance and Northeast Entrance, which runs through the northern portion of Yellowstone National Park, is open year-round, and is the only park road accessible by private cars and RVs in winter. Snowstorms can cause temporary closures during fall, winter, and spring. Call for current **road conditions** (tel. 307/344-2117). Due to limited snow-free seasons, construction happens in summer; you may encounter waits of 15-30 minutes in construction zones (find these online).

From North Entrance

Mammoth Village is 5 mi (8 km) south of the North Entrance, via the North Entrance Road (US-89; open year-round). The drive takes about 20 minutes.

From Northeast Entrance

Tower Junction and the park hub of Roosevelt are 30 mi (48 km) west of the Northeast Entrance (open year-round, but not accessible from the east in winter), via the Northeast Entrance Road. The drive can take up to one hour in the summer.

Mammoth Village to Tower Junction

From Mammoth Village, the two-lane Grand Loop Road travels east for 19 mi (31 km) across the Blacktail Deer Plateau to Tower Junction and the park hub of Roosevelt. The drive from Mammoth to Tower Junction can take one hour or more in summer.

From Norris Geyser Basin

From Norris Geyser Basin, the drive to Mammoth Village is 21 mi (34 km) north along Grand Loop Road. The drive can take an hour in summer.

From Canyon Village

From Canyon Village, Grand Loop Road climbs in a curvy 19 mi (31 km) from Canyon Junction over Dunraven Pass to Tower Junction at the hub of Roosevelt. The road closes mid-October-mid-June. This road will be closed for construction in 2021.

Parking

Find parking streetside in towns and villages or in parking lots at trailheads, lodges, picnic areas, and campgrounds in Yellowstone.

Mammoth Hot Springs

Parking in Mammoth Hot Springs can be crowded. Streetside parking is available by the visitors center, post office, and eateries. Five parking lots flank the Lower Terraces. Upper Terrace Drive has pullovers and two small parking lots; an additional lot is at the junction of Grand Loop Road and Upper Terrace Drive.

Lamar Valley

Lamar Valley has pullouts for parking, some paved and some gravel. Tiny overlook areas have a few parking spots, and trailheads have limited parking.

Gas

Gas stations (tel. 406/848-7548) are located at Mammoth (mid-May-mid-Oct.) and Tower Junction (June-Sept.). You can pay at the pump 24 hours a day with a credit card; in summer, you can also pay with cash.

Grand Prismatic Spring

OLD FAITHFUL AND THE GEYSER BASINS

THE WESTERN ARC OF YELLOWSTONE'S SUPERVOLCANO HOUSes a string of geyser basins that contain some of the world's most active hydrothermal features. Paint pots simmer with colorful microscopic creatures. Mud pots bubble like witches' cauldrons. Fumaroles blow off steam, and geysers spout scalding water.

Rumbling with geothermal gusto, Upper Geyser Basin has the largest concentration of geysers. Old Faithful draws crowds for its regular eruptions, and hot pools yield mesmerizing colors. For winter visitors, the otherworldly landscape vents copious steam.

Midway Geyser Basin houses two of Yellowstone's largest geothermal features: Grand Prismatic Spring and Excelsior Geyser. Lower Geyser Basin spreads across the largest piece of landscape, almost 11 square miles (28 sq km) of steaming portals from the earth's bowels. Norris Geyser Basin harbors the hottest hydrothermals and Steamboat Geyser, the world's tallest geyser.

This supervolcano arc is one of the most active geothermal zones in Yellowstone; it is also the most popular with throngs of visitors in summer. But nowhere will you see such utter uniqueness.

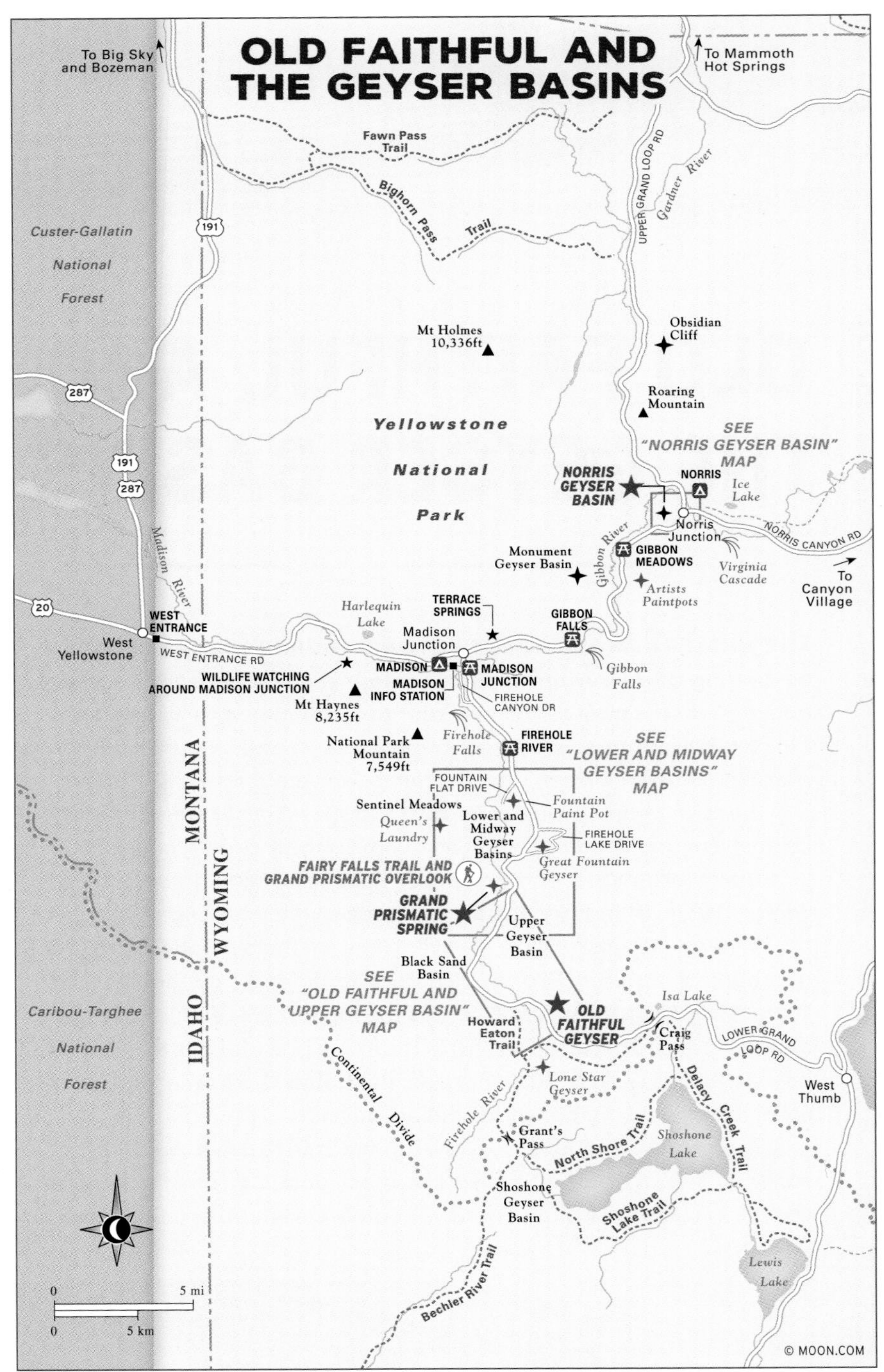
OLD FAITHFUL AND THE GEYSER BASINS
To Big Sky and Bozeman
To Mammoth Hot Springs
Fawn Pass Trail
Bighorn Pass Trail
UPPER GRAND LOOP RD
Gardner River
191
Custer-Gallatin National Forest
Mt Holmes 10,336ft
Obsidian Cliff
287
Roaring Mountain
Yellowstone National Park
SEE "NORRIS GEYSER BASIN" MAP
NORRIS GEYSER BASIN
NORRIS
Ice Lake
Norris Junction
NORRIS CANYON RD
Gibbon River
GIBBON MEADOWS
Monument Geyser Basin
Virginia Cascade
Artists Paintpots
To Canyon Village
Madison River
20
Harlequin Lake
TERRACE SPRINGS
GIBBON FALLS
WEST ENTRANCE
West Yellowstone
WEST ENTRANCE RD
Madison Junction
MADISON
MADISON JUNCTION
Gibbon Falls
WILDLIFE WATCHING AROUND MADISON JUNCTION
MADISON INFO STATION
Mt Haynes 8,235ft
FIREHOLE CANYON DR
National Park Mountain 7,549ft
Firehole Falls
FIREHOLE RIVER
SEE "LOWER AND MIDWAY GEYSER BASINS" MAP
MONTANA
FOUNTAIN FLAT DRIVE
Fountain Paint Pot
Sentinel Meadows
Queen's Laundry
Lower and Midway Geyser Basins
FIREHOLE LAKE DRIVE
Great Fountain Geyser
WYOMING
FAIRY FALLS TRAIL AND GRAND PRISMATIC OVERLOOK
GRAND PRISMATIC SPRING
Upper Geyser Basin
Black Sand Basin
SEE "OLD FAITHFUL AND UPPER GEYSER BASIN" MAP
Isa Lake
Caribou-Targhee National Forest
IDAHO
Howard Eaton Trail
OLD FAITHFUL GEYSER
Craig Pass
LOWER GRAND LOOP RD
West Thumb
Continental Divide
Lone Star Geyser
Delacy Creek Trail
Firehole River
Grant's Pass
North Shore Trail
Shoshone Lake
Shoshone Geyser Basin
Shoshone Lake Trail
Lewis Lake
Bechler River Trail
0 5 mi
0 5 km
© MOON.COM

TOP 3

★ **1. GRAND PRISMATIC SPRING:** The largest hot springs in the United States comprise vivid blue water surrounded by radiating browns and oranges (page 95).

★ **2. OLD FAITHFUL GEYSER:** This geyser spews hot water up to 185 ft (56 m) into the air about every 90 minutes—a regularity you can set your watch to (page 95).

★ **3. NORRIS GEYSER BASIN:** Walk through the hottest and most changeable geothermal basin in the park (page 101).

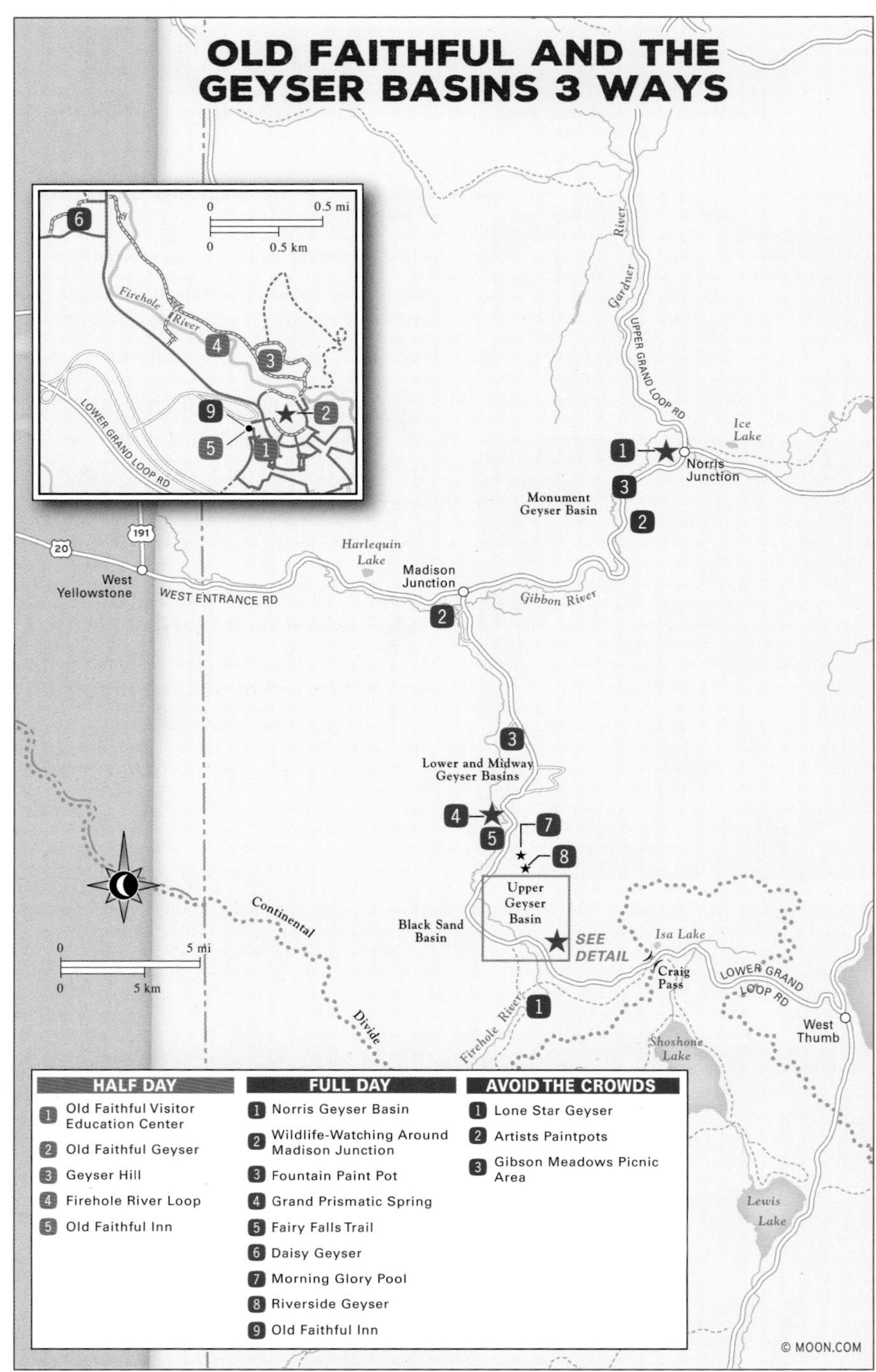
OLD FAITHFUL AND THE GEYSER BASINS 3 WAYS
0
0.5 mi
0
0.5 km
Firehole River
LOWER GRAND LOOP RD
Gardner River
UPPER GRAND LOOP RD
Ice Lake
Norris Junction
Monument Geyser Basin
191
20
Harlequin Lake
West Yellowstone
WEST ENTRANCE RD
Madison Junction
Gibbon River
Lower and Midway Geyser Basins
Upper Geyser Basin
Black Sand Basin
SEE DETAIL
Continental Divide
0
5 mi
0
5 km
Isa Lake
Craig Pass
LOWER GRAND LOOP RD
West Thumb
Firehole River
Shoshone Lake
Lewis Lake
HALF DAY
1 Old Faithful Visitor Education Center
2 Old Faithful Geyser
3 Geyser Hill
4 Firehole River Loop
5 Old Faithful Inn
FULL DAY
1 Norris Geyser Basin
2 Wildlife-Watching Around Madison Junction
3 Fountain Paint Pot
4 Grand Prismatic Spring
5 Fairy Falls Trail
6 Daisy Geyser
7 Morning Glory Pool
8 Riverside Geyser
9 Old Faithful Inn
AVOID THE CROWDS
1 Lone Star Geyser
2 Artists Paintpots
3 Gibson Meadows Picnic Area
© MOON.COM

OLD FAITHFUL AND THE GEYSER BASINS 3 WAYS

HALF DAY

If you only have a few hours, there's only one place to go. Head straight to Old Faithful and the Upper Geyser Basin.

1 Start off with a stop in the **Old Faithful Visitor Education Center** to learn when Old Faithful Geyser is scheduled to erupt and plan your time around that.

2 Catch the famous **Old Faithful Geyser** erupting roughly every 90 minutes or so. Plan to arrive about 30 minutes prior to the eruption if you want a seat in the arena.

3 Walk the loop around **Geyser Hill** to see smaller geysers and hot pools above the Firehole River.

4 Follow the boardwalk, if time permits, to the **Firehole River Loop.** Check out the activity at Grand Geyser, Grotto Geyser, and Castle Geyser. You'll also pass Beauty Pool and Chromatic Pool hot springs and hop back and forth across the Firehole River.

5 End by touring the immense lobby of **Old Faithful Inn,** a historic national park icon.

1

4

FULL DAY

A grand day in Yellowstone's geyser basins strings together the hottest and most changing basin with sights in the Lower, Midway, and Upper Geyser Basins. Between them, you can catch sight of wildlife. Parking lots often fill up at these popular sights between 9am and 4pm. You may need to bypass some temporarily and return later.

1 Loop around boardwalks through **Norris Geyser Basin** where two basins contain the fastest-changing and hottest volcanic features in Yellowstone. See the world's tallest and most acidic geysers in Back Basin, and stroll through Porcelain Basin to enjoy the colorful springs.

2 Head to **Madison Junction** and **watch for wildlife** such as bison around the confluence of the Gibbon and Firehole Rivers where they become the Madison River.

3 Tour the **Fountain Paint Pot** interpretive boardwalk in the Lower Geyser Basin, which views all four of Yellowstone's volcanic features: geysers, hot springs, fumaroles, and mud pots.

4 Admire the fiery arms surrounding the blue **Grand Prismatic Spring.** The huge steaming crater left from Excelsior Geyser exploding is impressive, too.

5 Climb to the Grand Prismatic Overlook off the **Fairy Falls Trail** to get a better vantage for viewing Grand Prismatic Spring.

6 Head south toward the Upper Geyser Basin area. Loop by **Daisy Geyser** to see the unique Punch Bowl.

7 Walk north along the main paved trail to see **Morning Glory Pool.**

8 Turn around and, on your way back, take in **Riverside Geyser.** Cross the Firehole River to head to Old Faithful area via the boardwalk. Catch an eruption of the famous geyser, if the timing is right.

9 Dine and spend the night in the **Old Faithful Inn.** You can also catch eruptions of Old Faithful Geyser from the second-story deck.

3

AVOID THE (HUGE) CROWDS

Yellowstone's geyser basins attract crowds curious to see volcanic activity. But a few places are less visited and hence less hectic. Visiting many of these places in early morning or evening also lessens the chances of crowds.

1 Take an early morning bike ride or hike along the Firehole River to **Lone Star Geyser.** It erupts about every three hours, but even if you miss the eruption, its large sinter cone is worth seeing.

2 Afterward, hop in your car and head toward Norris to get to **Artists Paintpots.** Marvel at bubbling mud pots and tiny colorful pools in nature's rendition of an artist's palette.

3 Pull over near the **Gibbon Meadows Picnic Area,** where the broad, flat meadows offer a chance to see bison, elk, moose, and Canada geese.

More Activities with Fewer Crowds

- Sentinel Meadows and Queen's Laundry hike
- Monument Geyser Basin hike
- Backpacking Bechler River Trail
- Winter snowcoach tours

BEST PLACE TO WATCH THE SUNSET

Head to **Great Fountain Geyser** on Firehole Lake Drive to watch the sunset. If the geyser, or its neighboring White Dome, is erupting, you can enjoy the backdrop of the setting sun. If Great Fountain isn't erupting, its water pools often still reflect the sunset.

HIGHLIGHTS

AROUND MADISON JUNCTION

Wildlife congregate in the lush meadows around the Gibbon and Madison Rivers. Along the **Madison River** and the **West Entrance Road,** pullouts permit viewing bison, elk, deer, and raptors. In fall, bull elk often round up harems along the river, their bugling echoing across the valley. At Madison Junction (14 mi/22.5 km from the West Entrance) adjacent to the Madison River Picnic Area parking lot, the **Madison Junior Ranger Station** is another good vantage point. North of Madison Junction above Gibbon Falls on the road to Norris, several pullouts offer views into **Gibbon Meadows,** where you can often see bison or elk herds.

Maintain a safe distance (at least 75-100 ft/23-30 m) from all wildlife and give them plenty of room. The animals may look tame, but gorings continue to occur when people get too close, especially while trying to take selfies or photos of others posed with bison.

LOWER GEYSER BASIN

Fountain Paint Pot

8 mi (13 km) south of Madison Junction (or north of Old Faithful)

At Fountain Paint Pot, an interpretive boardwalk loop (0.5 mi/0.8 km) tours all four types of hydrothermals: geysers, mud pots, hot springs, and fumaroles. Pick up the *Fountain Paint Pot Trail Guide* ($1) at the start of the trail.

At the boardwalk junction, look left into the blue **Celestine Pool** or right for the colorful bacterial mats of thermophiles (organisms that proliferate in hot water) formed in the runoff from the silica-rich, turquoise **Silex Spring** straight ahead. The trail then divides around pink and gray **Fountain Paint Pot,** bubbling more in the liquid clay of early summer but thicker by fall. (Its clay was used to paint the former hotel across the road.) The trail splits to circle **Red Spouter,** named for the red clay that acts like a mud pot, hot springs, or steam vent based on changing water amounts throughout the year. As the boardwalk continues west downhill, several geysers spurt and fume. When **Fountain Geyser** erupts, it can shoot water 20-50 ft in the air for longer than 20 minutes. The smaller neighboring **Clepsydra Geyser,** which sputters nonstop from several vents, can pause when Fountain erupts.

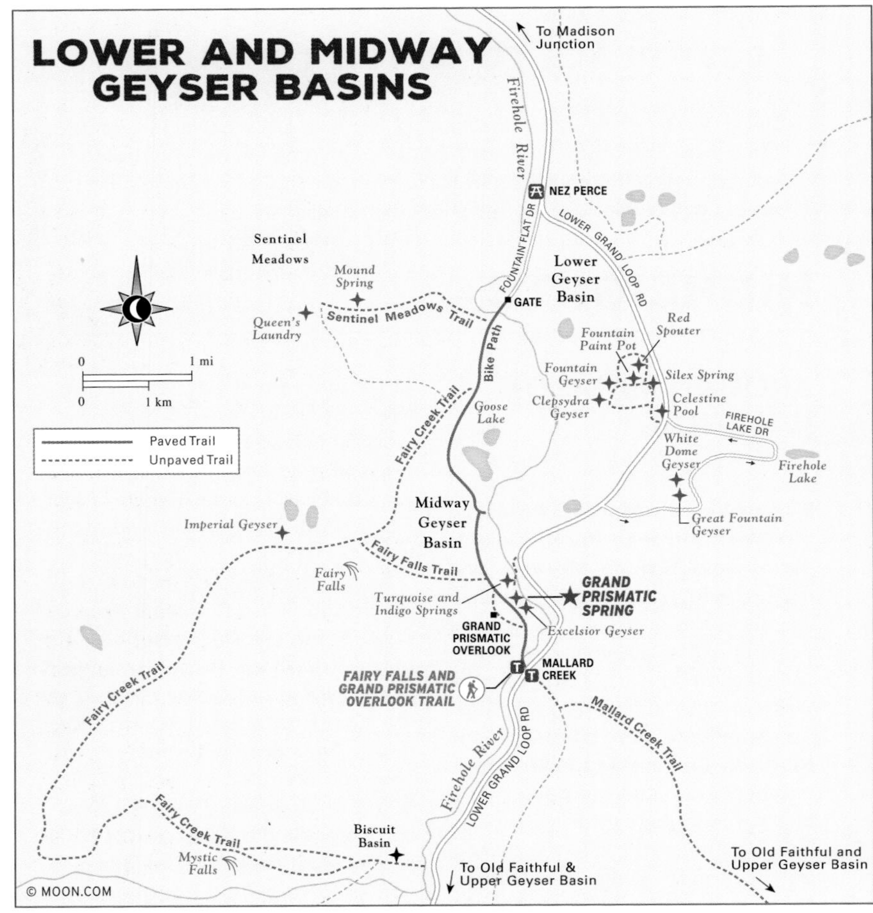

FIREHOLE LAKE DRIVE

Great Fountain Geyser

Located on the short, one-way Firehole Lake Drive (9.3 mi/15 km south of Madison Junction and 6.8 mi/10.9 km north of Old Faithful), Great Fountain Geyser shoots 75-220 ft (23-67 m) high every 10-14 hours. Unlike Old Faithful's short durations, Great Fountain's eruptions last about an hour, with short bursts of water interspersed between quiet periods. The geyser ushers in a long, dramatic prelude to erupting. Water floods the vent, and bubbles appear about 30 minutes later. As the water boils into giant 3-ft (1-m) bubbles followed by one big burp, the eruption begins. Check the NPS Yellowstone National Park app for predicted eruption time.

Adjacent to Great Fountain Geyser, **White Dome Geyser** goes off in shorter spurts from its 12-foot-tall sinter cone. Farther on, **Firehole Lake,** viewed from a boardwalk, is the largest hot spring in the area, heated via several vents.

MIDWAY GEYSER BASIN

6.5 mi (10.5 km) north of Old Faithful and about 10 mi (16 km) south of Madison

Midway Geyser Basin only has four thermal features, but they are huge. Two are the largest hot springs in Yellowstone. From the parking area (on the west side of the Grand Loop Road), a footbridge crosses the Firehole River to reach the Midway Geyser Basin boardwalk that loops 0.8 miles (1.3 km) past the four large hot springs.

★ Grand Prismatic Spring

At 370 ft (113 m) across and 121 ft (37 m) deep, Grand Prismatic Spring is the largest hot spring in Yellowstone and the third largest in the world. Enjoy the glorious hues: fiery arms of orange, gold, and brown thermophiles that radiate in a full circle from the yellow-rimmed, blue hot pool. Its 160°F (71°C) water discharges in all directions at 560 gallons per minute. See it from the boardwalk or the overlook loop on the **Fairy Falls Trail.**

Nearby, the largest feature here is the crystalline-blue **Excelsior Geyser Crater**, which puts out copious steam and spills down colorful thermophile communities into the Firehole River.

Old Faithful Geyser in winter

UPPER GEYSER BASIN

★ Old Faithful Geyser

Old Faithful Geyser anchors the Upper Geyser Basin. When Old Faithful erupts, it shoots up to 8,400 gallons of hot water as high as 185 ft (56 m). It's not the tallest geyser in the park, but it is one of the most regular, erupting about every 90 minutes for 1.5-5 minutes. Often, the geyser sputters for 20 minutes before erupting, spewing water that percolated into its

Beehive Geyser (left); Doublet Pool (right)

Fountain Paint Pot (top); Great Fountain Geyser (middle); Grand Prismatic Spring (bottom)

huge underground chamber 250-500 years ago. The eruption occurs when water forces upward through its 4-inch (10-cm) constriction. Expect massive crowds of people in summer, with benches surrounding the geyser filling 30 minutes in advance. Winter eruptions see only a handful of people. Old Faithful is behind the Old Faithful Visitor Education Center, which posts eruption times. A 0.7-mi (1.1-km) rubberized and pavement loop circles the famous geyser. You can also watch the geyser erupt from a seat on the deck of the nearby **Old Faithful Inn.** Check the NPS Yellowstone National Park app for next predicted eruption time or look on the sign at the visitors center.

Geyser Hill Loop

From the Old Faithful viewing area, head east across the Firehole River to climb the boardwalk and stairs that ring Geyser Hill, which is sprinkled with several active geysers. Geyser Hill is a 1.3-mi (2.1-km) walk from the visitors center, and a boardwalk connects it with the Firehole River Loop.

On the south section of this loop, turn left to view **Beehive Geyser,** which can shoot up 200 ft (60 m) but has an irregular schedule. The smaller nearby **Anemone** and **Plume Geysers** erupt regularly, the first about every 10 minutes and the second hourly. Continue north past Beehive to find the clear blue **Heart Spring** near the cones of the interconnected **Lion Group,** a family of geysers called Little Cub, Big Cub, Lioness, and Lion, the latter of which heralds eruptions with a roar. Turn right to access the upper part of this loop. Admire the radiant color and ledges of **Doublet Pool.** From here, a spur trail heads north to **Solitary**

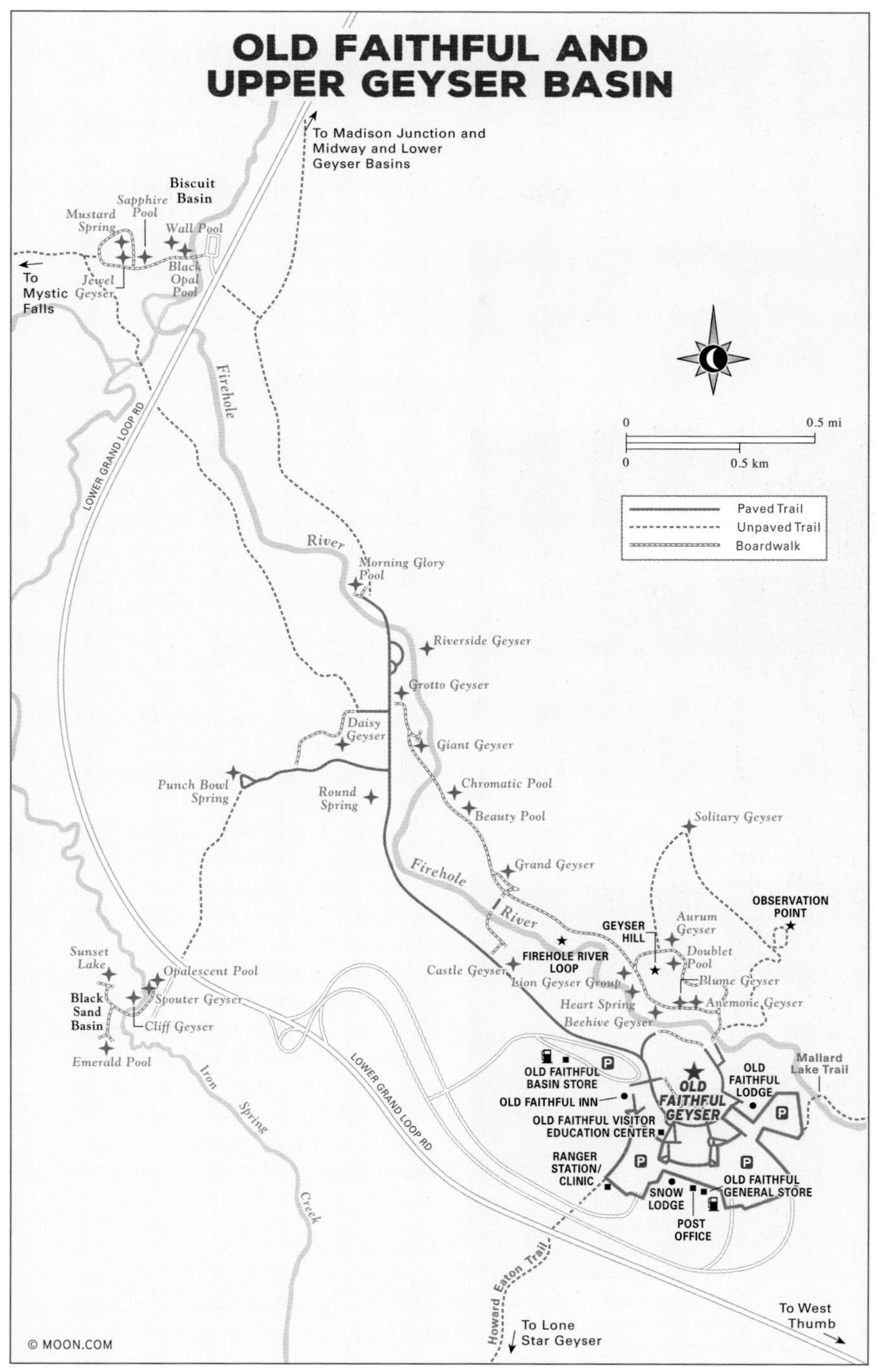
OLD FAITHFUL AND UPPER GEYSER BASIN
To Madison Junction and Midway and Lower Geyser Basins
Biscuit Basin
Sapphire Pool
Mustard Spring
Wall Pool
Black Opal Pool
Jewel Geyser
To Mystic Falls
Firehole
LOWER GRAND LOOP RD
0
0.5 mi
0
0.5 km
Paved Trail
Unpaved Trail
Boardwalk
River
Morning Glory Pool
Riverside Geyser
Grotto Geyser
Daisy Geyser
Giant Geyser
Punch Bowl Spring
Round Spring
Chromatic Pool
Beauty Pool
Solitary Geyser
Grand Geyser
Firehole
River
OBSERVATION POINT
GEYSER HILL
Aurum Geyser
Doublet Pool
FIREHOLE RIVER LOOP
Castle Geyser
Lion Geyser Group
Blume Geyser
Heart Spring
Anemone Geyser
Beehive Geyser
Sunset Lake
Opalescent Pool
Black Sand Basin
Spouter Geyser
Cliff Geyser
Emerald Pool
Iron Spring Creek
LOWER GRAND LOOP RD
OLD FAITHFUL BASIN STORE
OLD FAITHFUL INN
OLD FAITHFUL GEYSER
OLD FAITHFUL LODGE
Mallard Lake Trail
OLD FAITHFUL VISITOR EDUCATION CENTER
RANGER STATION/ CLINIC
SNOW LODGE
OLD FAITHFUL GENERAL STORE
POST OFFICE
Howard Eaton Trail
To Lone Star Geyser
To West Thumb
© MOON.COM

Punch Bowl (top); Emerald Pool (middle); Artists Paintpots (bottom)

Geyser, which surges with short 6-ft (2-m) bursts every 4-8 minutes.

Firehole River Loop

Northwest of Geyser Hill, the bigger Firehole River Loop crosses two bridges to take in the famous hot pools of the Upper Geyser Basin, plus more geysers, fumaroles, and springs. Check the Yellowstone Geyser App for next predicted eruption time or look on the sign at the visitors center.

At the southern start of this loop is **Castle Geyser,** a cone geyser built into the largest sinter formation in the world. About every 14 hours, Castle Geyser erupts for 20 minutes and then pumps out copious steam. Continue north and turn right to cross the Firehole River and reach **Grand Geyser,** a predictable fountain geyser that throws water 200 ft (60 m) skyward in several short bursts. To the north sit a pair of interconnected hot springs, **Beauty Pool** and **Chromatic Pool.** When the water level rises in one, it drops in the other.

As the boardwalk crosses the river again, you might get to see the erratic **Giant Geyser** throw water up 300 ft (90 m). At the junction with the paved trail, **Grotto Geyser** squirts water from its face-shaped cone for sometimes up to 24 hours. Continue north on the paved trail to **Riverside Geyser**, which shoots an arc of water at 6-hour intervals over the Firehole for about 20 minutes. The striking green, orange, and yellow **Morning Glory Pool** marks the turnaround point.

Daisy Loop

A small loop circles **Daisy Geyser,** which erupts every 2-4 hours. Check the NPS Yellowstone National Park

Riverside Geyser

app for the next predicted eruption time. Eruptions can last about five minutes with water shooting up at an angle. A spur loop takes in the raised sinter **Punch Bowl,** filled with boiling water.

BISCUIT BASIN

Separated from the main Upper Geyser Basin, Biscuit Basin holds a collection of smaller features, accessed by a 0.7-mi (1.1-km) boardwalk that ascends into the basin to circle hot pools, geysers, and fumaroles. After crossing the Firehole River on a footbridge, the boardwalk tours past **Black Opal Pool, Wall Pool,** and **Sapphire Pool.** The latter is the most commanding feature, a hot pool of crystal-clear 200°F (93°C) blue water that once used to be a geyser. At the junction, go either way to circle the basin. Highlights on the upper loop include the yellow **Mustard Spring** and **Jewel Geyser,** which shoots water up to 20 ft (6 m) in the air about every 10 minutes, a short enough time to wait to see it.

On Grand Loop Road, locate Biscuit Basin 2 mi (3.2 km) north of the Old Faithful turnoff and 3.8 mi (6.1 km) south of Midway Geyser Basin. From the Old Faithful Visitor Education Center, you can hike or bike to Biscuit Basin (5.9 mi/9.5 km round-trip). From the paved Upper Geyser Basin Trail, take the Daisy Geyser Loop at the second junction westward. At the next junction, turn north to reach Grand Loop Road. Hikers can cross the road onto the trail that continues to the back of the geyser basin. However, bikers must turn right onto the road to reach the parking lot.

BLACK SAND BASIN

In the Upper Geyser Basin, Black Sand Basin has a 0.6-mi (1 km) boardwalk across Iron Spring Creek with two short spurs that tour past small geysers and colorful hot pools. The basin acquired its name from the bits of obsidian that speckle the area. On the creek's edge, **Cliff Geyser** erupts up to 40 ft (12 m) from a small crater. Eruptions last 0.5-3 hours, with copious steam spewing out. At the boardwalk junction, turn right to see **Sunset Lake,** named for its yellow-orange rim, and left to see **Emerald Pool,** colored from its algae. Before hopping back in the car, walk a tiny spur off the north corner of the parking lot

Sapphire Pool (left); Black Sand Basin (right)

to see **Opalescent Pool,** fed by the almost constantly erupting **Spouter Geyser,** which flooded an area of lodgepoles. The dead trees are now known as **bobby socks trees** because of the white around their silica-soaked trunk bases.

Reach Black Sand Basin by driving Grand Loop Road 0.5 mi (0.8 km) northwest of the Old Faithful turnoff or 1.6 mi (2.6 km) south of Biscuit Basin. Hikers can walk (4.4 mi/7.1 km roundtrip) from Old Faithful Visitor Education Center via the paved trail to the first Daisy Geyser Loop turnoff and descend to cross Grand Loop Road at the geyser basin entrance.

ARTISTS PAINTPOTS

3.7 mi (6 km) south of Norris Junction, 9.8 mi (15.8 km) north of Madison Junction

Artists Paintpots gets its name from its bubbling gray mud pots that burp and spurt. Compared to the main geyser basins, fewer people stop here. The sunny gravel, dirt, boardwalk, and stair-step trail (1 mi/1.6 km) starts by cutting through lodgepoles. At the junction, turn in either direction; the remainder of the trail loops around the side of **Paintpot Hill,** full of small geysers, fumaroles, light blue pools, and red crusts. The base of the hill holds bubbling hot springs, clear hot pools, and streams with thermophiles, colorful organisms that proliferate in hot water. The famous paint pots at the top are formed of thicker clay; they emit gasses that scent the air with stinky hydrogen sulfide gas. By late summer, the mud pots thicken or dry up when less water feeds them.

★ NORRIS GEYSER BASIN

Of Yellowstone's thermal basins, Norris Geyser Basin is the hottest, measuring 459°F (237°C) at 1,087 ft (3,075 m) below the surface. With features 115,000 years old, it is the oldest geothermal basin. The most vigorous of the park's geyser basins, Norris has some features that change daily, many due to earthquakes. It also contains rare acidic geysers; you'll smell the rotten egg stench.

The *Norris Geyser Basin Trail Guide* ($1; available at visitors centers) can aid in touring the two self-guided interpretive boardwalks. Rangers also lead guided walks through the basins. From Norris Campground, a 1-mi (1.6-km) trail goes to Porcelain

Porcelain Basin (left); Steamboat Geyser (right)

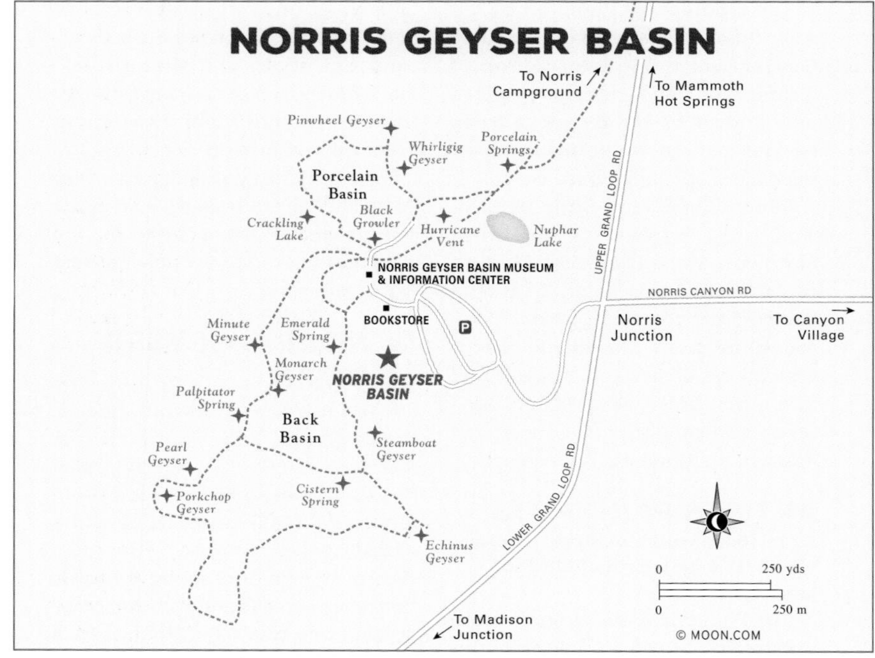

Basin. Due to the changing nature of the basins, boardwalks can be closed for reconstruction.

Back Basin

The thinly forested Back Basin double-loop (1.5 mi/2.4 km) houses two geysers that each hold world records: the tallest geyser and the largest acidic geyser. Heading south from the museum, the boardwalk first reaches **Emerald Spring,** with its striking blue color created from yellow sulfur minerals, near-boiling water, and colorful thermophiles. Continue south to unpredictable **Steamboat Geyser,** which shoots small bursts of water up to 40 ft (12 m) in the air. Its world-record eruptions of 300-400 ft/90-120 m happen infrequently, but 2018-2020 saw a record number of eruptions. The geyser links underground to the blue-green **Cistern Spring,** which puts out so much sinter that pipes often clog and force water to the surface in new pools. Turn left to stay on this outer loop as it winds past the red-orange-rimmed pool of **Echinus Geyser.** With unpredictable eruptions, it's the world's largest acidic geyser—on par with vinegar. After several hot springs, mud pots, and spitting geysers, **Porkchop Geyser** roils turquoise water but is more like a hot spring (it hasn't erupted since 1989 when it threw rocks). Due to superheating in this evolving basin, the park service rerouted the boardwalk to **Pearl Geyser** to avoid the 200°F (93°C) ground.

This outer loop completes at the junction near **Palpitator Spring.** Continue north through the Back Basin past **Minute** and **Monarch Geysers** to return to the visitors center junction.

Porcelain Basin

The wide-open Porcelain Basin is named for its color. Two loops of the 0.5-mi (0.8-km) boardwalk cross the acidic basin that contains the park's highest concentration of silica; thermophiles add brilliant splashes of green or red. From the museum junction, turn left past turquoise **Crackling Lake,** a hot pool that bubbles along the edges of the basin. The loop brings you to the defunct **Pinwheel Geyser** and active **Whirligig Geyser,** which spills into a runoff stream full of orange iron oxide and green thermophiles. A smaller boardwalk loop heads left past roaring **Hurricane Vent** and colorful **Porcelain Springs,** a changeable hot pool that waffles from water action to dry. Complete the loop and return to the museum by heading south, passing **Black Growler,** a noisy vent belching copious steam up to 280°F (138°C). You can also follow the trail from Porcelain Springs to the **Museum of the National Park Ranger** near the campground (1 mi/1.6 km).

SCENIC DRIVES

WEST ENTRANCE ROAD

DRIVING DISTANCE: 14 mi (22.5 km) one-way
DRIVING TIME: 30 minutes one-way
START: West Yellowstone
END: Madison Junction

For an evening wildlife-watching drive, take the West Entrance Road (late Apr.-early Nov.) east from West Yellowstone to Madison Junction. The road parallels the **Madison River,** with sprawling meadows that fill with bison in summer and elk herds in fall. Pullouts allow places to watch, but don't become so enamored with the megafauna that you miss eagles in the trees or bobcats hunting along the river.

LOWER GRAND LOOP ROAD

DRIVING DISTANCE: 96 mi (154 km) round-trip
DRIVING TIME: 4 hours round-trip
START/END: Madison Junction

Lower Grand Loop Road links **Madison, Norris, Canyon Village, West Thumb,** and **Old Faithful** to take in loads of wildlife-watching plus Norris Geyser Basin, Grand Canyon of the Yellowstone, Hayden Valley, Yellowstone Lake, West Thumb Geyser Basin, and the Old Faithful complex. Driving the entire loop (mid-May-early Nov.) will take four hours; add more time for scenic stops and walks along the geyser basins.

Follow the West Entrance Road from Madison Junction to Norris Junction (14 mi/22.5; 30 min; mid-Apr.-early Nov.). From Madison, the road loops past **Terrace Springs** to parallel the **Gibbon River.** The road climbs north through a canyon housing **Gibbon Falls** as it ascends out of the supervolcano caldera. Blue **Beryl Spring** spews steam in the canyon before reaching **Gibbon Meadows,** where bison and elk congregate and **Artists Paintpots** sits amid trees. At Norris Junction, turn left for **Norris Geyser Basin** or right to Canyon Village.

Zip east over the forested road from Norris to **Canyon Village**

West Entrance Road follows the Madison River (top); bison along Gibbon River (middle); Nez Perce Creek (bottom)

(12 mi/19.5 km; 30 min; late Apr.-early Nov.) and south to access **Grand Canyon of the Yellowstone.** Head south along the Yellowstone River, curving around the shores of Yellowstone Lake to **West Thumb** (37 mi/60 km; 90 min; mid-May-early Nov.).

From West Thumb, turn west to Old Faithful (17 mi/27 km; 45 min; mid-May-early Nov.). The route bounces twice over the **Continental Divide,** the highest point at 8,391 ft (2,558 m). **Isa Lake,** located at **Craig Pass,** has the unique status of flowing toward both the Pacific Ocean and the Gulf of Mexico. After descending Craig Pass, the road passes **Old Faithful** and the **Upper Geyser Basin** before completing the loop north to Madison (16 mi/26 km; 45 min; late Apr.-early Nov.).

NEZ PERCE NATIONAL HISTORIC TRAIL

DRIVING DISTANCE: 132 mi (212 km) one-way
DRIVING TIME: 3.5 hours one-way
START: West Entrance
END: Northeast Entrance

In 1877, the Nez Perce, or Nee-Me-Poo, fled their ancestral land in Oregon, chased by the U.S. Army that sought to move them from their treaty-designated homeland to an Idaho reservation. On foot and horseback, about 750 Nez Perce, including children, traveled 1,170 mi (1,800 km) on a mountainous, convoluted route through Washington, Idaho, Montana, Wyoming, and back through Montana to reach Canada. They made it within 40 miles of the border when a five-day battle ended in the surrender of the Nez Perce and survivors being sent to Oklahoma Indian Territory.

Today, the sacred Nez Perce National Historic Trail goes through Yellowstone, which took the Nee-Me-Poo 13 days to cross. From West Yellowstone, turn south on Grand Loop Road at Madison Junction to reach Yellowstone Lake, where the route heads north on Grand Loop Road to Tower Junction before exiting the park via the Northeast Entrance Road. The drive, which approximates the flight of the Nez Perce, takes about 3.5 hours without stops. For detailed information on the driving tour, including stops and hikes, download the brochure and map prior to reaching Yellowstone: www.fs.usda.gov/Internet/FSE_DOCUMENTS/stelprd3823849.pdf. Please note that a portion of Grand Loop Road on the north side of Dunraven Pass will be closed in 2021 for construction, forcing the route to be completed in two different segments.

BEST HIKES

SENTINEL MEADOWS AND QUEEN'S LAUNDRY

DISTANCE: 3.8 mi (6.1 km) round-trip
DURATION: 2 hours round-trip
ELEVATION CHANGE: 45 ft (14 m)
EFFORT: Easy to moderate
TRAILHEAD: Fountain Flat Drive parking lot, south of Madison

From the trailhead, walk south on the old road to the bridge over the Firehole River. To the west, the riverside Ojo Caliente hot spring pours water down yellow sulfur channels. Cross the bridge to find the trail junction on the right. Turn west to walk through grasslands, crossing Fairy and Sentinel Creeks. In wet seeps, the trail can disappear. At **Sentinel Meadows,** thermal features come into view; the first is **Mound Spring,** the largest. Several smaller cones spread around the meadows. (Use caution in exploring the basin, as thermal features can be dangerous.) Follow the trail south between the forest and the multiple smaller cones. The next major thermal is **Queen's Laundry Geyser,** at 1.9 mi (3.1 km). On top of the sinter mound is an old, roofless log structure that was built in 1881 to serve as the bathhouse for soaking in the hot spring. To protect the spring, and for safety, soaking is now taboo.

While you can hike out and back on this trail, other options include adding on **Imperial Geyser** and **Fairy Falls** or bicycling **Fountain Flat Drive** to trailheads and locking up bikes to walk to destinations. Bear activity closes this trail in spring until Memorial Day weekend.

OBSERVATION POINT

DISTANCE: 2.1 mi (3.4 km) round-trip
DURATION: 1 hour round-trip
ELEVATION CHANGE: 237 ft (72 m)
EFFORT: Moderate
TRAILHEAD: Old Faithful Visitor Education Center

Most hikers coordinate the walk up to Observation Point with an eruption of Old Faithful Geyser. From the overlook, you can look down on the masses of people surrounding the geyser and watch it blow, but the steam plume sometimes occludes the water spouting, depending on wind direction. In winter, when the ground is snow-covered, wear snowshoes or boot cleats (rent from the Bear's Den in the Snow Lodge). While hiking time is short, the wait for Old Faithful to erupt may be long.

From the Old Faithful Visitor Education Center, circle the east side of Old Faithful Geyser heading toward **Geyser Hill** and cross the Firehole River. After crossing the bridge, turn right at the sign for **Observation Point.** The trail switchbacks uphill for 0.5 mi (0.8 km), making a small loop at the top. At the point, claim your spot in the trees to watch Old Faithful erupt. In winter, you may be the only one there, but in summer, you'll join a crowd. To descend, walk down the loop and then continue westward on the trail through the forest to **Solitary Geyser.** From the geyser, a dirt trail connects south with the boardwalk on Geyser Hill near Aurum Geyser. Go east on the boardwalk to retrace your route across the Firehole River and back to Old Faithful.

MYSTIC FALLS AND BISCUIT BASIN OVERLOOK

DISTANCE: 2.4-8 miles (3.8-12.9 km) round-trip
DURATION: 1-4 hours round-trip
ELEVATION CHANGE: 135-545 ft (41-166 m)
EFFORT: Moderate
TRAILHEADS: Biscuit Basin parking area, 2 mi (3 km) northwest of Old Faithful, or access from Old Faithful Visitor Education Center

At Biscuit Basin, a short boardwalk loop provides hiking access to Mystic Falls and the overlook trail. Bears close the trail in spring until **late May.** With sparse shade, the route can be hot in summer.

From Biscuit Basin parking area, follow the **boardwalk trail** to the back of the basin and take the short spur west. Turn right and hike 0.4 mi (0.6 km) through young lodgepoles and meadows to a junction. Take the left fork and ascend into the canyon along the Little Firehole River to **Mystic Falls,** a 70-foot (20-m) waterfall that feeds a series of cascades. For the shortest hike (2.4 mi/3.8 km), retrace your steps to Biscuit Basin.

For a 3.9-mile (6.3-km) loop, continue west from the falls toward the Biscuit Basin Overlook. Climb the south-facing switchbacks to reach another junction at the forested

Queen's Laundry (left); Sentinel Meadows (right)

Old Faithful Geyser from Observation Point (left); Mystic Falls (right)

summit. Turn right to reach **Biscuit Basin Overlook** (a left turn goes to Fairy Falls). As the trail crosses the ridge and descends, you'll get multiple views of Biscuit Basin, the Firehole River, and steam rising across the Upper Geyser Basin. Descend the trail and turn left at the fork to return to the Biscuit Basin boardwalk.

From Old Faithful, hiking to Biscuit Basin, the falls, and the overlook is 8 mi (13 km) round-trip. Follow the trail system through the Upper Geyser Basin to connect to Biscuit Basin across Grand Loop Road.

MONUMENT GEYSER BASIN

DISTANCE: 2.8 mi (4.5 km) round-trip
DURATION: 2.5 hours round-trip
ELEVATION CHANGE: 637 ft (194 m)
EFFORT: Strenuous, but short
TRAILHEAD: On Grand Loop Road 4.7 mi (7.6 km) south of Norris Junction and 8.7 mi (14 km) northeast of Madison Junction. Parking lot sits on the west side of the road at the south end of the bridge over the Gibbon River.

Monument Geyser Basin takes more effort than the popular hydrothermal basins, but the reward is fewer people and a boardwalk-free basin that has a more natural look. At almost 8,000 ft (over 2,400 m) in elevation, the basin features multiple cylindrical sinter cones created from now-defunct geysers. The basin's namesake **Monument Geyser,** once called "Thermos Bottle" for its shape,

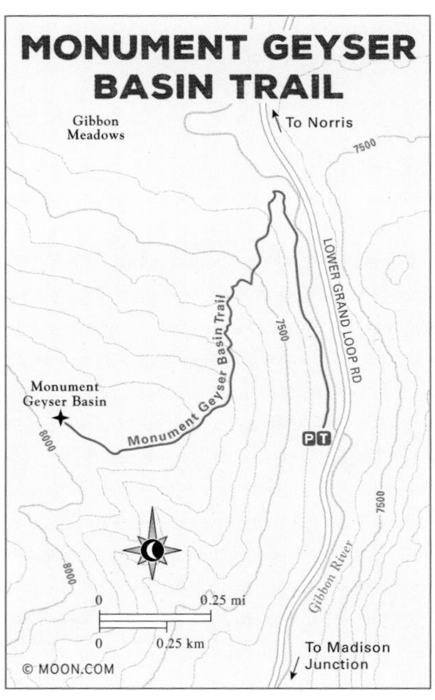

TOP HIKE

FAIRY FALLS AND GRAND PRISMATIC OVERLOOK

Distance: 1.7-9 mi (2.7-14.5 km) round-trip
Duration: 1-5 hours round-trip
Elevation change: 88-129 ft (27-39 m)
Effort: Easy to moderate
Trailheads: Fairy Falls parking area off Grand Loop Road

Directions: The Fairy Falls parking area is off the Grand Loop Road, 11.5 mi (18.5 km) south of Madison Junction or 4.5 mi (7.2 km) north of Old Faithful. At 197 ft (60 m), Fairy Falls is the park's fourth-highest waterfall, and it provides a scenic year-round destination for hikers, bikers, and skiers. A spur loop en route adds an overlook of Grand Prismatic Spring, with its cobalt hot spring and fiery arms of thermophiles. Bears close this trail in spring until **late May.**

From **Fairy Falls Trailhead,** cross the Firehole River and hike the abandoned road. To climb to the overlook of **Grand Prismatic Spring,** take the signed spur to ascend 105 ft (32 m) in elevation to the platform. (To hike only to the overlook is 1.7 mi/2.7 km round-trip.) From there, descend westward to reach another junction on the main **Fairy Falls Trail.** Continue west for 0.2 mi (0.3 km) on the main trail to the signed junction for the falls. Hike 1.5 mi (2.4 km) through a young lodgepole forest to the base of the falls. In summer, the falls plunge ribbon-like into a pool; in winter, it's an ice sculpture. Plan 3.5 hours for the 6.8-mi (11.1 km) round-trip to the falls, including Grand Prismatic Spring Overlook. In winter, cross-country skiers can catch a snowcoach shuttle from Old Faithful to ski from the parking area. To hike from Old Faithful, allow 5 hours for the 9-mi (14.5-km) round-trip.

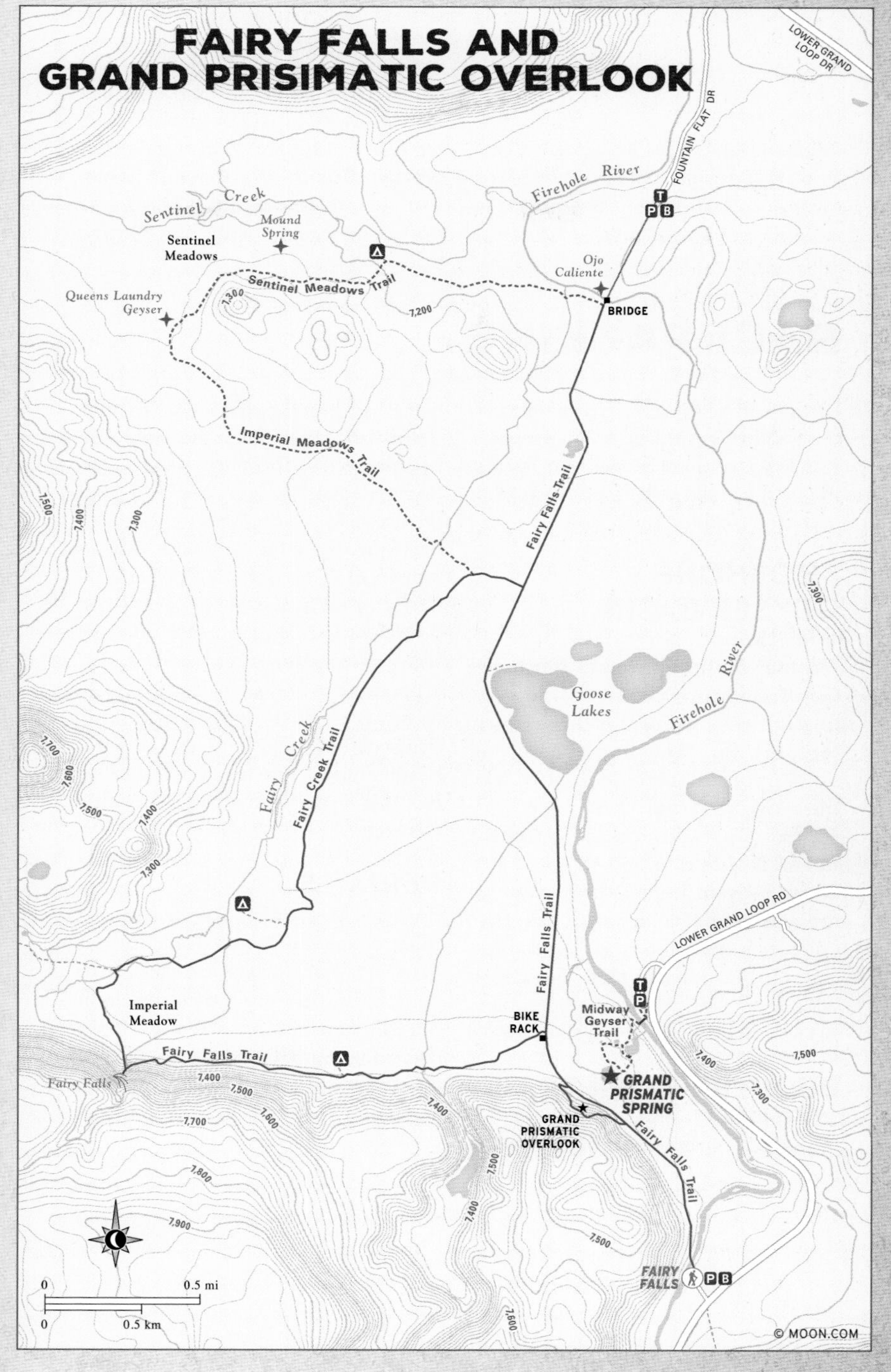
FAIRY FALLS AND
GRAND PRISIMATIC OVERLOOK
LOWER GRAND LOOP DR
FOUNTAIN FLAT DR
Firehole River
Sentinel Creek
Mound Spring
Sentinel Meadows
Sentinel Meadows Trail
Queens Laundry Geyser
Ojo Caliente
BRIDGE
Imperial Meadows Trail
Fairy Falls Trail
Fairy Creek
Fairy Creek Trail
Goose Lakes
Firehole River
LOWER GRAND LOOP RD
Imperial Meadow
BIKE RACK
Midway Geyser Trail
Fairy Falls Trail
Fairy Falls
GRAND PRISMATIC SPRING
GRAND PRISMATIC OVERLOOK
Fairy Falls Trail
FAIRY FALLS
0
0.5 mi
0
0.5 km
© MOON.COM

is a 10-ft-tall (3-m-tall) cone that spewed a steady stream of 194°F (90°C) water.

The trail runs north along the **Gibbon River** for 0.5 mi (0.8 km) and stays in sight of the road before swinging southwest. Switchbacks ascend a ridge sparsely forested with lodgepoles. Near the ridgetop, the trail broadens into an overlook with views of **Mt. Holmes** and **Gibbon Meadows.** As the route travels northwest, the sulfur smell heralds the barren landscape of **Monument Geyser Basin.** Use caution while exploring the cones and steam vents before retracing your steps back down the trail.

BACKPACKING

For a short backpacking trip, head to Shoshone Geyser Basin. More experienced distance hikers can tackle the king of Yellowstone backpacking trips, the Bechler River Trail.

SHOSHONE GEYSER BASIN

18 mi (29 km)

This two-day trip travels to Shoshone Geyser Basin, the largest backcountry geyser basin, with 110 hydrothermal features, and **Shoshone Lake**, the second largest lake in the park. Via the Howard Eaton Trail from Old Faithful, the route crosses the **Continental Divide** at 8,050-ft (2,454-m) **Grant's Pass** before dropping to the west end of Shoshone Lake. Use caution touring the boardwalk-free basin to see **Minute Man Geyser;** it will spout 10-40 ft (3-12 m) high every 1-3 minutes during active phases.

BECHLER RIVER TRAIL

30 mi (48 km)

In the park's remote southwest, this backpacking trip gets you farther away from day hiker hordes. The Bechler River Trail descends into Bechler River Canyon and the land of waterfalls. The point-to-point trail leads from the Lone Star Geyser Trailhead to the Bechler Ranger Station and takes 3-5 days, plus eight hours for the shuttle back. Due to snow and water levels, permit reservations are only available from July 15 onward. While elevation gain is minimal (980 ft/300 m), crossing the Continental Divide twice and fording multiple streams and the river adds difficulty.

PERMITS

Backpackers must obtain permits ($3/person, children 8 and younger free) for assigned backcountry campsites. Permits are available in person 48 hours in advance from the backcountry offices. For more information, see the *Essentials* chapter.

BIKING

ROAD BIKING

Yellowstone park roads offer prime road cycling, with rolling terrain along the Madison River, a big climb from Madison to Norris, and a slightly lesser grade to Old Faithful and the Continental Divide. Lack of road shoulders means that cyclists should be skilled enough to bike with traffic at their elbows. Plows clear pavement on the **West Entrance to Madison** (14 mi/22.5 km) and **Madison to Mammoth Hot Springs** (35 mi/56 km) late March-mid-April. During this time, these roads open to cyclists yet remain closed to vehicles. Confirm road status online (www.nps.gov/yell) and carry all supplies (including pepper spray for bears), as no services are open. After traffic thins in fall, riding from West Yellowstone to Old Faithful is a prime time to hear elk bugling.

MOUNTAIN BIKING

Mountain bikes are only permitted on three shared hiker-biker routes in the Old Faithful area. These wide, level remnants of old asphalt roadbeds are perfect places for family biking.

Fountain Flat Road

4 mi (6.4 km) one-way; late May-early Nov.

Fountain Flat Road links the Fountain Flat Drive parking lot with the Fairy Falls Trailhead (park at either end). En route between Goose Lake and Grand Prismatic Spring, park bikes in the rack to walk to Fairy Falls.

Old Faithful Inn to Biscuit Basin

5 mi (8 km) round-trip

A round-trip ride connects Old Faithful Inn with Biscuit Basin. Start at Hamilton's Store (1 Old Faithful Rd.; tel. 406/586-7593) to ride the paved path along the south side of

Lone Star Geyser

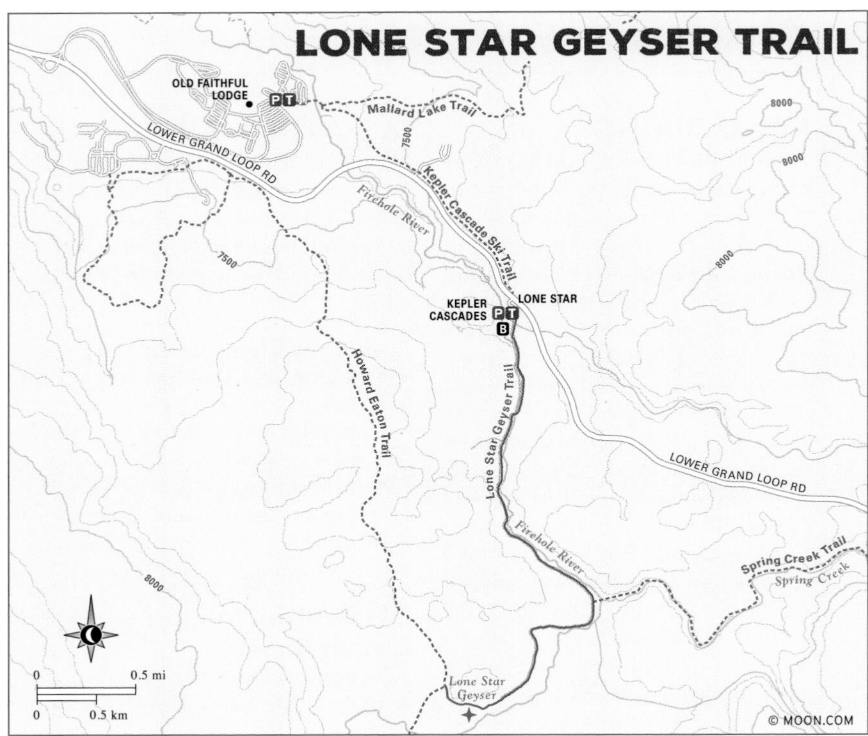

the Firehole River for 1.2 mi (1.9 km). Turn left onto the second Daisy Geyser Loop entrance, then turn right onto a single-track trail that leads to Grand Loop Road near Biscuit Basin.

Lone Star Geyser Trail

4.8 mi (7.7 km) round-trip

The Lone Star Geyser Trail offers a pleasant forest ride along the Firehole River to **Lone Star Geyser,** a 12-ft-tall (4-m-tall) pink and gray sinter cone. Spouting up to 40 ft (12 m) in the air, the geyser erupts about every 3 hours with spurts lasting 30 minutes. If you see the geyser go off, add the date and time to the logbook in the old interpretive stand. Park at Lone Star Geyser Trailhead or **Kepler Cascades.**

RENTALS

SNOW LODGE

tel. 307/344-7311; www.yellowstonenationalparklodges.com; daily late May-early Sept.

In Old Faithful, the Snow Lodge rents bikes for adults and children, including helmets ($8-10/1 hour, $20-30/4 hours, $30-40/8 hours). Add on kiddie trailers or bike trains for $5-20.

WINTER SPORTS

When snow covers the geyser basins, every pore in the landscape emits copious steam, creating an otherworldly peek at nature. Due to colder winter temperatures, the scenes take on more drama than in summer. It's the one season where you are guaranteed front-row seats to see Old Faithful Geyser.

CROSS-COUNTRY SKIING AND SNOWSHOEING

Groomed Routes and Trails

Winter turns the Yellowstone landscape into an otherworldly scene of snow broken by steaming geothermals. Park roads between West Yellowstone and Old Faithful are closed to wheeled vehicles but open for skiing and snowshoeing.

At **Old Faithful,** the park service grooms several roads for skate and classic skiing or snowshoeing. One groomed ski trail ascends a gentle grade to **Lone Star Geyser,** while a less-traveled loop tours through the cabins of **Old Faithful Lodge** with views of the Firehole River. The park service also grooms a trail from **Old Faithful Inn** to **Morning Glory Pool,** but geothermal hot spots cause meltouts; you may have to remove skis in order to walk across the bare pavement. In addition, all summer hiking trails turn into ungroomed winter ski and snowshoe trails, including Biscuit Basin and Fairy Falls, and trails around the geyser basins, though boardwalks can get icy.

Rentals, Shuttles, and Guides

BEAR'S DEN

tel. 307/344-7311; www.yellowstonenationalparklodges.com; 7:30am-5pm daily mid-Dec.-Feb.

At Old Faithful's Snow Lodge, the Bear's Den rents cross-country ski packages (skis, boots, and poles $17-27), snowshoes ($14-20), and boot cleats for walking on ice ($3-5). The shop also waxes skis, repairs gear, teaches lessons, and guides ski and snowshoe trips by reservation. One ski or snowshoe tour goes to **Lone Star Geyser** (11:45am-5pm Mon. and Fri.; $56). Snowcoaches

cross-country skiing from Lone Star Geyser (left); snowcoach tour to Old Faithful (right)

also go to Grand Canyon of the Yellowstone (7:45am-6pm; $287) for guided **Ski Tours** (Tues., Thurs., and Sun.) and **Snowshoe Tours** (Wed. and Sat.). **Snowcoach shuttles** from Snow Lodge (by reservation only; $24 adults, $12 kids) can drop you off at several trailheads. Make reservations for guided trips and shuttles when booking your lodging.

WEST YELLOWSTONE VISITOR INFORMATION CENTER SNOWSHOE WALK

Yellowstone Ave. and Canyon St., West Yellowstone; tel. 307/344-2876; 10am-noon Sat.-Sun. late Dec.-early Mar.; free

Because West Yellowstone sits on the park boundary, skiers and snowshoers can also tour the **Riverside Trail** along the Madison River inside the park. The 9-mi (14.5-km) trail has three loops. Sometimes you can see bison, bald eagles, trumpeter swans, and foxes. From the West Yellowstone Visitor Information Center, park rangers lead a 2-mi (3.2 km) snowshoe walk into the park. Bring your own snowshoes.

SNOWMOBILING

Inside the park, the snowmobile season runs **mid-December to mid-March.** You can go with commercial concessionaires or self-guided via the annual lottery for limited permits (apply in Sept.). Daily, guided snowmobile tours travel roads inside Yellowstone on new, quieter, less stinky machines required by the park.

Guided tours ($270-280 per machine) and rentals ($150-260 per machine) are available through **Yellowstone Vacations** (415 Yellowstone Ave.; tel. 800/426-7669; www.yellowstonevacations.com), **Backcountry Adventures** (224 N. Electric St.; tel. 406/646-9317 or 800/924-7669; www.backcountry-adventures.com), and **Two Top Yellowstone Winter Tours** (645 Gibbon Ave.; tel. 406/646-7802; www.twotopsnowmobile.com). Insulated snowsuits, gloves, boots, and helmets rent for $15-30.

From West Yellowstone, the tour to **Old Faithful** is 65 mi (105 km) round-trip. You'll have time to get off the snowmobile to tour geyser basins and walk around Old Faithful. The Grand Canyon of the Yellowstone tour is a 90-mi (145-km) round-trip. Roads are groomed daily, but for inexperienced riders, it's a long day. Tours into the park are limited to 10 snowmobiles and usually launch at 8am for the 8-hour ride. Rates do not include park entrance fees, meals, taxes, or 15 percent guide gratuities. Make reservations for park tours six months in advance.

SNOWCOACH TOURS

Designed for snow travel, most snowcoaches are heated sightseeing buses or vans equipped with huge wheels or tracks. In certain snow conditions, they sway and bounce, especially for backseat riders. Led by interpretive guides, coaches stop at sights where visitors can photograph geysers or wildlife. Wear warm layers of winter clothing and boots for walking in snow. Snowcoach tours **require reservations;** book tours 6-12 months in advance at the same time you make your lodging reservations. Rates for trips do not include entrance fees into the park, lunch, or tips for drivers (15 percent).

From Old Faithful

Xanterra (tel. 307/344-7311; www.yellowstonenationalparklodges.com; daily mid-Dec.-Feb.; kids age 3-11 half price) operates all the tours launching inside the park from Old Faithful Snow Lodge on snowcoach minibuses with oversized tires. Shorter daily tours (2-4.5 hours; $57-78) go wildlife-watching, evening sightseeing, and geyser-exploring; destinations include West Thumb Geyser Basin, Firehole Basin, and Madison River. Full-day tours ($258-276), which include a box lunch, visit Grand Canyon of the Yellowstone or go on a photo safari. These tours are only for visitors staying at Old Faithful Snow Lodge; make reservations at the same time you book your lodging.

FOOD

Lodge eateries are all operated by **Xanterra** (tel. 307/344-7311; www.yellowstonenationalparklodges.com), where casual attire is appropriate. All restaurants are open daily in season; spring and fall hours shorten and sometimes menu offerings do too. For traveling, all lodges sell deli lunches to go or items to create your own lunch.

Old Faithful has two full-service restaurants: the dining room at Old Faithful Inn and the Obsidian Room in Snow Lodge. Both venues serve beer, wine, and cocktails. Their short menus have flexible choices for light eaters or multi-course dining, select organic ingredients, and local and regional sourcing, plus vegan, vegetarian, gluten-free, and kid-friendly options. You can customize many breakfast items, salads, and sandwiches with toppings for an additional cost.

STANDOUTS

Old Faithful Inn Dining Room

daily early May-mid-Oct.

In the historic hotel, the Old Faithful

Old Faithful Inn Dining Room

GEYSER BASINS FOOD OPTIONS

NAME	LOCATION	TYPE
★ **Old Faithful Inn Dining Room**	Old Faithful Inn	sit-down restaurant
Bear Pit Lounge	Old Faithful Inn	sit-down restaurant
Bear Paw Deli	Old Faithful Inn	quick meals and take-out
Obsidian Dining Room	Snow Lodge at Old Faithful	sit-down restaurant
Geyser Grill	Snow Lodge at Old Faithful	cafeteria-style and take-out
Old Faithful Lodge Cafeteria	Old Faithful	cafeteria-style and take-out
Bake Shop	Old Faithful	quick meals and take-out
Old Faithful General Store	Old Faithful	café
Old Faithful Basin Store	Old Faithful	café

Inn Dining Room is an experience of ambience. The log dining room, with its immense fireplace and woven twig chairs, harkens back to another era. **Breakfast** (6:30am-10am daily; $6-15) serves up traditional egg and griddle dishes. **Lunch** (11:30am-2:30pm daily; $10-18) has burgers, sandwiches, and salads. Breakfast and lunch are first-come, first-served.

Dinner (4:30pm-10pm; $10-40) mixes lighter, flexible options with entrée specialties such as pork osso bucco, pasta, fish, and quail. Dinner reservations are required; without one, waits of one hour or longer are common. Make reservations by phone or online up to one year in advance when booking lodging at the inn. Those not staying at the inn can make reservations 60 days in advance.

For faster service, **buffets** (breakfast and lunch $14-18 adults, $7-9 kids, dinner $33 adults, $12 kids) are offered at all meals. Lunch has a Western buffet with trout, pulled pork, and barbecue-style sides. Dinner rolls out the prime rib.

BEST PICNIC SPOTS

Between the West Entrance, Old Faithful, and Norris, plenty of picnic areas offer places to eat an alfresco meal.

FOOD	PRICE	HOURS
casual American (breakfast/lunch); contemporary American (dinner)	moderate	6:30am-10am, 11:30am-2:30pm, dinner 4:30pm-10pm daily early May-mid-Oct. (reservations required for dinner)
pub food	moderate	11:30am-11pm daily
sandwiches and salads	budget	6am-6pm daily
casual American (breakfast/lunch); contemporary American (dinner)	moderate	6:30am-10:30am, 11:30am-3pm, 5pm-10:30pm daily late Apr.-late Oct. and mid-Dec.-Feb.
casual American	moderate	6:30am-9pm daily early June-Oct. (closes 8pm in fall), 11am-3pm daily mid-Dec.-mid-Mar.
casual American	budget	11am-9pm daily mid-May-Sept.
baked goods and casual American	budget	6:30am-9pm (till noon in Sept.) daily mid-May-Sept.
casual American and groceries	budget	7:30am-8:30pm daily May-Oct.
fast food and groceries	budget	early May-late Sept.

You must bring your own firewood to use fire grills where provided.

Gibbon Meadows

On Lower Grand Loop Road between Madison Junction and Norris Junction, north of Artists Paintpots

Visit Artists Paintpots, and then drive 0.5-mile (0.8km) north to this picnic area with tables and an accessible vault toilet. Between the two locations, the broad meadows usually have bison or elk. The picnic area sits along the meandering Gibbon River, which offers fishing or a place to splash on a hot day.

Gibbon Falls near the picnic area

GEYSER BASINS CAMPGROUNDS

NAME	LOCATION	SEASON
★ Madison	Madison Junction	late Apr.-mid-Oct.
★ Norris	Norris Geyser Basin	mid-May-late Sept.

Gibbon Falls

On Lower Grand Loop Road between Madison Junction and Norris Junction, south of Gibbon Falls

Pair up picnicking here with a stop to see Gibbon Falls, 0.5 mile (0.8 km) north. This partly forested area has picnic tables and an accessible vault toilet adjacent to a bend in the Gibbon River, where bison often migrate.

Madison Junction

At the junction of the West Entrance Road and Lower Grand Loop Road, just south of Madison Junction

Adjacent to the Madison River, this large picnic area offers excellent fly-fishing and the historic Madison Information Station, which hosts Junior Ranger Programs. The location is also good for spotting bison and elk. Facilities include tables, accessible flush toilets, and a few fire grills.

Firehole River

On Lower Grand Loop Road between Old Faithful and Madison Junction

On the Firehole River, this popular picnic area has tables and an accessible vault toilet. Cast for trout in the river or just enjoy the river's ambiance.

Nez Perce

On Lower Grand Loop Road between Old Faithful and Madison Junction, at the north end of Fountain Flat Road

With picnic tables, a few fire grills, and an accessible vault toilet, this picnic area on the Nez Perce National Historic Trail sits at the confluence of Nez Perce Creek and the Firehole River. You can fish for native trout, explore both waterways, watch for wildlife including birds, or picnic after bicycling Fountain Flat Road.

SITES AND AMENITIES	RV LIMIT	PRICE	RESERVATIONS
278 sites; some can accommodate RVs; tent pads at some sites; flush toilets; accessible sites available	up to 40 ft/12 m	$27	yes
100 sites; some can accommodate RVs; tent pads at some sites; flush toilets; accessible sites available	30 ft/9 m	$20	no

CAMPING

This area holds two outstanding campgrounds: Madison is closest to Old Faithful, while Norris is closer to Mammoth and Canyon Village. Both campgrounds have flush toilets, potable water, picnic tables, fire rings with grills, food storage boxes, tent pads (at some sites), firewood and ice sales, evening ranger programs, accessible sites, and shared biker-hiker campsites ($5-8/person).

Reservations and Tips

Only Madison takes reservations (tel. 307/344-7311 advance reservations, tel. 307/344-7901 same-day reservations; www.yellowstonenationalparklodges.com), which open a year in advance. To get a spot in the summer at no-reservation Norris, arrive by 7am to be ready for a site that opens.

STANDOUTS

Madison Campground

At Madison Junction, below National Park Mountain, Madison Campground has 278 sites on a flat plain spread around 10 loops. The Madison River flows past the campground, attracting anglers for iconic fly-fishing; wildlife-watchers often spot bison and elk. In fall, elk bugling fills the air. At the campground's west end, G and H loops have 65 sunny sites for tents only.

Norris Campground

Across from Norris Geyser Basin at 7,555 ft (2,303 m) on the Upper Grand Loop's southwest corner, Norris Campground has 100 sites spread

Madison Campground

GEYSER BASINS LODGING

NAME	LOCATION	SEASON
★ Old Faithful Inn	Old Faithful	May-early Oct.
Old Faithful Lodge	Old Faithful	early May-Sept.
★ Snow Lodge	Old Faithful	late Apr.-late Oct., mid-Dec.-Feb.

around a steep hillside. Loop A campsites are flatter and have views of surrounding meadows that often contain elk, bears, moose, or sandhill cranes. Bison often walk through campsites and bed down here. Prime walk-in tent sites line Solfatara Creek. The adjacent **Museum of the National Park Ranger** contains exhibits about early rangers, and nearby hiking trails lead to Norris Geyser Basin, Ice Lake, and north along Solfatara Creek.

LODGING

Reservations

Competition for **Old Faithful reservations** (Xanterra; tel. 307/344-7311; www.yellowstonenationalparklodges.com; May-Oct., mid-Dec.-Feb.) is fierce. Plan ahead and **book 13-18 months in advance** for summer stays. Only the Snow Lodge is open in winter; book it 9 months ahead. You may be able to pick up last-minute reservations due to cancellations, but choices for room types will be limited. The highest rates are mid-June through early September; spring and fall have lower rates. Add on 14 percent tax and utility fee.

STANDOUTS

Old Faithful Inn

May-early Oct.; $145-522 rooms, $790-1,070 suites

Built with logs, tree limbs, and rhyolite stone from the surrounding landscape, Old Faithful Inn is worthy of wows. With a steep-pitched roof and gabled dormers, the lobby vaults five stories high and is centered around an 85-ft-tall (26-m-tall) stone fireplace and handcrafted clock built from wood, copper, and iron. Today, this National Historic Landmark is the most-requested lodge in the park and houses 327 guest rooms in two wings.

The Old House, or the main log lodge, was built in 1903-1904, with the east wing added in 1913-1914 and west wing in 1927-1928. It is reputed to be the largest log building in the world, with distinctive log architecture. Room styles, sizes, and ambience are a throwback to the last century. No elevators access the upper floors of the Old House. The two more modern (but still dated) wings are 3-4 stories tall with elevators. The Old House also contains the immense lobby, dining room, lounge, snack bar, and gift shop. Walk around the lobby balcony to take in all the historical intricacies, and watch Old Faithful Geyser erupt from the deck. Daily **tours** (hours

OPTIONS	PRICE
rooms and suites	rooms starting at $145
rooms and cabins	$110-185
rooms and cabins	rooms starting at $140; prices higher in winter

vary, early May-early Oct.; free) are available.

Snow Lodge

late Apr.-late Oct. $130-350; mid-Dec.-Feb. $140-400

Built in 1989-1999 with modern Western architecture, Snow Lodge sits behind the visitors center with no views of the geyser basin and partially surrounded by parking lots. Snow Lodge is the most modern hotel at Old Faithful. The 134 rooms are larger and have modern-style bathrooms and furnishings. Cabins are a few minutes' walk from the lodge; you might encounter wildlife en route to breakfast. Wireless Internet is available in the lobby and main lodge. The lodge has a restaurant, grill café, lounge, gift shop, and winter ice rink and ski shop.

Hotel-style rooms with one king or two queen beds and log furnishings are in the three-story main lodge. Motel-style rooms cluster in plain duplex or quad buildings. Larger cabins have two queen beds per room with some rooms adjoining, while smaller cabins have one or two double beds. In winter, slide your bags to your room on plastic sleds, or use the bell service.

In winter, the park road to Old Faithful is closed. **Snowcoaches** ($130 adults one-way, kids half-price) travel from Mammoth to the Snow Lodge twice daily in each direction for the four-hour trip.

Snow Lodge in winter

bald eagle

INFORMATION AND SERVICES

The main hub for services near the geyser basins is the **Old Faithful** area, where the Old Faithful Visitor Education Center, Old Faithful Inn, two general stores, a post office, and other services can be found.

Entrance Stations

West Entrance

$35/vehicle, $30 motorcycles, $20 hike-in/bike-in/ski-in

Located on US-20 on the east edge of West Yellowstone, Montana, the West Entrance is the **busiest entrance in the park.** From the West Entrance, the park hub of Madison lies 14 mi (23 km) east and Old Faithful is 30 mi (48 km) southeast. The West Entrance is open to cars and RVs mid-April to early November; in winter (mid-Dec.-mid-Mar.), the road closes but is accessible to snowmobiles and snowcoaches.

In summer, due to West Yellowstone's high volume of lodging and proximity to Old Faithful, the West Entrance sees more than 100,000 visitors each month; in July, more than 4,000 visitors enter each *day* (that's more than double some of the other park entrance stations). If visiting in **summer** (especially July), stop at the West Yellowstone Visitor Information Center in West Yellowstone first to buy your park entrance pass, which will allow you to enter the faster entrance line for vehicles with passes (usually the left lane). In summer, plan to enter the park before 9:30am or after 3pm because cars clog the four entrance lanes midday, often creating 30-minute waits as traffic backs up into town. You can also buy your **entrance pass in advance** online at www.yourpassnow.com.

Visitors Centers

Three national park visitors centers service this area. You can get maps, information, ranger program schedules, and updates on wildlife sightings and geyser basins at all of them. Be aware that hours usually shorten in spring and fall.

Madison Information Station

tel. 307/344-7381; www.nps.gov/yell; 9am-6pm daily late May-early Oct.

A National Historic Landmark, the small Madison Information Station is housed in a historic stone cabin overlooking the Madison River near Madison Junction. Also known as the Madison Junior Ranger Station, this is where naturalists put on short presentations about wildlife and ecology for families. In winter, a wood-sided trailer in the adjacent parking lot serves as the information station (and sells hot chocolate).

Norris Geyser Basin Museum & Information Station

tel. 307/344-7381; www.nps.gov/yell; 9am-5pm daily mid-May-mid-Oct.

At the entrance to Norris Geyser Basin, the Norris Geyser Basin Museum & Information Station houses exhibits on geothermal features. Rangers lead several programs, including walks into the geyser basin. Completed in 1930, the log-and-stone building is a National Historic Landmark. A **Yellowstone Forever** bookstore (tel. 406/848-2400, www.yellowstone.org) is housed in an adjacent building.

Old Faithful Visitor Education Center

Old Faithful Village; tel. 307/344-2751; www.nps.gov/yell; 8am-8pm daily June-Sept., 9am-5pm daily late Apr.-May, Oct.-early Nov., and mid-Dec.-mid-Mar.

Are geysers, hot springs, fumaroles, and mud pots really that different? Find out what makes them each distinct at The Old Faithful Visitor Education Center, located adjacent to Old Faithful Geyser. Interactive exhibits let you see how each works, and kids have a special room with hands-on exhibits. Stop in here to get geyser eruption predictions, which are also available online, (@Twitter.com/GeyserNPS), and on the NPS Yellowstone National Park app (download before you leave home). The center also shows a lineup of rotating films, and a daily film schedule of movies about the park is posted outside the theater. Several naturalist-led tours depart from here, including tours of the facility. Kids can get Junior Ranger booklets ($3) and are sworn in after completion to receive a patch. **Yellowstone Forever** (tel. 406/848-2400; www.yellowstone.org) runs a bookstore inside.

TRANSPORTATION

Getting There

Only two-lane roads tour this area of Montana and Wyoming. Inside and outside the park, roads cut through wildlife habitats. Be on the lookout for deer, pronghorn, elk, bison, and other wildlife jumping out onto the road. Driving into Old Faithful can be confusing, as one-way roads enter and depart the complex. Look for signage at junctions. **Roads to Old Faithful are closed November-mid-April or May.** Due to limited snow-free seasons, construction happens in summer; you may encounter 15- to 30-minute waits in these zones (specific construction sites are listed online).

From West Entrance

From the West Entrance, the road goes 14 mi (23 km) to Madison Junction, where you can drive northwest 14 mi (23 km) to Norris Junction or south 16 mi (26 km) to Old Faithful. Driving each of these roads can take 35-45 minutes due to wildlife jams and traffic. These roads close early November to mid-April. From Norris Geyser Basin to Old Faithful, the drive takes about one hour—longer with heavy traffic or bison jams.

From North Yellowstone

From Mammoth Hot Springs, the drive south on Grand Loop Road to Norris Geyser Basin is 21 mi (34 km). The route takes about 45 minutes without stops. This

Porcelain Basin at Norris Geyser Basin

route closes early November to mid-April.

From Canyon and Lake Country

From Canyon Village, the drive to Norris Geyser Basin is 12 mi (19 km) along Norris Canyon Road. It takes about 30 minutes. This route closes November-mid-April.

From West Thumb, the drive to Old Faithful is 17 mi (27 km) along Lower Grand Loop Road. It takes 45 minutes. This route closes November-early May.

In Winter

With roads snow-covered in winter, the only way to reach Old Faithful is via snowcoach. If you plan on spending the night at Snow Lodge at Old Faithful, make reservations when you book your lodging. Otherwise, visiting Old Faithful in winter requires a snowcoach tour from North Yellowstone or outside the park.

Parking

At many of the geyser basins, parking lots fill to capacity in summer. Sometimes, you may loop around several times to find a free spot; you also may need to skip a sight and return later when parking frees up. Many lots have small, tight parking spaces, sharp corners, and lack of turnaround area, which may be difficult for large RVs. You may need to park elsewhere and hike to access geyser basins.

Old Faithful and Upper Geyser Basin

For overnight visitors staying at lodges, check in first and park where the front desk directs. For day visitors, two giant parking lots are available, both equal distance from Old Faithful Geyser. They pack out in summer; row signs will help you remember where you parked. The smaller parking lot with 342 spaces (including 28 ADA-designated and 29 RV spaces) is southwest of the visitors center, in between Snow Lodge and Old Faithful Inn. The larger parking lot with 674 spaces (11 ADA-designated and 32 RV spaces) is on the east side of the complex near Old Faithful Lodge. Both lots fill up 11am-5pm. To see Old Faithful Geyser, you must walk about five minutes or so from the parking lots, as no road passes by it. RVs are not permitted to park overnight in the lots.

Midway and Lower Geyser Basin

Midway Geyser Basin's small parking lot fits only 55 vehicles, including spaces for 12 designated ADA cars and 12 RVs. Due to popularity, the lot gets very busy 9am-9pm. If possible, plan to visit in the early morning, or you may have to check for parking availability periodically. The Fairy Falls Trailhead parking lot that leads to Grand Prismatic Overlook and Fairy Falls crowds 10am-6pm. It has no RV parking and only one ADA-designated space.

In the Lower Geyser Basin, the parking lot at Fountain Paint Pot is less congested, but it can still fill up 9am-5pm. Parking on Firehole Lake Drive for Great Fountain Geyser fills about 30 minutes before a scheduled eruption.

Norris Geyser Basin

The parking lot at Norris is busiest 10am-6pm. The lot has 143 spaces, including 5 ADA-designated spaces and 17 RV spaces around the outer edges. Overflow parking is available (rangers at Norris Junction will direct you to it), and it requires a 0.5-mile (1.2-km) walk to reach the basin.

Wildlife-Watching

For watching-wildlife, use pullouts rather than stopping in the middle of the road or driving off the road and onto meadows. Congestion at pullouts varies by time and location, depending on what wildlife is present.

Gas

A gas station is located at **Old Faithful** (late Apr.-late Oct.). You can pay at the pump 24 hours with a credit card.

Yellowstone Lake

CANYON AND LAKE COUNTRY

SCULPTED BY A GLACIER, WATER, EARTHQUAKES, AND WIND, the Grand Canyon of the Yellowstone is one of the park's most striking features. Prominent points allow visitors to gape down to the Yellowstone River far below and the Upper and Lower Falls plunging over their precipices. Inspiration Point has accessible overlooks, Artist Point takes in the classic canyon view, and trails with steep stairways climb down to other viewing platforms.

Upstream at 7,732 feet, Yellowstone Lake is the largest freshwater high-elevation lake in North America. Rimmed with a handful of steaming thermals, the lake holds islands and remote bays that offer boaters, canoers, and kayakers plenty of places for solitude. Scenic drives tour miles and miles of shoreline where picnic areas offer places to enjoy the water, but be prepared for frigid temperatures.

Between the two locales, bison often create traffic jams in Hayden Valley. This wildlife-rich zone, bisected by the meandering Yellowstone River, is also home to elk, wolves, and trumpeter swans. Don't forget the binoculars; you'll definitely want them here.

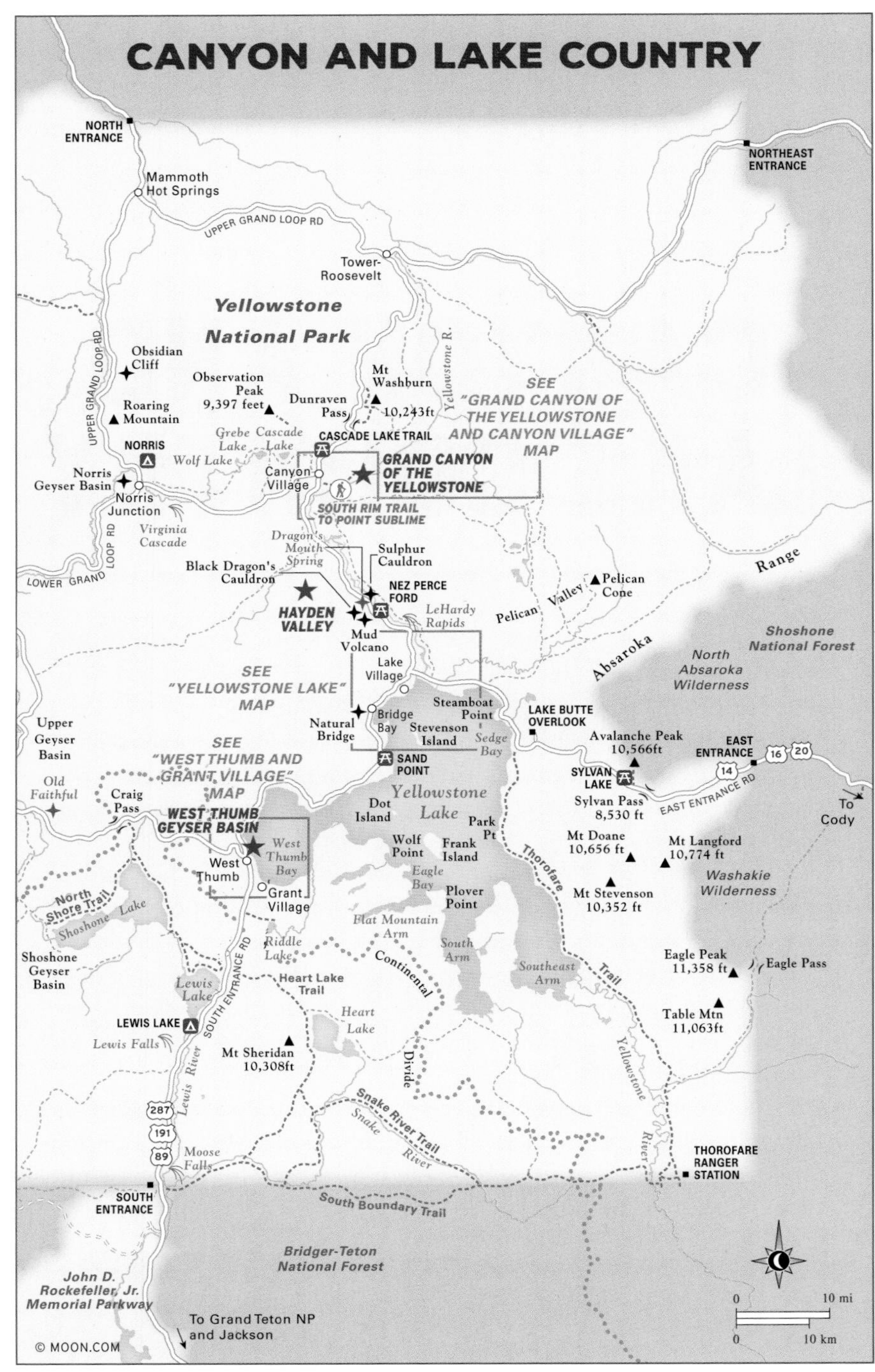
CANYON AND LAKE COUNTRY
NORTH ENTRANCE
Mammoth Hot Springs
UPPER GRAND LOOP RD
Tower-Roosevelt
NORTHEAST ENTRANCE
Yellowstone National Park
Obsidian Cliff
Observation Peak 9,397 feet
Mt Washburn 10,243ft
Dunraven Pass
Yellowstone R.
SEE "GRAND CANYON OF THE YELLOWSTONE AND CANYON VILLAGE" MAP
Roaring Mountain
Grebe Lake
Cascade Lake
CASCADE LAKE TRAIL
NORRIS
Wolf Lake
GRAND CANYON OF THE YELLOWSTONE
Canyon Village
Norris Geyser Basin
Norris Junction
SOUTH RIM TRAIL TO POINT SUBLIME
Virginia Cascade
Dragon's Mouth Spring
Sulphur Cauldron
Black Dragon's Cauldron
LOWER GRAND LOOP RD
NEZ PERCE FORD
Pelican Cone
Range
HAYDEN VALLEY
LeHardy Rapids
Pelican Valley
Mud Volcano
Absaroka
Shoshone National Forest
North Absaroka Wilderness
SEE "YELLOWSTONE LAKE" MAP
Lake Village
Steamboat Point
LAKE BUTTE OVERLOOK
Upper Geyser Basin
Natural Bridge
Bridge Bay
Stevenson Island
Sedge Bay
Avalanche Peak 10,566ft
EAST ENTRANCE
16
20
SEE "WEST THUMB AND GRANT VILLAGE" MAP
SAND POINT
SYLVAN LAKE
14
EAST ENTRANCE RD
Old Faithful
Craig Pass
Yellowstone Lake
Dot Island
Sylvan Pass 8,530 ft
To Cody
WEST THUMB GEYSER BASIN
Park Pt
Wolf Point
Frank Island
Mt Doane 10,656 ft
Mt Langford 10,774 ft
West Thumb
West Thumb Bay
Eagle Bay
Thorofare Trail
Washakie Wilderness
Mt Stevenson 10,352 ft
Grant Village
Plover Point
North Shore Trail
Shoshone Lake
Flat Mountain Arm
South Arm
Riddle Lake
Continental Divide
Southeast Arm
Eagle Peak 11,358 ft
Eagle Pass
Shoshone Geyser Basin
Heart Lake Trail
SOUTH ENTRANCE RD
Lewis Lake
Table Mtn 11,063ft
Heart Lake
LEWIS LAKE
Lewis Falls
Mt Sheridan 10,308ft
Yellowstone River
Lewis River
287
Snake River Trail
Snake River
191
89
Moose Falls
THOROFARE RANGER STATION
SOUTH ENTRANCE
South Boundary Trail
Bridger-Teton National Forest
John D. Rockefeller, Jr. Memorial Parkway
To Grand Teton NP and Jackson
0
10 mi
0
10 km
© MOON.COM

TOP 3

★ **1. GRAND CANYON OF THE YELLOWSTONE:** From 10 overlooks, view the thunderous Upper or Lower Falls and the colorful canyon (page 135).

★ **2. HAYDEN VALLEY:** Second only to Lamar Valley in wildlife-watching, this vast sagebrush meadow holds bison, elk, waterfowl and other animals (page 139).

★ **3. WEST THUMB GEYSER BASIN:** This geyser basin contains steaming hot pools and yields views across Yellowstone Lake to the Absaroka Mountains (page 140).

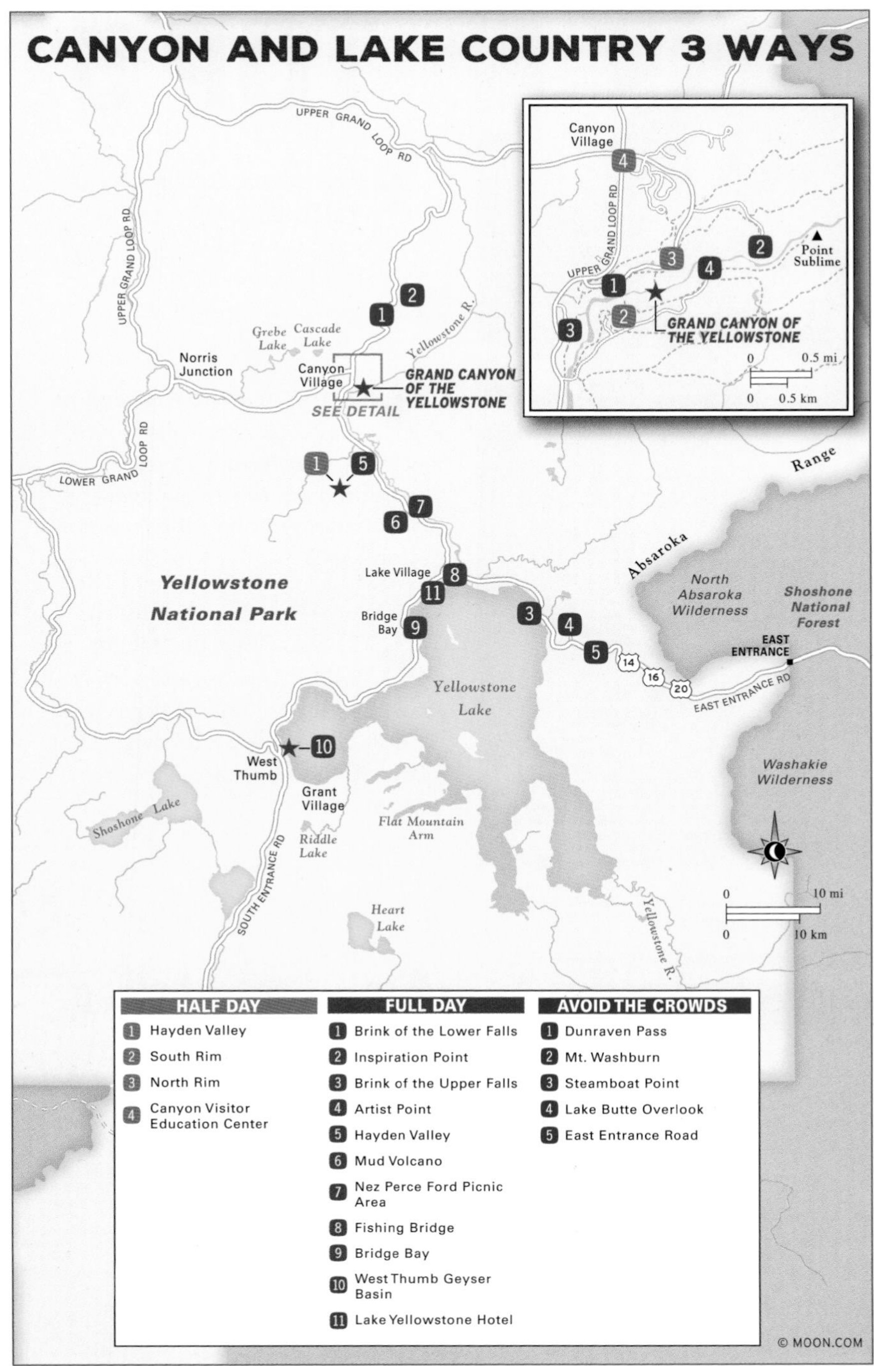
CANYON AND LAKE COUNTRY 3 WAYS
UPPER GRAND LOOP RD
Canyon Village
Point Sublime
GRAND CANYON OF THE YELLOWSTONE
0 0.5 mi
0 0.5 km
Grebe Lake
Cascade Lake
Norris Junction
Canyon Village
SEE DETAIL
Yellowstone R.
LOWER GRAND LOOP RD
Range
Absaroka
North Absaroka Wilderness
Shoshone National Forest
EAST ENTRANCE
EAST ENTRANCE RD
Yellowstone National Park
Lake Village
Bridge Bay
Yellowstone Lake
West Thumb
Grant Village
Riddle Lake
Flat Mountain Arm
Shoshone Lake
SOUTH ENTRANCE RD
Heart Lake
Washakie Wilderness
0 10 mi
0 10 km
HALF DAY
1 Hayden Valley
2 South Rim
3 North Rim
4 Canyon Visitor Education Center
FULL DAY
1 Brink of the Lower Falls
2 Inspiration Point
3 Brink of the Upper Falls
4 Artist Point
5 Hayden Valley
6 Mud Volcano
7 Nez Perce Ford Picnic Area
8 Fishing Bridge
9 Bridge Bay
10 West Thumb Geyser Basin
11 Lake Yellowstone Hotel
AVOID THE CROWDS
1 Dunraven Pass
2 Mt. Washburn
3 Steamboat Point
4 Lake Butte Overlook
5 East Entrance Road
© MOON.COM

CANYON AND LAKE COUNTRY 3 WAYS

HALF DAY

With minimal time, concentrate on two adjacent features in Yellowstone: Hayden Valley and Grand Canyon of the Yellowstone. Bring the binoculars and cameras.

1 Pull out the binoculars for wildlife-watching in **Hayden Valley** and expect to get caught in a bison jam. Bison, elk, and trumpeter swans are common, but wolves and bears also come through the area.

2 Head a few miles north to the Grand Canyon of the Yellowstone. Make two stops along the **South Rim:** one to see the thundering Upper Falls and the other to take in the famous view of the Lower Falls and canyon from Artist Point.

3 Backtrack to the main road, and drive up to the **North Rim** of the Grand Canyon of the Yellowstone. Climb to Lookout Point and descend to Red Rock Point for full views of the Lower Falls. Stop further at Grand View Point and Inspiration Point to peer into the canyon at the Yellowstone River far below.

4 Visit the **Canyon Visitor Education Center** to learn more about geology, and stop for a bite in one of the Canyon Village eateries.

2

1

FULL DAY

Plan an early start for the day in order to find parking at Grand Canyon of the Yellowstone. In order to cap off your day at the Lake Yellowstone Hotel, make reservations a year or more in advance.

1 Head first to Grand Canyon of the Yellowstone's North Rim. Stop at **Brink of the Lower Falls** and descend switchbacks to stand at the lip of the roaring waterfall in the canyon.

2 Then, drive to the overlooks at **Inspiration Point** to enjoy the canyon color.

3 Get back to Grand Loop Road and head south to **Brink of the Upper Falls.** Walk down to the viewing platform for a different perspective on the canyon's smaller waterfall.

4 Take South Rim Drive to the end, and pick up the classic view of the canyon from **Artist Point.**

5 Next, keep the binoculars handy for a drive through **Hayden Valley.** Look for waterfowl including Canada geese and trumpeter swans in the waterways, plus bison, elk, and deer in the sagebrush meadows.

6 On your way to Yellowstone Lake, stop at **Mud Volcano.** You'll smell this volcanic basin before you see it. Lower and upper loops go to otherworldly features that belch steam.

7 Take a lunch break at nearby **Nez Perce Ford Picnic Area,** where you can have a riverside picnic.

8 After a few more miles of driving, you'll hit Yellowstone Lake. Stroll across historic **Fishing Bridge,** which crosses over the Yellowstone River at the outlet of Yellowstone Lake. It's a good place to spot native trout spawning.

9 Hop aboard a boat tour from **Bridge Bay.** It's the easiest way to get out on Yellowstone Lake and see a few islands.

10 Explore the boardwalk loops at **West Thumb Geyser Basin,** a unique volcanic area that flanks Yellowstone Lake.

11 Return back up-lake to the **Lake Yellowstone Hotel,** a National Historic Landmark on the shore of Yellowstone Lake, to dine and spend the night.

1

AVOID THE CROWDS

To avoid crowds, get an early start or explore roads in the evening.

1 In the early morning, drive the curves up to **Dunraven Pass** for viewing alpine wildflower meadows and sometimes spotting bears or coyotes.

2 Hike or bike to the summit of **Mt. Washburn** to survey the Yellowstone landscape. On a clear day, you'll see the Teton Mountains to the south. (While you will encounter other hikers and bikers on Mt. Washburn, it's less crowded because of the exertion needed to reach the high-elevation summit.)

3 Head toward Yellowstone Lake, and enjoy the less-visited northern shoreline, including **Steamboat Point** with the steaming Steamboat Springs.

4 Take a side trip to **Lake Butte Overlook** for an expansive view of Yellowstone Lake.

5 In early evening, drive the **East Entrance Road** to rugged Sylvan Pass high in the Absaroka Mountains. Enjoy the lupine-lined road on the curvy descent back westward.

More Activities with Fewer Crowds

- Backpacking Heart Lake and Mt. Sheridan
- Boating on Yellowstone Lake
- Paddling on Yellowstone Lake, Lewis Lake, or Shoshone Lake

1

4

HIGHLIGHTS

★ GRAND CANYON OF THE YELLOWSTONE

South of Canyon Village are three entrances to Grand Canyon of the Yellowstone, the iconic 20-mi-long (30-km-long) canyon cut through lava rhyolite. The **Yellowstone River** chewed a colorful swath 1,000 ft (300 m) deep and 0.75 mi (1 km) wide through the landscape. The river plunges over the **Upper Falls** before thundering down the **Lower Falls,** the tallest (and most famous) falls in the park. Roads and trails with multiple overlooks flank the North and South Rims. If you have only a few minutes, stop at **Artist Point** on the South Rim or **Lookout Point** on the North Rim.

Some overlooks have short, easy paved routes, while others have descents that require strenuous climbs back up. The 8,000-ft (2,400-m) elevation may cause labored breathing for those coming from sea level. Prepare for crowds in summer: Tour buses disgorge swarms of visitors, parking lots are congested, and restrooms have long lines. Visit in early morning or evening for fewer people. Pick up a trail guide ($1) at visitors centers.

North Rim

The one-way **North Rim Drive** (east side of Lower Grand Loop Rd., 1.2 mi/1.9 km south of Canyon Junction) visits four signed overlooks of the canyon, Yellowstone River, and the 308-ft (94-m) Lower Falls.

The first stop is **Brink of the Lower Falls,** where a paved walkway with stairs leads to an overlook for views. To reach the actual brink requires a steep 357-ft (109-m) drop in elevation through multiple switchbacks to the platform, where underfoot you can feel the thundering of almost 40,000 gallons of water per second plummeting over the lip.

The second stop accesses **Lookout Point** via a quick paved ascent to an overlook of the Lower Falls and canyon. Just before the overlook, a 0.4-mi (0.6-km) switchback-and-boardwalk stairway trail plunges 315 ft (96 m) in elevation to

Lower Falls and Grand Canyon of the Yellowstone from Artist Point (left); Upper Falls of Yellowstone River (right)

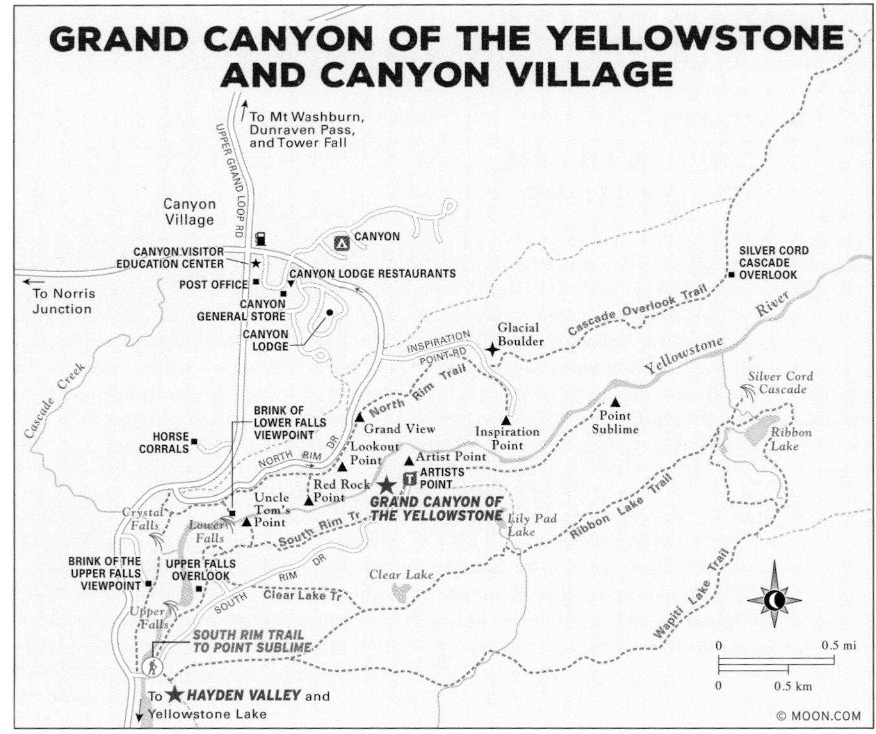

Red Rock Point, a perch closer to the Lower Falls.

The third stop on North Rim Drive is **Grand View,** a paved descent of 127 ft (39 m) in elevation to the overlook.

Near the end of North Rim Drive, turn right onto the two-lane road to reach the rebuilt **Inspiration Point** for the fourth and more distant view upcanyon. While the Lower Falls is not visible, the four newly rebuilt Inspiration Point rock-and-steel walkway platforms (three are wheelchair-accessible) offer spiraling views of the canyon and river.

From Lower Grand Loop Road (0.4 mi/0.6 km south of North Rim Dr.), turn east at the signed road to **Brink of the Upper Falls.** Walk 0.1 mi (160 m) upstream to a left turn for the short descent to the platform at the brink. The falls mesmerize with a roaring 109-ft (33-m) plunge.

South Rim

From **South Rim Drive** (1 mi/1.6 km south of Canyon Junction), cross the Chittenden Bridge to reach two main signed parking areas that have viewpoints of the canyon, Yellowstone River, Upper Falls, and Lower Falls. At **Uncle Tom's Point** (west side of the drive), park and follow the easy paved walkway to the **Upper Falls viewpoint** that faces the 109-ft (33-m) waterfall. North of the parking lot, a 0.25-mi (0.4-km) trail follows switchbacks and steel stairways to drop 500 ft (150 m) in elevation to **Uncle Tom's overlook**, a small steel platform yielding the closest view of the 308-ft (94-m) **Lower Falls.** Most visitors count the

328 metal stairs as they slog back up. South Rim Drive terminates at the parking lot for **Artist Point.** An easy, paved walkway leads to the classic view of the canyon and Lower Falls.

FISHING BRIDGE

East Entrance Rd. near the junction with Lower Grand Loop Rd.

Where the Yellowstone River exits Yellowstone Lake, the original log Fishing Bridge was erected over the waterway in 1902. The current bridge replaced it in 1937, with walkways on both sides to accommodate hordes of anglers going after cutthroat trout. Due to threats to the trout population from lake trout and overfishing, angling is no longer allowed on the bridge, but visitors can still watch spawning trout June-early July.

East of Fishing Bridge, **Pelican Creek** (East Entrance Rd.) offers prime wildlife-watching. Early morning and evening are best for spotting waterfowl, bald eagles, elk, moose, or bears. Twisting in slow eddies, the creek turns through a 2-mi-long (3-km-long) wetland that stretches 0.3 mi (0.4 km) wide. Use pullouts adjacent to the new bridge over the creek for the best places to scan for wildlife with binoculars.

Pelican Creek

YELLOWSTONE LAKE

At 7,733 ft (2,357 m), the natural Yellowstone Lake is the largest water body in Yellowstone National Park and the largest high-elevation freshwater lake in North America. Its stats

rocky shore of Yellowstone Lake

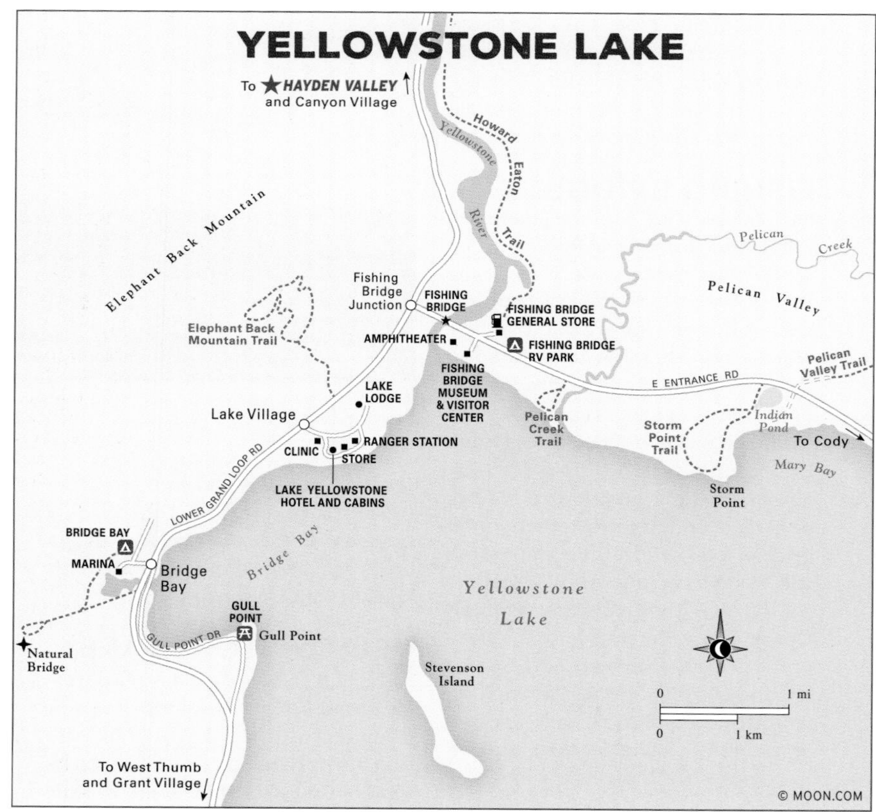

are impressive: 20 mi long by 15 mi wide (32 km long by 24 km wide), covering 136 square mi (352 square km) and diving to its deepest spot at 410 ft (125 m). With the exception of thermal areas, the lake freezes over with 3 ft (1 m) of ice in winter and often doesn't melt out until late May or early June, which means chilly water for swimming. Snowmelt causes the water to rise to its highest level in early June, flooding some south-end beaches and closing Gull Point Drive. Boating usually starts in mid-June. During summer and fall, afternoon winds frequently whip the lake into whitecaps.

Located partly inside the Yellowstone Caldera, the northern section of the lake has its origins in volcanic activity and lava flows—hence the springs at **Steamboat Point**—while the southern arms were formed from glaciers. The lake's thermal activity includes geysers, fumaroles, and hot springs. West Thumb Geyser Basin is the most accessible of these; the largest is a 2,000-ft-long (600-m-long) vent at the lake bottom that bulges up 100 ft (30 m).

The lake's six islands and shoreline attract wildlife. Look for trumpeter swans, pelicans, ducks, eagles, herons, and other shorebirds.

Bridge Bay Boat Tours

To get out on Yellowstone Lake, take the **Yellowstone Lake Scenic Cruise**

BEST PLACE TO WATCH THE SUNSET

From the East Entrance Road, the paved side spur of Lake Butte Road (1 mi/1.6 km; no RVs or trailers) climbs through the remains of a 2002 forest fire to 8,348-ft (2,544-m) **Lake Butte Overlook.** Here, you can see for miles, taking in the Absaroka Mountains and Yellowstone Lake. On clear days, you can spot the Teton Mountains in the distance to the south.

sunset from Lake Butte Overlook

(1 hour; departs 5-7 times daily mid-June-early Sept.; $19 adults, $11 children). From Bridge Bay Marina, the *Lake Queen* circles Stevenson Island, home to ospreys, eagles, ducks, herons, and other shorebirds. The interpretive tour fills you in on the lake's history, geology, and natural history while the enclosed boat shelters passengers from strong afternoon lake winds. Reservations are highly recommended midsummer. Plan to arrive at the marina 15 minutes prior to launch.

★ HAYDEN VALLEY

Wildlife-Watching

Occupying almost 50 square mi (130 square km) between Canyon and Fishing Bridge, Hayden Valley once held an arm of Yellowstone Lake. Today, it contains prime wildlife-watching. Look for coyote, moose, bison, elk, raptors, grizzly bears, trumpeter swans, wolves, and hordes of Canada geese. (Use the multiple pullovers to watch wildlife.) The **Yellowstone River** meanders through the sagebrush and grass valley, giving it a bucolic feel. No off-trail travel is allowed, and most waterways are closed to fishing in order to protect the sensitive area. Bring binoculars, spotting scopes, and cameras. Drive slowly; bison jams are frequent.

Mud Volcano

Before you see Mud Volcano, you'll smell the rotten-egg scent of hydrogen sulfide gas billowing from the earth. A 0.7-mi (1.1-km) boardwalk and trail tours several thermal

Hayden Valley (top); Dragon's Mouth Spring (middle); sunrise at West Thumb Geyser Basin (bottom)

features; the two most prominent ones are on the lower and shorter boardwalk loop. Mud Volcano is a 17-ft-deep (5-m-deep) burbling pot of watery clay that especially amuses kids when they can stand the stench. Nearby, hot steam from 170°F (77°C) water belches from **Dragon's Mouth Spring.** At the high end of the longer paved and stair-step boardwalk loop, **Black Dragon's Cauldron** stretches nearly 200 ft (60 m) across, bubbling up from a crack with the dark color created from iron sulfides. Pick up a trail guide ($1) at Mud Volcano.

At a pullout across the road to the north is one of the park's most acidic hot springs. On par with battery acid, **Sulphur Cauldron** boils with yellow color created from sulfur and bacteria.

★ WEST THUMB GEYSER BASIN

0.1 mi (0.2 km) northeast of West Thumb Junction

On West Thumb Bay in Yellowstone Lake, the West Thumb Geyser Basin is a smaller caldera within the larger Yellowstone Caldera. The geyser basin dumps more than 3,100 gallons of hot water daily into the lake and contains three geysers and 11 hot springs, plus fumaroles and mud pots. Two loops (0.8 mi/1.3 km) guide visitors around the thermal features.

The larger boardwalk loop cruises the lakeshore, where early park visitors once cooked fish in **Fishing Cone.** The striking turquoise and emerald **Abyss Pool** may be one of the deepest in the park at 53 ft (16 m). **Twin Geyser** has two vents that shoot water as high as 75 ft (23 m). Many of the colorful hot pools derive their hues from heat-happy thermophiles. Pick up a trail guide ($1) on the boardwalk.

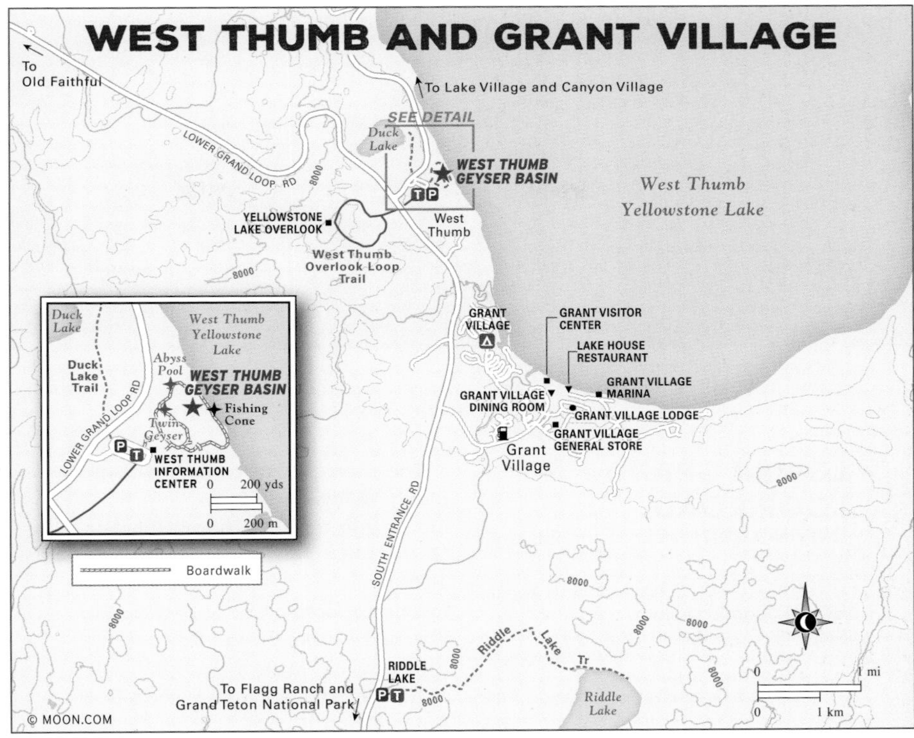

SCENIC DRIVES

EAST ENTRANCE ROAD

DRIVING DISTANCE: 27 mi (43 km) one-way
DRIVING TIME: 1 hour one-way
START: East Entrance Station
END: Fishing Bridge

From the East Entrance Station, the East Entrance Road (late-May–early Nov.) climbs a steep road through cliffs overlooking Middle Creek. Near the head of the valley, a pullout affords views down into the glacier-carved terrain. Amid howling winds, 8,524-ft (2,598-m) **Sylvan Pass** cuts through a rocky slot in the Absaroka Mountains. A small summit parking lot offers a place to scan the hillsides for bighorn sheep and peruse long, thin waterfalls.

On the descent, use second gear to avoid burning your brakes. At **Sylvan** and **Eleanor Lakes,** small pullouts allow photo ops. Thick lupine flanks the road as it plunges through the remains of a 2002 forest fire. For a giant view, take the 1-mi (1.6-km) paved side spur of **Lake Butte Road** (no RVs or trailers) to **Lake Butte Overlook.** After reaching the north shore of **Yellowstone Lake,** the road curves around **Steamboat Point,** a collection of puffing, noisy fumaroles, and **Mary Bay,** a volcanic caldera, to reach **Fishing Bridge.**

Dunraven Pass (left); Natural Bridge (right)

LOWER GRAND LOOP ROAD

DRIVING DISTANCE: 96 mi (155 km) one-way
DRIVING TIME: 4 hours one-way
START: Canyon Village
END: Old Faithful

The Lower Grand Loop Road (late May-early Nov.) links the Grand Canyon of the Yellowstone, Hayden Valley, Yellowstone Lake, West Thumb Geyser Basin, Old Faithful, and Norris Geyser Basin. Stops for touring geyser basins will add to your time.

Between Canyon Village and Fishing Bridge (16 mi/26 km; 45 min), the road tours the ultra-scenic **Hayden Valley,** cut by the meandering **Yellowstone River.** The valley usually has scads of **wildlife:** bison, elk, deer, and sometimes bears or wolves. For the best wildlife-watching, drive through Hayden Valley in the early morning or at dusk. Expect slow going where wildlife jams stall traffic. South of Hayden Valley, the smelly volcanic features of **Mud Volcano** and **Sulphur Cauldron** shoot steam across the road. **LeHardy Rapids** offers a place to spot harlequin ducks in early summer.

The scenic drive continues south along **Yellowstone Lake** from Fishing Bridge to West Thumb Junction (21 mi/34 km; 45 min). Stop in Lake Village to view the historic **Lake Yellowstone Hotel.** Continuing south, the road passes **Bridge Bay** and the trailhead to **Natural Bridge.** South of Bridge Bay, the conifer-lined **Gull Point Drive** (2.1 mi/3.4 km; often closes late May-June due to flooding) leads to **Gull Point Picnic Area,** where a long sandbar extends out into the lake at Gull Point—a good place for fishing and beachcombing with views across the lake to the Absaroka Mountains. South of Gull Point Drive, multiple **picnic areas** and pullouts offer places to enjoy the lake; prepare for afternoon wind. **West Thumb Geyser Basin** is on the left just before West Thumb Junction.

From West Thumb, the Lower Grand Loop Road heads west through lodgepole pine and spruce forests toward **Old Faithful** (17 mi/27 km; 45 min), reaching a south-side overlook that has trees occluding part of distant **Shoshone Lake.** The route pops out twice over the **Continental Divide,** the highest point at 8,391 ft (2,558 m). **Isa Lake,** located at **Craig**

Pass, has the unique status of flowing toward both the Pacific Ocean and the Gulf of Mexico. After Craig Pass, the road descends into **Old Faithful.**

DUNRAVEN PASS

DRIVING DISTANCE: 19 mi (35 km) one-way
DRIVING TIME: 40 minutes one-way
START: Canyon Junction
END: Tower Junction

On Upper Grand Loop Road north of Canyon Village, 8,859-ft (2,700-m) Dunraven Pass is the highest drive-to point in Yellowstone. Those coming from sea level will feel sluggish and short of breath just stepping a few feet from the car at scenic pullouts. The pass crosses the Washburn Range right at the base of **Mt. Washburn.** To reach the 10,243-ft (3,122-m) summit of Mt. Washburn and the lookout requires hiking or mountain biking.

From Canyon Junction drive north, climbing into open hillsides. The best viewpoint south of Dunraven Pass is 4.4 mi (7 km) up the road. At **Dunraven Pass** (4.8 mi/7.7km), the road launches into a curvy 7 percent descent to Tower Junction; shift into second gear to save your brakes. Sweeping views take in the Absaroka Mountains, herds of bison, and high meadows of wildflowers.

Dunraven Pass usually opens in **late May** but still has snow on the sides of the road. It will be **closed throughout 2021** for construction.

BEST HIKES

MT. WASHBURN

DISTANCE: 5.4-6.4 mi (8.7-10.3 km) round-trip
DURATION: 4 hours round-trip
ELEVATION CHANGE: 1,400-1,483 ft (427-452 m)
EFFORT: Strenuous by elevation
TRAILHEADS: For the south trail: Dunraven Pass Trailhead parking area on the east side of Grand Loop Road, 5.4 mi (8.7 km) north of Canyon Junction. For the north trail: 10.3 mi (16.6 km) north of Canyon Junction, drive 1.3 mi (2.1 km) up Chittenden Road to reach the parking area.

At 10,243 ft (3,122 m), the Mt. Washburn Lookout yields a 360-degree panorama with big views. On a clear day, hikers can see the Grand Canyon of the Yellowstone, Yellowstone Lake, and even the Tetons. The Chittenden Trail is steeper and has a bit more elevation gain than the Dunraven Pass Trail, but both high-elevation trails climb up switchbacks in a steady plod on former roads. The sheer elevation leaves big crowds behind.

The **Dunraven Pass Trail** (6.4 mi/10.3 km; hikers only) traverses across a southern slope before swinging north at 9,100 ft (2,775 m). It then makes four switchbacks up a west slope to crest a long ridge for a scenic walk that finishes with a 360-degree circle to Mt. Washburn Lookout. In upper elevation cliffs and meadows, look for bighorn sheep.

The steeper **Chittenden Trail** (5.4 mi/8.7 km; bicycles allowed) ascends just below a ridge with a few switchbacks thrown in to work up the slope. On the final ridge, the trail swings east and then switchbacks west for the last steps to the summit of Mt. Washburn.

At the summit, **Mt. Washburn Lookout** is an ugly three-story cement

TOP HIKE
SOUTH RIM TRAIL TO POINT SUBLIME

Distance: 5.1 mi (8.2 km) round-trip
Duration: 3 hours round-trip
Elevation change: 250-750 ft (75-230 m)
Effort: Easy to strenuous
Trailheads: South trailhead: Wapiti Picnic Area on South Rim Drive, on the east side of the bridge over the Yellowstone River. North trailhead: Artist Point parking lot at terminus of South Rim Drive

The South Rim Trail has multiple overlooks of the Grand Canyon of the Yellowstone. From the Wapiti Picnic Area, a 0.4-mi (0.6-km) forested walk heads north, following the Yellowstone River to the first viewpoint at the **Upper Falls.** A spur trail drops 15 ft (5 m) to the viewpoint. After circling north on the bluff for snippets of views, the strenuous **Uncle Tom's Trail** plunges 500 ft (150 m) down paved switchbacks and 328 metal stair steps (that you have to climb back up) to an overlook. Skip this if you want the easy walk.

Past Uncle Tom's Trail, the route continues east through the forest, with several viewpoints along the canyon rim, until it reaches the Artist Point

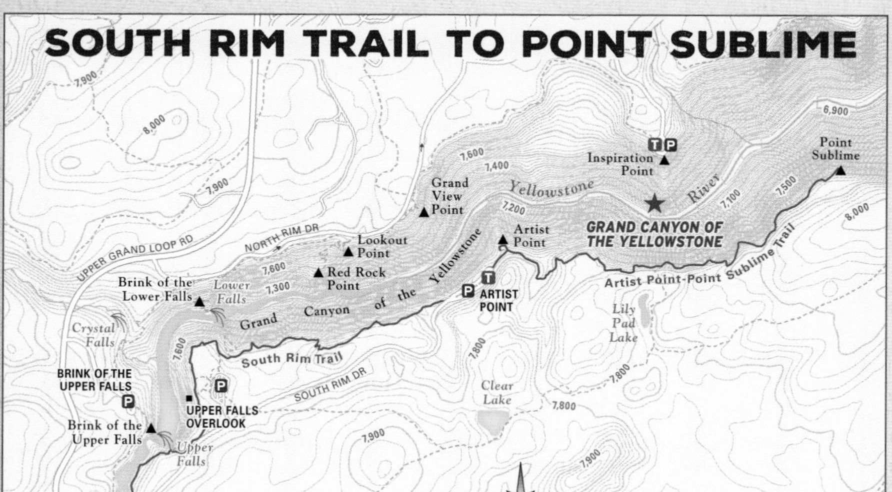

SOUTH RIM TRAIL TO POINT SUBLIME

parking lot. Walk northeast through the parking lot to reach the **Artist Point Trailhead** and continue 0.1 mi (160 m) to the scenic point. From Artist Point, the dirt trail continues east 0.75 mi (1.2 km) to **Point Sublime,** and you leave many of the crowds behind. On this section, exposed overlooks (no railings) require caution to take in the depth of the canyon. The Lower Falls drops out of view, but the canyon walls and hoodoos become far more colorful with smears of reds and pinks above the frothy blue water. The trail dead-ends at Point Sublime at a log railing where the forest claims the canyon.

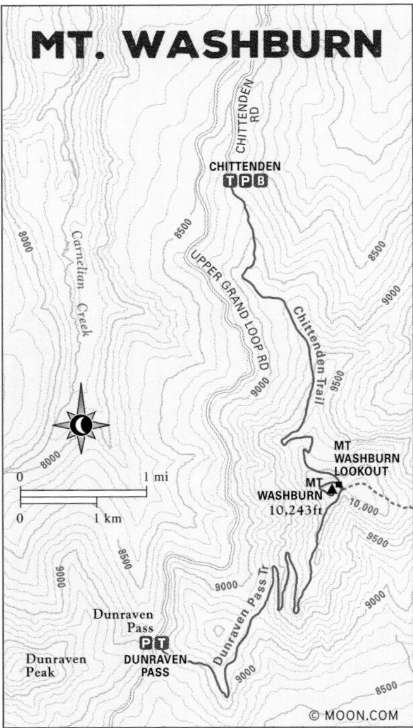

block covered in radio equipment. Visitors can access only two levels: An observation room with windows on three sides has interpretive displays and a viewing scope, and a windy deck offers views. Restrooms are available.

Slopes may be **snow-covered in June** but burst with alpine wildflowers by July. Due to afternoon thunderstorms, plan to **descend before early afternoon.** Even though the treeless trail looks hot, **bring warm clothing;** the alpine tundra summit is often windy and cold. Due to the trail's popularity, you'll have company at the lookout.

CASCADE LAKE AND GREBE LAKE

DISTANCE: 4.4-8 miles (7-13 km) round-trip
DURATION: 2.5-4 hours round-trip
ELEVATION CHANGE: 60-350 ft (18-107 m)
EFFORT: Easy
TRAILHEAD: Cascade Picnic Area on Grand Loop Road, 1.3 mi (2.1 km) north of Canyon Junction or Grebe Lake Trailhead on the Canyon-Norris Road, 3.8 miles (6 km) west of Canyon Junction

Spring snowmelt can make this trail muddy in marshy areas on this first portion of the Chain of Lakes Trail. June and July usually bring on bluebells, prairie smoke, and elephant's head lousewort in the meadows. Prepare for swarms of mosquitoes throughout summer.

From Cascade Picnic Area, a relatively flat route crosses through large meadows made marshy by myriad streams. (Some streams have footbridges, while others don't.) Before reaching Cascade Lake, the easternmost lake in the Chain of Lakes, you'll pass a trail junction to Observation Peak. A bit farther, **Cascade Lake** (4.4 mi/7 km round-trip) is cradled in a basin surrounded by meadows. Lily pads cover its southwest end, and you may see trumpeter swans.

Continuing around the north side of Cascade Lake, the Chain of Lakes Trail enters a loose forest broken by meadows. The trail rolls gently up to reach **Grebe Lake** (8 mi/12.9 km round-trip), the largest of the Chain of Lakes. It holds rainbow trout and arctic grayling that lure anglers. Meadows and marshes surround the scenic lake. When high water abates after June, beaches appear on the north shore.

Grebe Lake also has an alternate trailhead on Canyon-Norris Road west of Canyon Junction. From this trailhead, hike northward through a lodgepole forest that is fast regrowing from the 1988 fires. Portions of

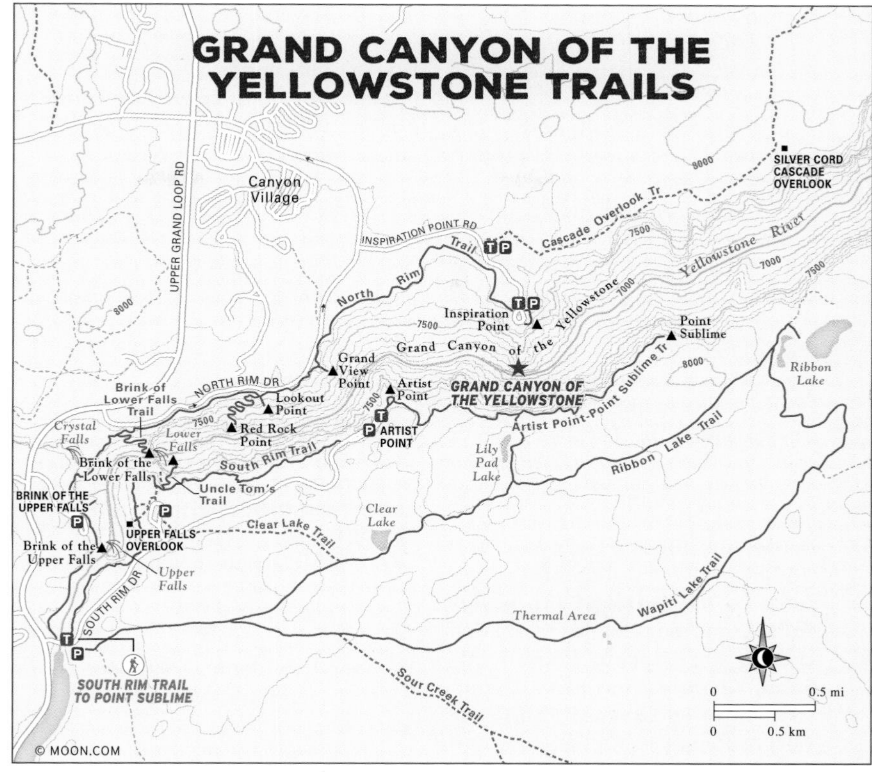

the trail are dusty, hot, and open. After arcing over a gentle hump, the trail reaches the lake's southeast side (6.6 mi/10.6 km round-trip), then arcs north around the lake.

NORTH RIM OF GRAND CANYON OF THE YELLOWSTONE

DISTANCE: 3.8-6.6 mi (6.1-10.6 km) one-way
DURATION: 3-4 hours one-way
ELEVATION CHANGE: 250-1,500 ft (75-460 m)
EFFORT: Easy to strenuous
TRAILHEAD: Wapiti Lake Trailhead on South Rim Drive, on the west side of the bridge over the Yellowstone River
DIRECTIONS: Park at Wapiti Picnic Area on the east side of South Rim Drive. Walk back across the Chittenden Bridge over the Yellowstone River to find the trailhead heading north.

This trail is not about backcountry solitude, but rather tremendous views of the Grand Canyon of the Yellowstone. A combination of paved and dirt trails link together multiple overlooks; some include steel stairways and boardwalks down to overlook platforms. You can start at either the north or south end to hike the entire trail, or shorten the distance by driving some segments. (In several places, the trail pops out to cross parking lots on North Rim Drive.) Spur trails also drop down switchbacks and steep stairways to viewing platforms; all require climbing back up. Completing all the spurs adds a climb of nearly 1,500 ft (460 m) in elevation and 2.8 more mi (4.5 km).

To start at the **south end** of the North Rim Trail, cross Chittenden Bridge to follow the Yellowstone River downstream (heading north). In 0.4 mi (0.6 km), the trail reaches the first viewpoint at **Brink of the Upper Falls.** A spur trail drops 42 ft (13 m) to an overlook of the 109-ft (33-m) falls. Continue north, passing the parking lot for Brink of the Upper Falls, to the 130-ft (40-m) **Crystal Falls** as it spews from a slot in the North Rim cliffs. Next, the 308-ft (94-m) **Lower Falls** comes into view; follow the trail to a junction where a spur plummets 600 ft (185 m) down switchbacks and stairs to the **Brink of the Lower Falls.** Climb back up and continue east to the **Lookout Point Trailhead,** where a short trail goes up 25 ft (8 m) to **Lookout Point.** Just west, a longer trail plunges 500 ft (150 m) in 0.4 mi (0.6 km) down switchbacks and steep stairs to **Red Rock Point.** Returning to the North Rim Trail, continue north to **Grand View Point,** where a short, paved trail drops about 150 ft (45 m) to the viewpoint. Past Grand View Point, the trail curls northeast about 1.3 mi (2.1 km) to the **Inspiration Point** parking lot, where you can take in canyon views from four viewpoints.

To hike the trail in reverse, start at the **north end** by parking at Inspiration Point. For the 3.8-mi (6.1-km) one-way hike, leave a car at either the Inspiration Point or Wapiti Picnic Area parking lot. Or return the way you came for a 7.6-mi (12.2-km) out-and-back hike.

STORM POINT

DISTANCE: 2.3 mi (3.7 km) round-trip
DURATION: 1.5 hours round-trip
ELEVATION CHANGE: 40 ft (12 m)
EFFORT: Easy
TRAILHEAD: Indian Pond pullout on the East Entrance Road, 3 mi (4.8 km) east of Fishing Bridge

This loop hike offers wildlife-watching from an impressive point on the north shore of Yellowstone Lake. Grizzlies frequent the area, which can sometimes close the trail (check trail status at Fishing Bridge Ranger Station). Look for waterfowl at Indian Pond, marmots at Storm Point, and bison in the meadows. Winds can

Red Rock Point (left); Storm Point Trail on Yellowstone Lake (right)

rage across the point, so bring an extra layer.

From the pullout at **Indian Pond,** the trail cuts across a sagebrush meadow for 0.2 mi (0.3 km) to a fork. The left fork heads straight toward **Mary Bay,** an ancient caldera on Yellowstone Lake, before swinging into the forest to reach the rocky **Storm Point** that juts out into the lake and takes the brunt of winds from the south. From Storm Point, you can see Stevenson Island and Mt. Sheridan in the distance. The trail continues west along broken rock and sandy bluffs reminiscent of an ocean coast with sandy beaches and driftwood. Clusters of yellow arrowleaf balsamroot flank the trail as it cuts back into the woods, where winds make the conifers clatter and creak. The trail returns to the fork in the meadow and the pullout.

YELLOWSTONE LAKE OVERLOOK

DISTANCE: 2 mi (3.2 km) round-trip
DURATION: 1.5 hours round-trip
ELEVATION CHANGE: 194 ft (59 m)
EFFORT: Easy
TRAILHEAD: West side of the West Thumb Geyser Basin parking lot

The Lake Overlook Trail climbs from the start, beginning in a meadow and entering a forest. In 0.3 mi (0.5 km), the trail crosses the **South Entrance Road** and reaches a **fork.** Turn left and continue hiking south up to a meadow with red paintbrush and yellow buckwheat in early summer; the panoramic views of Yellowstone Lake and the Absaroka Mountains unfold. Sit on the **bench** to enjoy the view, and climb a **short spur** behind the bench about 30 ft (9 m) for a peekaboo view of the Tetons. Complete the loop to return to the parking lot.

BACKPACKING

Backpacking in canyon and lake country takes you close to water, with treks going to Heart and Shoshone Lakes, both very popular with permits in high demand, and along Chain of Lakes Trail, which is a favorite among anglers. The best is the multiday Heart Lake and Mt. Sheridan trip.

HEART LAKE AND MT. SHERIDAN

21 mi (34 km)

Competition for permits is keen for Heart Lake, which is closed until July because it's a prime grizzly habitat. For a 21-mi (34-km) round-trip trek, spend two nights at **Heart Lake** and climb the steep 2,700-ft (825-m) vertical trail up **Mt. Sheridan** on the middle day. Campsite 8H1 is the most secluded; campsites 8H5 and 8H6 are closest to the Mt. Sheridan Trail.

summit of Mt. Sheridan

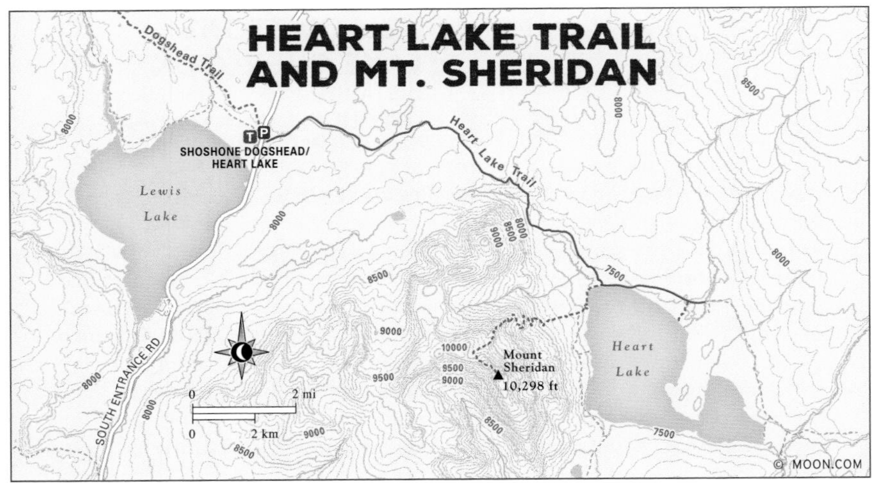

PERMITS

Backpackers must obtain permits ($3/person, children 8 and younger free) for assigned backcountry campsites. Permits are available in person 48 hours in advance from the backcountry offices at Canyon Village, Lake Village, or Grant Village. For more information, see the *Essentials* chapter.

BIKING

ROAD BIKING

During spring, after roads are plowed (late Mar.-early Apr.), the **South Entrance Road to West Thumb** (22 mi/35 km) and the **East Entrance Road to Sylvan Pass** (6 mi/9.5 km) are open to bicycles but remain closed to vehicles until May. In November, the roads once again close to vehicles but remain open for bicycling. Cyclists can ride until snow covers the road.

MOUNTAIN BIKING

Mountain bikes are only permitted in a few locations, mostly on old roadbeds; they are not allowed on trails. Mountain bikers can explore shorter routes that are especially good for kids. At **Lake Village,** a 1-mi (1.6-km) slice of road runs from Lake Yellowstone Hotel to Grand Loop Road south of Lake Junction. Although short, the level ride is scenic along the waterfront of Yellowstone Lake. At Bridge Bay, mountain bikers can ride an old 1-mi (1.6-km) road to **Natural Bridge**.

Mt. Washburn Lookout

5.4 mi (8.7 km) round-trip

The most challenging mountain-bike ride goes to Mt. Washburn Lookout. From the Chittenden Road parking lot, bikers grunt 2.7 mi (4.3 km) up to the lookout. The difficulty level is compounded by the 10,243-ft (3,122-m) summit elevation, but the return trip sails downhill. (The Dunraven Pass route is not open to bikers.)

BOATING AND PADDLING

BOATING

Yellowstone Lake

With 141 mi (227 km) of shoreline and six islands, Yellowstone Lake offers expansive water for boating, angling, island touring, and overnighting. Touring the east shore of the lake is best in the morning, as afternoon winds can push heavily onto the shore. In the South and Southeast Arms, no-wake zones marked by buoys reduce travel speeds.

Two marinas operated by Xanterra (tel. 307/344-7311; www.yellowstonenationalparklodges.com) tuck into sheltered bays. **Bridge Bay Marina** has a boat launch with cement ramp, docks, moorage, rentals, store, and boat gas. The marina has separate parking zones designated for day use and overnighters. On the West Thumb, **Grant Village Marina** (mid-June-Oct.) has a boat launch with a cement ramp, docks, and boat slips, but no services.

Four docks allow places to tie up for land explorations: at the south end of Frank Island, Wolf Point, Eagle Bay, and Plover Point. Priority for tying up is for overnighters with permits; day-use boaters must be accommodating. Motorized boats can overnight at 32 primitive **campsites;** some are anchoring sites for sleeping aboard.

Be aware of **boating closures.** Thermal areas, hotel beaches, and Yellowstone Lake's outlet are closed. **Stevenson** and **Frank Islands** are closed mid-May to mid-August to protect nesting birds, although you can still tour the waters around the islands.

Sailboaters should check into launch sites for keel and mast requirements. At Bridge Bay, you may need to lower the mast in order to go under a bridge to reach the lake. At Grant Village, lake levels in late summer may not be deep enough for keels.

Lewis Lake

Lewis Lake is prized for its beauty, quiet ambience, and fishing for brown trout. Though it is smaller than Yellowstone Lake, afternoon winds still churn up waves. Most winds come from the west or southwest, so you'll find more sheltered boating along the west shore.

The lake connects with the larger **Shoshone Lake** via the **Lewis Channel;** however, motorized boats are not permitted up the channel beyond the signed closure. If you have an outboard motor, you can detach the motor and chain it up with a lock onshore at the sign to row upstream.

A **boat launch** with a cement ramp and dock is adjacent to the Lewis Lake Campground, accessed from a well-signed turnoff on the South Entrance Road. Parking areas are designated for day-use and overnight boaters.

Rentals

BRIDGE BAY MARINA

June-Oct. for boat launch, daily mid-June-early Sept. for rentals and charters

The marina rents 18-ft boats with 40-horsepower outboard motors ($60/hour, first-come, first-served). They also run a reservation charter service ($103/hour) for guided fishing or sightseeing.

PADDLING

Paddle sports allow boaters to access some of the most scenic waterways in Yellowstone, particularly Shoshone Lake and the South and Southeast Arms of Yellowstone Lake. The quiet plop of the paddle into the water offers a chance to hear the cry of an eagle in the trees or the snap of twigs from a bear walking along shore.

The water is frigid—bring a paddling jacket and pants or wetsuit. Winds crop up huge and fast with whitecaps, so stick to shoreline paddles or wait until winds subside rather than crossing open water. Since onshore winds batter eastern shores, stick to western shorelines for more sheltered paddling.

Boating regulations are available online (www.nps.gov/yell), including required boat, fishing, and backcountry camping permits. **No kayak, canoe, or paddleboard rentals are available inside Yellowstone National Park.** Bring your own or rent in Jackson Hole.

Yellowstone Lake

Paddlers can launch from multiple locations to tour the shoreline of Yellowstone Lake. To launch from developed boat ramps, go to Bridge Bay Marina or Grant Village Marina. You can carry your boat or paddleboard to launch from any Yellowstone Lake picnic area, at Sedge Bay on the north shore, or from Gull Point Drive along the west shore between Lake Village and West Thumb.

Be aware that paddling around thermal areas, hotel beaches, and wildlife preserves is restricted. In the Southeast Arm nonmotorized zone, the Molly Islands are a bird sanctuary; beaching boats is prohibited. Travel at least 0.5 mi (0.8 km) out to protect this wild zone.

For prized overnight paddle trips, **campsites** are strung around the lake, with 10 coveted sites in the quiet nonmotorized zones of South and Southeast Arms. These bays with paddler-accessible campsites have abundant wildlife and birds. You can also overnight in Flat Mountain Bay

Bridge Bay

and the smaller Wolf and Eagle Bays, but you will share water with motorboaters. To avoid paddling the long distance across open water, make advance reservations for a **shuttle** from Bridge Bay Marina (reservations tel. 307/344-7311, summer shuttle office tel. 307/242-3893; www.yellowstonenationalparklodges.com; mid-June-mid-Sept.; $214/2 hours), which can take up to six people with gear and a few canoes or kayaks. Make a shuttle reservation also for pickup at a predetermined day, time, and location. For overnight trips, rental canoes ($53/night) are available.

Lewis Lake

Higher than Yellowstone Lake, the much smaller Lewis Lake sits at 7,830 ft (2,387 m). While it offers pleasant day paddling, most paddlers use it as a waterway to access the Lewis Channel and Shoshone Lake, both nonmotorized zones. Unless the lake is dead calm, take a shoreline route rather than crossing open water. On many days, winds start at 10am and the trees along the western shore provide a little shelter; the eastern shore takes the brunt of winds pushing on shore.

A **boat launch** with a cement ramp and dock is at the south end of Lewis Lake, adjacent to the campground. Park in the appropriate zone for day-use or overnight parking. A second, more difficult launch (due to onshore winds) is along the northeast shore of the lake. Look for a parking pullout about 1.6 mi (2.6 km) north of the boat launch; it has a short pebble-beach access.

Shoshone Lake

Shoshone Lake is on every serious paddler's bucket list: It has seclusion, wildlife, a geyser basin, an access via a river channel (after paddling across Lewis Lake), and no road or motorized boat access. Lewis Channel is about 3 mi (4.8 km) long as the crow flies, but river convolutions make the route longer. Paddle up the slow-moving stream for the first 2 mi (3.2 km) to encounter the challenge: wading the last mile due to the water moving too fast to paddle upstream or being too shallow.

Wading the upper portion of the **Lewis Channel** is easier if you bring a 15-ft (5-m) rope to pull your boat. Early summer paddlers (into early July) will need a wetsuit or drysuit to cope with the cold, deep (up to 4 ft/1 m) runoff of the high-water season. If that sounds too challenging, wait until August when the water warms slightly and lowers in depth. With a sturdy pair of water shoes to protect your feet on rocks, you can wade the last mile in calf-deep water.

Shoshone Lake is divided into two sections by **the Narrows,** a pinch in

Lewis Lake

the shoreline squeezing the lake to a half mile wide. The Narrows provides the best place to cross open water, if you must do so. Otherwise, the southeast shore is the safest travel route; winds hammer the east shore with waves up to 3 ft (1 m). To visit **Shoshone Geyser Basin,** with 80 active geysers, beach boats at the landing area denoted with an orange marker. Find the area in a small bay in the northwest corner of the lake, where a trail connects to the geyser basin. You can overnight at one of 16 boating **campsites** on the north or south shore.

WINTER SPORTS

SNOWMOBILING

The Yellowstone snowmobile season runs **mid-December to early March.** Several companies guide **snowmobile tours** (www.nps.gov/yell) to Grand Canyon of the Yellowstone, launching from West Yellowstone, Gardiner, Mammoth Hot Springs, and Flagg Ranch. You can go on your own with a **permit** (www.recreation.gov; early Sept.-early Oct.) from the annual lottery and an approved BAT (Best Available Technology) snowmobile. Snowmobile rentals are only available in West Yellowstone, Gardiner, and Jackson.

TOURS

At Grand Canyon of the Yellowstone, you can tour snowy canyon rim trails to enjoy the frozen splendor of the giant chasm; all snow-covered roads become winter ski and snowshoe routes in winter. Bring your own cross-country skis and snowshoes; rentals are only available at Old Faithful, Mammoth Hot Springs, West Yellowstone, and Jackson. Find winter trail maps online (www.nps.gov/yell) and at visitors centers. Snowcoaches are required to reach many trails, so most skiers and snowshoers tour with guides.

Canyon Snowcoach Tours

Xanterra; tel. 307/344-7311; www.yellowstonenationalparklodges.com; mid-Dec.-Feb.; $287

Cross-country ski and snowshoe tours of Grand Canyon of the Yellowstone depart from **Old Faithful Snow Lodge** several days weekly for a 10-hour adventure. A two-hour snowcoach ride gets you to the canyon, where a guide leads you along the canyon rim to see the Upper and Lower Falls. Ski tours go about 6 mi (10 km); snowshoe tours travel 3 mi (5 km). Advanced beginners can handle the easy routes. Lunch is included; reservations are required.

Yellowstone Expeditions

536 Firehole Ave., West Yellowstone; tel. 406/646-9333 or 800/728-9333; http://yellowstoneexpeditions.com; late Dec.-early Mar.; $1,260-2,200/person double occupancy

Yellowstone Expeditions leads cross-country ski and snowshoe tours from their yurt camp. This is a bucket-list trip (especially during a full moon). Located at 8,000 ft (2,400 m) about 0.5 mi (0.8 km) from Grand Canyon of the Yellowstone, the camp is the only overnight winter facility on the park's east side. Two large yurts serve as the dining room and kitchen, which rolls out yummy meals. A sauna soothes muscles after skiing, and a heated restroom building has a hot shower and large pit toilet rooms. Sleeping is in two-person heated huts. Guides lead daily ski tours from camp or after a short shuttle. Packages (four, five, or eight days) include snowcoach transportation from West Yellowstone and on daily ski treks, lodging, sleeping bags with flannel sheets, meals, and guide service. Rental skis or snowshoes are available. January rates are lowest, when daylight hours are shortest. Tip 20 percent.

Cross-country ski and snowshoe tours go to Grand Canyon of the Yellowstone in winter.

FOOD

Dining is limited to restaurants and cafés operated by Xanterra and Delaware North Company; each concessionaire offers different menus. Mid-June to early September, expect long waits (up to an hour or so) at some restaurants. Canyon Lodge M66 Grill, Lake Yellowstone Hotel Dining Room, and Grant Village Dining Room **require dinner reservations;** book **12-18 months in advance** when you make your lodging reservations. Those not staying in the lodges can make dinner reservations 60 days in advance. In all park restaurants, dress is casual and kiddie menus are available. All restaurants are open daily within their season. In spring and fall, hours may shorten. For traveling, all lodges sell deli lunches to go or items to create your own lunch.

STANDOUTS

Canyon General Store

2 Canyon Village Loop Rd.; tel. 406/586-7593; www.yellowstonevacations.com; 7:30am-8:30pm daily mid-Apr.-late Oct.; $5-14

The Canyon General Store has a large soda fountain diner with red stools set around four huge peninsula counters. Music from the 1950s adds a retro feel. The diner serves breakfast until 10:30am, followed by lunch and dinner with burgers, sandwiches, fries, salads, soda fountain ice-cream treats (made with Wilcoxson's ice cream from Montana), and Junior Ranger meals for kids, too.

Lake Yellowstone Hotel Dining Room

daily mid-May-early Oct.

Lake Yellowstone Hotel is the headliner place to dine. Surrounded on three sides by large windows with peekaboo views of the lake, the Lake Yellowstone Hotel Dining Room clusters tables around white columns that echo the exterior architecture of the colonial building. Order **breakfast** (6:30am-10am; $5-17) off the menu; if you're in a hurry, go for the buffet. Specialties include eggs Benedict on crab cakes and huckleberry-cream-cheese-stuffed French

CANYON AND LAKE COUNTRY FOOD OPTIONS

NAME	LOCATION	TYPE
Canyon Lodge M66 Bar & Grill	Canyon Village	sit-down restaurant
Canyon Lodge Eatery	Canyon Village	cafeteria-style
Canyon Lodge Falls Café	Canyon Village	take-out
★ Canyon General Store	Canyon Village	café
Fishing Bridge General Store	Fishing Bridge	café and take-out
Lake Village General Store	Lake Village	café and take-out
★ Lake Yellowstone Hotel Dining Room	Lake Yellowstone Hotel at Lake Village	sit-down restaurant
Deli at Lake Yellowstone Hotel	Lake Yellowstone Hotel at Lake Village	take-out
Wylie's Canteen	Lake Lodge at Lake Village	cafeteria
★ Grant Village Dining Room	Grant Village	sit-down restaurant
Grant Village Lake House Restaurant	Grant Village Marina	sit-down restaurant
Grant Village Grill	Grant Village	take-out
Grant Village General Store	Grant Village	café, grocery, and take-out

FOOD	PRICE	HOURS
Western American	moderate	6:30am-10am, 5pm-10pm daily mid-May-mid-Oct. (reservations required for dinner)
Asian and American	budget	6:30am-10am, 11:30am-3pm, 4:30pm-10pm daily mid-May-mid-Oct.
casual American	budget	6am-9pm daily mid-May-early Sept.
diner-style food	budget	7:30am-8:30pm daily mid-Apr.-late Oct.
diner-style food	budget	daily late May-early Oct.
casual American	budget	daily mid-May-late-Sept.
contemporary American	moderate-splurge	6:30am-10am, 11:30am-2:30pm, 5pm-10pm daily mid-May-early Oct. (reservations required for dinner)
deli food	budget	7am-8pm daily mid-May-early Oct.
casual and Western American	moderate	6:30am-9:30pm daily early June-early Sept.
casual and contemporary American	moderate	6:30am-10am, 11:30am-2:30pm, 5pm-10pm daily late May-Sept. (reservations required for dinner)
buffet (breakfast) and Western American (dinner)	moderate	6:30am-10:30am, 5pm-9pm daily late May-late Sept.
diner-style food	budget	7:30am-8:30pm daily late May-Sept.
diner-style food and groceries	budget	daily late May-Sept.

toast. **Lunch** (11:30am-2:30pm; $10-18) features burgers, sandwiches, salads, noodle bowls, and trout. **Dinner** (5pm-10pm; $15-40) offers multiple courses with appetizers, soups, and salads followed by entrées of fresh fish, bison, elk, lamb, salads, or burgers. The wine list includes western and international vintages. Reservations are not accepted for breakfast or lunch, but advance reservations *are* required for dinner and should be made when booking your lodging 12-18 months in advance. (If you are not staying in Lake Yellowstone Hotel, make reservations 60 days in advance.)

Grant Village Dining Room

daily late May-Sept.

Tucked in the forest, the Grant Village Dining Room is a vaulted room with a wood ceiling and large-paned windows looking out on the lake through trees. **Breakfast** (6:30am-10am; $5-15) can be ordered from the menu; for a quicker meal, choose the breakfast buffet. **Lunch** (11:30am-2:30pm; $10-15) includes salads, burgers, sandwiches, and fish entrées. **Dinner** (5pm-10pm; $16-33) starts with appetizers, salads, and soups before moving on to specialties of trout, prime rib, bison meatloaf, and eggplant. Beer, cocktails, and wine are available. Dinner reservations are required and should be made when booking your room in Grant Village Lodge 12-18 months in advance; if staying elsewhere, make reservations 60 days in advance.

BEST PICNIC SPOTS

Scads of picnic areas line Grand Loop Road between Dunraven Pass and Yellowstone Lake. The lake brims with 13 sites with the best located on the west shore, which is more protected from winds that batter the north shore.

Cascade Lake Trail

Between Canyon Junction and Dunraven Pass, at the trailhead to Cascade Lake

This large picnic area has tables, several fire rings with grills (bring firewood), and an accessible vault toilet. Best of all, before or after picnicking, you can hike through wildflower meadows to Cascade Lake.

Nez Perce Ford

Between Canyon Junction and Fishing Bridge Junction, south of Hayden Valley

Set along the scenic Yellowstone

Lake Yellowstone Hotel Dining Room (top); Grant Village Dining Room (bottom left); Sylvan Lake Picnic Area (bottom right)

River, this large picnic area offers quick access to wildlife-watching in Hayden Valley, exploring Mud Volcano, and spotting harlequin ducks in May–June at LeHardy Rapids. It has picnic tables and a vault toilet. The site is also part of the Nez Perce National Historic Trail.

Sylvan Lake

On the East Entrance Road, west of Sylvan Pass

Split between the shore of shallow Sylvan Lake and across the road along a creek in the trees, this picnic spot offers scenery and fishing for cutthroat trout. Facilities include tables and a vault toilet.

Gull Point

On Yellowstone Lake south of Bridge Bay, on Gull Point Drive

Tucked in the trees on Gull Point, this large picnic area offers a way to explore the shore of Yellowstone Lake. You can fish, play in the water protected by a spit from the lake's big waves, skip rocks, or enjoy the scenery with a backdrop across the lake of the Absaroka Mountains. Facilities include picnic tables and a vault toilet.

Sand Point

On Yellowstone Lake between Bridge Bay and West Thumb Junction

This large picnic area has tables and a vault toilet. But its claim to fame is its long sandy beach, accessed via a short trail. It's one of the few sandy beaches on Yellowstone Lake and offers a shallow place to swim with slightly warmer water.

bluebells and wildflowers around Cascade Lake

CAMPING

Campgrounds have flush toilets, cold running water, potable water, coin-op ice machines, and evening amphitheater programs. With the exception of Fishing Bridge, they also have picnic tables, fire rings, firewood for sale, dishwashing stations, bear boxes, tent pads, and shared campsites for hikers and bikers ($5-8/person). For RVs, only a few campsites fit rigs or combos of 40 ft (12 m) or more. The only campground with full hookups for RVs is Fishing Bridge.

Reservations

Of the five campgrounds on the park's east side, four accept **reservations** (tel. 307/344-7311; www.yellowstonenationalparklodges.com). For summer, book reservations a year in advance at Canyon, Fishing Bridge, Bridge Bay, and Grant Village. Call to pick up campsites from last-minute cancellations. Camping fees cover six people or one family; taxes and utility fees are added on.

Tips

Campgrounds here that take reservations have a maximum RV length of 40 ft (12 m) for a **very limited** number of campsites. Smaller RVs have more options for campsites. Some campsites are in hilly sections and may not be level. For seniors with senior federal lands passes, campsites are discounted 50 percent, except for Fishing Bridge RV Park.

STANDOUTS

Bridge Bay Campground

North of Bridge Bay Marina; mid-May-late Sept.; $27

At 7,784 ft (2,373 m), Bridge Bay Campground flanks a hillside across the road from Yellowstone Lake. With 432 campsites in 12 loops swooping through meadows and forests, the campground is the largest in the park. The five huge front loops sit on a large, sunny, sloped meadow with some views of the water, distant Absaroka Mountains, and neighboring campers. The meadows are green in June, brown in August. The back loops circle through conifers with more shady sites. Bridge Bay Marina has a boat launch, rentals, scenic cruises, store, RV dump station, and ranger station. Separate trails for bikers and hikers lead 1 mi (1.6 km) to Natural Bridge, a rock arch above Bridge Creek.

Lewis Lake Campground

South Entrance Rd.; tel. 307/344-7381; www.nps.gov/yell; late June-early Nov.; $15

Boaters, anglers, and paddlers favor the primitive first-come, first-served sites at Lewis Lake Campground. Located on Lewis Lake at 7,830 ft (2,387 m), this quiet campground is close to the South Entrance, hence it's the first campground for those

Lewis Lake Campground

CANYON AND LAKE COUNTRY CAMPGROUNDS

NAME	LOCATION	SEASON
Canyon Campground	Canyon Village	late May-late Sept.
Fishing Bridge RV Park	Yellowstone Lake	early May-late Sept.
★ **Bridge Bay Campground**	Yellowstone Lake	mid-May-late Sept.
Grant Village Campground	Yellowstone Lake	early June-mid-Sept.
★ **Lewis Lake Campground**	Lewis Lake	late-June-early Nov.

heading north from Grand Teton National Park and Jackson Hole. The campground flanks a forested hillside with 85 campsites and is one of the last in the park to fill; in peak season, all sites are claimed by 9am. RVs are limited to 25 ft (8 m), and generators are not allowed. The campground has vault toilets. When temperatures reach freezing, drinking water may be shut off. Paddlers can tour up the Lewis Channel to Shoshone Lake. Near the lake's north end, trails lead to Shoshone Lake and Heart Lake. Lewis Falls sits 1 mi (1.6 km) south.

LODGING

Park lodges and cabins do not have televisions, radios, or air-conditioning; a few have mini-fridges. Rooms have private bathrooms in two styles: a tub/shower combination or shower only. When booking, clarify your room needs and confirm whether there is an elevator; a few rooms and cabins meet ADA standards. Cell phone reception is usually available at the lodge or nearby. Internet access is limited. Add 14 percent tax and utility fee.

SITES AND AMENITIES	RV LIMIT	PRICE	RESERVATIONS
270 tent and RV sites; flush toilets; showers; laundry; RV dump station	40 ft/12 m	$32	yes
310 RV sites for hard-sided vehicles only; RV hookups (electrical, water, and sewer); flush toilets; shower house; laundry; RV dump station	40 ft/12 m (95 ft/28.9 m after 2021); some double sites can include towed and towing unit parked side by side	$80	yes
432 tent and RV sites; flush toilets; RV dump station	40 ft/12 m	$27	yes
430 sites; flush toilets: showers; laundry; RV dump station	40 ft/12 m	$32	yes
85 tent and RV sites; vault toilets; drinking water	25 ft/8 m; generators not allowed	$15	no

Reservations

The four in-park lodging options are open only in summer. Lake Yellowstone Hotel is the most requested of the three for its location, architecture, and historical ambience. Reservations (tel. 307/344-7311; www.yellowstonenationalparklodges.com) are a must and should be booked **12-18 months in advance.**

Tips

Lake Yellowstone Hotel and Canyon Lodge are the most popular, thanks to location and facilities that have been built or renovated recently. If you want to stay in these locations, make reservations as soon as they accept them.

STANDOUTS

Canyon Lodge and Cabins

mid-May-mid-Oct.; $221-450 lodge and cabin rooms, $660-805 suites

With more than 500 rooms in a huge complex, Canyon Lodge and Cabins has hotel rooms in multistory lodges or motel rooms in cabins. It is the largest facility in the park and has the newest accommodations. Five three-story, stone-and-wood lodge buildings built in 2016 replaced the low-end cabins. These lodges have recycled-glass bathroom counters, electric car charging stations, and keycard-accessed lights. Two other lodges, Cascade and Dunraven, were built in the 1990s. Rooms typically have 1-2 doubles or queens, and two-bedroom suites have a king room, queen

CANYON AND LAKE COUNTRY LODGING

NAME	LOCATION	SEASON
★ **Canyon Lodge and Cabins**	Canyon Village	mid-May-mid-Oct.
★ **Lake Yellowstone Hotel and Cabins**	Lake Village	mid-May-early Oct.
Lake Lodge Cabins	Lake Village	early June-early Sept.
Grant Village Lodge	Grant Village	late May-late Sept.

room, and sofa-sleeper in a sitting room. Some rooms have refrigerators. All lodges except Cascade have elevators to access upper floors. Older cabins in four- or six-unit buildings have motel-style rooms with two queens. The complex includes several restaurants, gift shops, a visitors center, and wireless Internet in the lobby.

Lake Yellowstone Hotel and Cabins

mid-May-early Oct.; $220-590 cabins and rooms, $601-800 suites

Built in 1891, Lake Yellowstone Hotel and Cabins is a striking colonial building with tall Ionic columns, a bright yellow exterior, and an entrance facing the lake. The three-story hotel, also called Lake Hotel, sports 15 fake balconies added in 1903 for looks rather than usability, and later additions of the portico, dining room, and sunroom gave the hotel more distinction. Named a National Historic Landmark in 2015, it is the oldest operating hotel in Yellowstone.

Lake Yellowstone Hotel and Cabins

OPTIONS	PRICE
hotel and motel rooms, suites	rooms starting at $221
hotel rooms, suites, cabins	rooms starting at $220
motel rooms, cabins	rooms starting at $170
hotel rooms	rooms starting $295

Lake Yellowstone Hotel is a historical experience—not a luxury resort. With the history and delightful location come minimal amenities and little soundproofing between rooms. Make **dinner reservations** when you book, as the dining room packs out with waiting lines. The sunroom is the place to lounge with views of the lake. Nearby, a gated old roadway offers a mile of walking along the shore.

The complex has **three types of accommodations:** hotel rooms and suites in the historic lodge, hotel rooms in an older lodge, and cabins. Historic hotel rooms include a king or 1-2 queen beds. Superior rooms face the lake, while standard rooms face the parking lot, kitchen, buildings, or trees. Two high-end suites have multiple rooms. Behind the hotel are economical options with no lake views.

The two-story **Sandpiper Lodge** has hotel rooms with 1-2 double beds. The yellow 1920s duplex cabins have two double beds and small showers. Amenities include a dining room, bar, deli, a business center, and Internet in the hotel rooms.

Yellowstone River

INFORMATION AND SERVICES

There are a few hubs for services in Canyon and Lake Country. The park hub of **Canyon Village** sits at an east-side junction connecting Upper and Lower Grand Loop Roads. It is 12 mi (19.5 km) east of Norris, 19 mi (31 km) south of Tower Junction, and 16 mi (26 km) north of Yellowstone Lake and Fishing Bridge.

The park hub of **Fishing Bridge** is home to Fishing Bridge Historic District and the 1931 Fishing Bridge Museum and Visitor Center, a National Historic Landmark. Other facilities include Fishing Bridge RV Park, Yellowstone General Store, and a gas station.

Lake Village (signed spur road 1.5 mi/2.4 km south of Fishing Bridge Junction) is a cluster of visitor services on the northwest end of Yellowstone Lake. The yellow colonial Lake Yellowstone Hotel is a National Historic Landmark built in 1891 that offers lodging and dining. Follow the beach road to pull over at the overlook in front of the octagonal Yellowstone General Store, built in 1919 and housing historical photos.

Near West Thumb Junction, **Grant Village** provides the most southern services in the park, with a campground, lodging, restaurants, stores, and a marina for launches onto Yellowstone Lake. The junction is 21 mi (34 km) south of Fishing Bridge, 17 mi (27 km) east of Old Faithful, and 22 mi (35 km) north of the South Entrance.

Entrance Stations

$35 vehicle, $30 motorcycles, $20 hike-in/bike-in/ski-in

Two entrance stations provide access to the Lake Yellowstone region; they are 70 mi (113 km) apart. You can also buy your **entrance pass in advance** online at www.yourpassnow.com. The entrance roads into the park are generally open spring-fall; winter access (mid-Dec.-early Mar.) is only via snowmobile at both entrances or by snowcoach from the south at Flagg Ranch outside the park boundary. Both entrances close to cars early November to mid- or late May.

South Entrance

mid-May-early Nov.

The South Entrance is on US-89/191/287 south of Lewis Lake at the boundary between Yellowstone and John D. Rockefeller, Jr. Memorial Parkway. If coming from Grand Teton National Park, you will drive through this entrance. The closest park hub is Grant Village and West Thumb, 21-22 mi (34-35 km) north; Old Faithful is 17 mi (27 km) farther west.

East Entrance

late May-early Nov.

The East Entrance sits on the east side of Sylvan Pass on US-20. Cody, Wyoming, is 53 mi (85 km) east of the entrance station, and Fishing Bridge on Lake Yellowstone is 27 mi (43 km) west.

Visitors Centers

Four visitor information centers dot the canyon and lake area; all contain **Yellowstone Forever** stores (tel. 406/848-2400; www.yellowstone.org) selling books, field guides, and maps. Hours shorten in spring and fall, and services are limited at the beginning and end of the season.

Canyon Visitor Education Center

Canyon Village; tel. 307/344-7381; www.nps.gov/yell; 8am-6pm daily May-early Nov.

Canyon Visitor Education Center is the place to learn about the major earth forces that shaped Yellowstone's landscape: volcanoes, earthquakes, glaciers, and water. Highlights include a huge relief model of the park that traces its geologic history, a 9,000-pound rotating kugel ball that shows volcanic hot spots around the globe, and one of the world's largest lava lamps to show how magma works. You can even check the strength of the current earthquakes resounding underground. Interactive exhibits, murals, films, and photos tell the story. The visitors center also contains a **backcountry office** (8am-4:30pm daily June-Aug.).

Fishing Bridge Museum and Visitor Center

Fishing Bridge Historic District; tel. 307/344-7381; www.nps.gov/yell; 8am-7pm daily late May-early Sept.

Located on the north end of Yellowstone Lake, the log-and-stone Fishing Bridge Museum and Visitor Center tucks into the trees on the East Entrance Road, less than a mile from the historic Fishing Bridge. Built in 1931, the small museum is now a National Historic Landmark and contains bird and waterfowl specimens plus other wildlife. Their outdoor amphitheater has naturalist presentations.

West Thumb Information Center

West Thumb Geyser Basin; tel. 307/344-7381; www.nps.gov/yell; 9am-5pm daily late May-early Oct.

Located on West Thumb Geyser Basin off Yellowstone Lake, West Thumb Information Center is a small log building with exhibits. This is where you can ask about the 100-ft-high (30-m-high) bulge growing on the floor of Yellowstone Lake due to activity from faults and hot springs.

Grant Visitor Center

Grant Village; tel. 307/344-7381; www.nps.gov/yell; 8am-7pm daily late May-early Oct.

Grant Visitor Center has exhibits and a movie that detail the role of fire via the story of 1988, the fieriest summer in the park's history.

TRANSPORTATION

Getting There

Two-lane roads are the standard in Yellowstone. Throw in curves, wildlife, and scenery, and drivers need to pay attention. Use pullouts for sightseeing or wildlife-watching rather than stopping in the middle of the road. Traffic gets extremely congested on summer afternoons on North Rim and South Rim Drives at Grand Canyon of the Yellowstone. Avoid the mayhem by visiting earlier or later in the day. Stop at picnic areas to use toilets to avoid long restroom lines at the canyon. Due to limited snow-free seasons, construction happens in summer; you may encounter waits of 15-30 minutes in these zones (specific construction sites are listed online).

From South Entrance

The forested South Entrance Road connects the South Entrance of Yellowstone with Grant Village and West Thumb and is open mid-May-early November. The road passes the Lewis River, Lewis Falls, and Lewis Lake, and the 22-mi (35-km) drive takes 45 minutes.

From East Entrance

From the East Entrance Station, the East Entrance Road (open late May-early Nov.) is a steep climb through Sylvan Pass and then a descent with wide views, reaching Fishing Bridge after 27 mi (43 km), about 1 hour of driving. East Entrance Road meets Lower Grand Loop Road a little after passing the visitor center.

From North Yellowstone

From Tower Junction, the drive to Canyon Village on Upper Grand Loop Road is 19 mi (31 km) and takes 45 minutes. This road will be closed for construction in 2021.

From Old Faithful

From Old Faithful, the Lower Grand Loop Road (open late May-early Nov.) heads east over Craig Pass and through forests to West Thumb, a 17-mi (27-km), 45-minute drive.

Around Canyon and Lake Country

To get between West Thumb Junction, Fishing Bridge, and Canyon Village, take Lower Grand Loop Road (open late May-early Nov.)

- **Between West Thumb Junction and Fishing Bridge:** 21 mi (34 km); 45 minutes
- **Between Fishing Bridge and Canyon Village:** 16 mi (26 km); 45 minutes

Parking

Parking lots cram full in summer. RVs will find limited parking at some locations. At trailheads such as Dunraven Pass, as well as all trailheads around Grand Canyon of the Yellowstone, claim a spot by 9am.

Grand Canyon of Yellowstone

Grand Canyon of the Yellowstone is one of the park's most congested locations in summer. If possible, plan your visit for early morning or evening to avoid the big midday crowds.

The parking lot for Canyon Village and Canyon Visitor Education Center is busiest noon-4pm. The large parking lot includes 14 ADA-designated spaces and 19 RV spots.

The North Rim Road is busiest 11am-4pm. All overlooks have parking lots with at least one ADA-designated space, but not necessarily RV spaces. The largest lot is located at Brink of the Lower Falls Trailhead, which has 139 parking spaces (including 5 that are ADA-designated and 12 for RVs).

Brink of the Upper Falls parking lot sees the lightest use. If other lots are full, try going here.

The two popular stops on South Rim Road are often crowded 10am-6pm: Artist Point has 109 spaces (5 ADA-designated and 9 for RVs, including tour buses), and Uncle Tom's has 92 spaces (4 ADA-designated and 8 for RVs). For hikers, the Wapiti Parking Lot often only fills noon-3pm, offering access for trailheads to the North Rim, South Rim, and Clear and Ribbon Lakes.

Hayden Valley

For watching-wildlife, use pullouts rather than stopping in the middle of the road or driving off the road on meadows. Congestion at pullouts varies by time and location, depending on what wildlife is present. Hayden Valley has a few small parking lots overlooking the Yellowstone River.

Gas

Gas stations (tel. 406/848-7548) are located at **Canyon Village** (early May-late Oct.), **Fishing Bridge,** and **Grant Village** (mid-May-late Sept.). You can pay at the pump 24 hours a day with a credit card.

view of the Tetons from Signal Mountain

GRAND TETON NATIONAL PARK

IN GRAND TETON NATIONAL PARK, SAWTOOTH SPIRES CLAW the sky in one of the youngest mountain ranges in the Rockies. Towering thousands of feet culminating in the Grand Teton itself, these peaks command attention from almost every location in the park. They were likely first summited by Native Americans, who gave them spiritual value. The Snake River people—Northern Paiute, Bannock, and Shoshone—named the trio of Grand, Middle, and South Tetons the "Hoary-headed Fathers."

Wildlife abounds in the Tetons. Bison, elk, moose, pronghorn, and deer populate the fields. Bald eagles and great blue herons fish the Snake River, also home to river otters and muskrats. Grizzly bears roam the forests, and shrieking pikas inhabit high-elevation talus slopes.

Snuggled at the base of the peaks, glacial lakes string along the valley floor, offering picturesque places to hike, paddle, and fish. Boating on Jackson Lake, floating the Wild and Scenic Snake River, pedaling paved pathways, and skiing winter slopes are all enjoyed beneath the skyscraping grandeur of the Tetons.

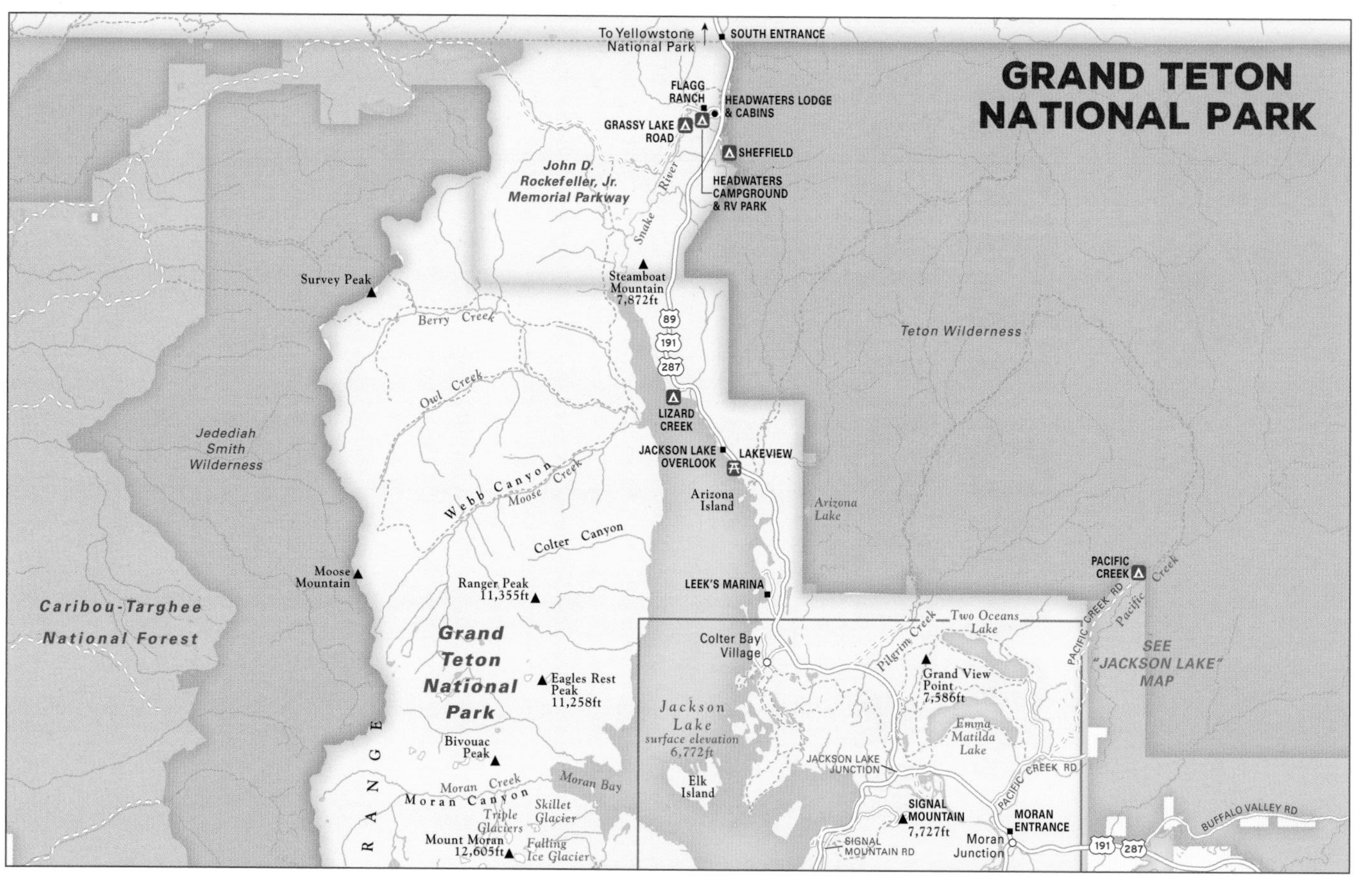
GRAND TETON NATIONAL PARK
To Yellowstone National Park
SOUTH ENTRANCE
FLAGG RANCH
HEADWATERS LODGE & CABINS
GRASSY LAKE ROAD
SHEFFIELD
HEADWATERS CAMPGROUND & RV PARK
John D. Rockefeller, Jr. Memorial Parkway
Snake River
Steamboat Mountain 7,872ft
89
191
287
Survey Peak
Berry Creek
Owl Creek
Teton Wilderness
LIZARD CREEK
JACKSON LAKE OVERLOOK
LAKEVIEW
Jedediah Smith Wilderness
Webb Canyon
Moose Creek
Arizona Island
Arizona Lake
Colter Canyon
Moose Mountain
Ranger Peak 11,355ft
LEEK'S MARINA
PACIFIC CREEK
PACIFIC CREEK RD
Pacific Creek
Caribou-Targhee National Forest
Grand Teton National Park
Two Oceans Lake
Pilgrim Creek
Colter Bay Village
SEE "JACKSON LAKE" MAP
Grand View Point 7,586ft
Eagles Rest Peak 11,258ft
Jackson Lake surface elevation 6,772ft
Emma Matilda Lake
Bivouac Peak
JACKSON LAKE JUNCTION
RANGE
Moran Creek
Moran Bay
Elk Island
Moran Canyon
Skillet Glacier
Triple Glaciers
SIGNAL MOUNTAIN 7,727ft
MORAN ENTRANCE
BUFFALO VALLEY RD
Mount Moran 12,605ft
Falling Ice Glacier
SIGNAL MOUNTAIN RD
Moran Junction

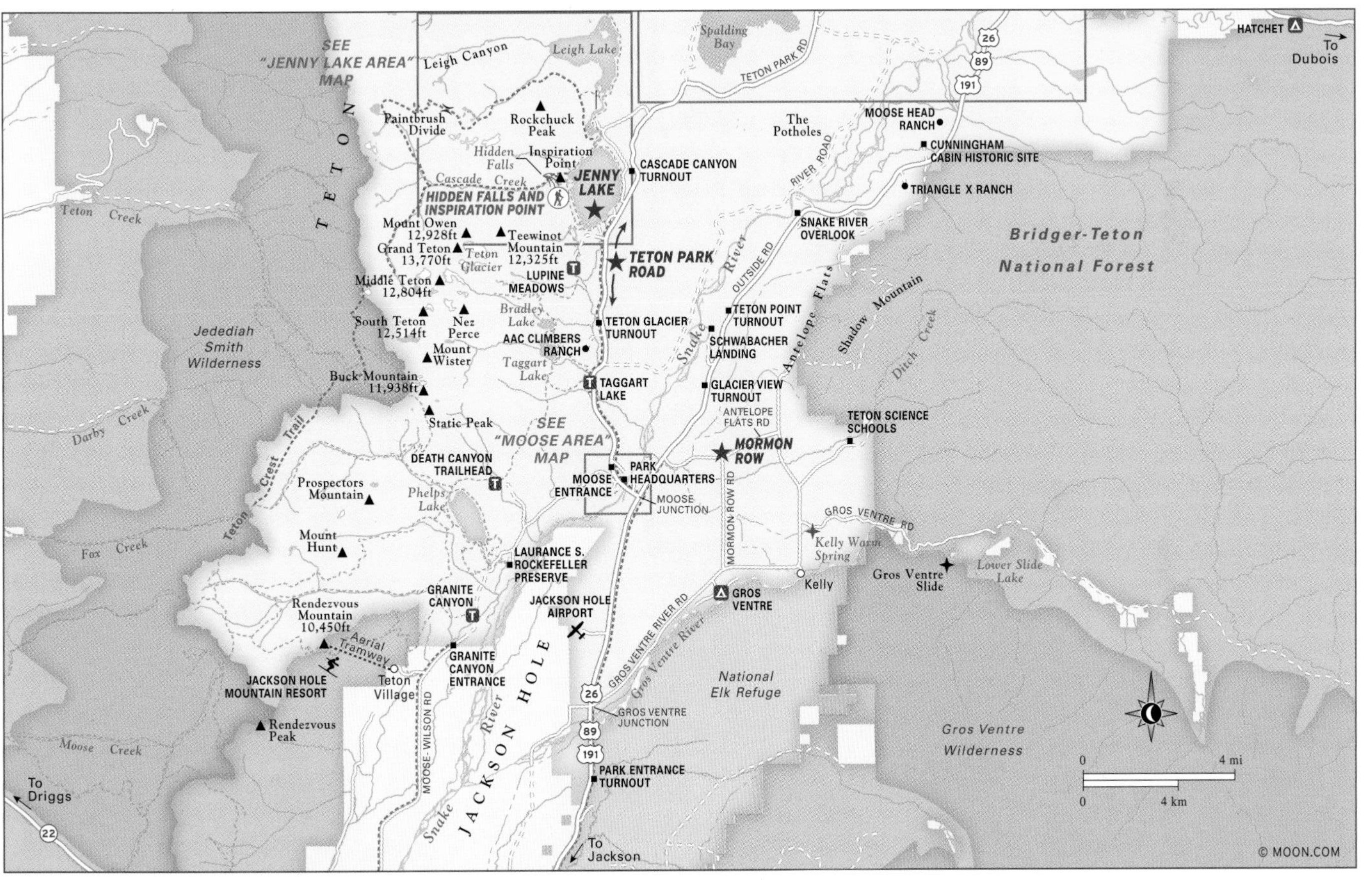

HATCHET
To Dubois
Bridger-Teton National Forest
CUNNINGHAM CABIN HISTORIC SITE
TRIANGLE X RANCH
MOOSE HEAD RANCH
SNAKE RIVER OVERLOOK
The Potholes
RIVER ROAD
TETON PARK RD
Spalding Bay
CASCADE CANYON TURNOUT
TETON PARK ROAD
JENNY LAKE
Leigh Lake
Leigh Canyon
Rockchuck Peak
Inspiration Point
Hidden Falls
Cascade Creek
HIDDEN FALLS AND INSPIRATION POINT
Paintbrush Divide
SEE "JENNY LAKE AREA" MAP
TETON
Teewinot Mountain 12,325ft
Mount Owen 12,928ft
Grand Teton 13,770ft
Teton Glacier
Middle Teton 12,804ft
South Teton 12,514ft
Nez Perce
Mount Wister
Buck Mountain 11,938ft
Static Peak
LUPINE MEADOWS
Bradley Lake
Taggart Lake
AAC CLIMBERS RANCH
TETON GLACIER TURNOUT
TAGGART LAKE
SEE "MOOSE AREA" MAP
TETON POINT TURNOUT
SCHWABACHER LANDING
GLACIER VIEW TURNOUT
OUTSIDE RD
Snake River
Antelope Flats
Shadow Mountain
Ditch Creek
TETON SCIENCE SCHOOLS
ANTELOPE FLATS RD
MORMON ROW
MORMON ROW RD
PARK HEADQUARTERS
MOOSE JUNCTION
MOOSE ENTRANCE
DEATH CANYON TRAILHEAD
Phelps Lake
LAURANCE S. ROCKEFELLER PRESERVE
GRANITE CANYON
GRANITE CANYON ENTRANCE
JACKSON HOLE AIRPORT
JACKSON HOLE
MOOSE-WILSON RD
Teton Village
Aerial Tramway
Rendezvous Mountain 10,450ft
JACKSON HOLE MOUNTAIN RESORT
Rendezvous Peak
Prospectors Mountain
Mount Hunt
Teton Crest Trail
Jedediah Smith Wilderness
Teton Creek
Darby Creek
Fox Creek
Moose Creek
To Driggs
GROS VENTRE RD
Kelly Warm Spring
Kelly
GROS VENTRE
Gros Ventre Slide
Lower Slide Lake
Gros Ventre Wilderness
National Elk Refuge
Gros Ventre River
GROS VENTRE RIVER RD
GROS VENTRE JUNCTION
PARK ENTRANCE TURNOUT
To Jackson
0
4 mi
0
4 km
© MOON.COM

2

TOP 3

★ **1. MORMON ROW:** This former settlement has the perfect backdrop—the Teton Mountains (page 183).

★ **2. JENNY LAKE:** Idyllic Jenny Lake is perfect for hiking, paddling, and fishing (page 185).

★ **3. TETON PARK ROAD:** Called the Inside Road, this scenic drive takes you right under the Teton Mountains (page 192).

3

GRAND TETON NATIONAL PARK 3 WAYS

HALF DAY

With limited time, you'll want to head to Teton Park Road to enjoy the close-up views of the Tetons. In summer, plan to go early to be able to find parking at Jenny Lake. Make reservations in advance for the boat tour.

1 Start with a drive on scenic **Teton Park Road** below the Tetons. Enjoy the views of the toothy peaks.

2 Head to **Jenny Lake** first. Tour the accessible paved Discovery Trail that loops out to several overlooks along the shoreline of Jenny Lake.

3 The Discovery Trail also connects with the boat dock where you can board the **Jenny Lake Boating Tour.** Circle the scenic lake at the base of the Tetons via this narrated cruise.

4 Afterward, keep heading up Teton Park Road. Stop at the **Mt. Moran Turnout** for more photos.

5 Drive up to Jackson Point Overlook atop **Signal Mountain** for expansive views of Jackson Hole, Jackson Lake, and the Teton Mountains.

6 Celebrate the scenery with lunch on the deck at **Signal Mountain Lodge** overlooking Jackson Lake.

5

4

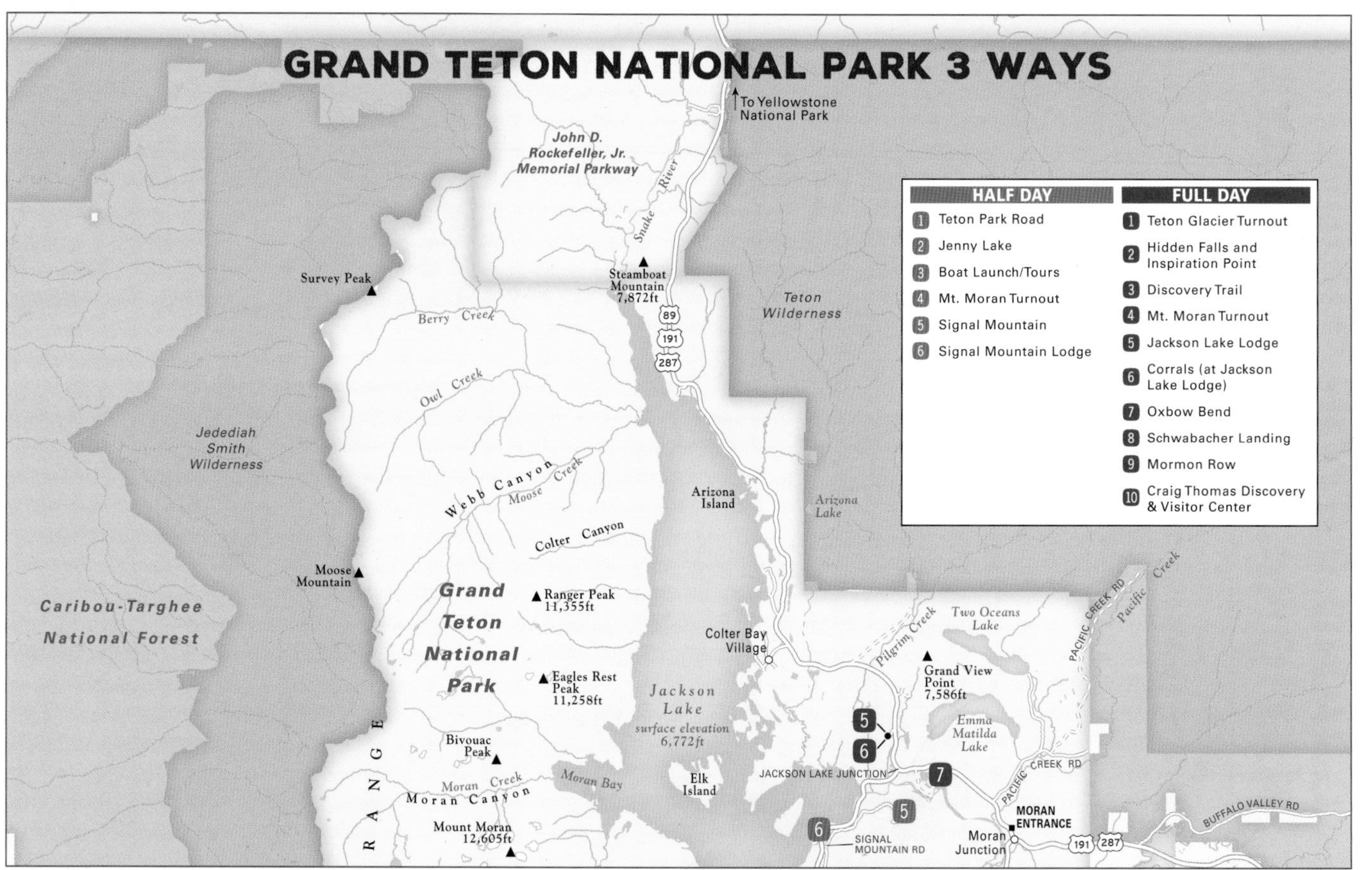
GRAND TETON NATIONAL PARK 3 WAYS
HALF DAY
1 Teton Park Road
2 Jenny Lake
3 Boat Launch/Tours
4 Mt. Moran Turnout
5 Signal Mountain
6 Signal Mountain Lodge
FULL DAY
1 Teton Glacier Turnout
2 Hidden Falls and Inspiration Point
3 Discovery Trail
4 Mt. Moran Turnout
5 Jackson Lake Lodge
6 Corrals (at Jackson Lake Lodge)
7 Oxbow Bend
8 Schwabacher Landing
9 Mormon Row
10 Craig Thomas Discovery & Visitor Center
To Yellowstone National Park
John D. Rockefeller, Jr. Memorial Parkway
Snake River
Steamboat Mountain 7,872ft
89
191
287
Teton Wilderness
Survey Peak
Berry Creek
Owl Creek
Jedediah Smith Wilderness
Webb Canyon
Moose Creek
Colter Canyon
Arizona Island
Arizona Lake
Moose Mountain
Caribou-Targhee National Forest
Grand Teton National Park
Ranger Peak 11,355ft
Eagles Rest Peak 11,258ft
Colter Bay Village
Jackson Lake
surface elevation 6,772ft
Pilgrim Creek
Two Oceans Lake
Grand View Point 7,586ft
Emma Matilda Lake
PACIFIC CREEK RD
Pacific Creek
Bivouac Peak
Moran Creek
Moran Canyon
Moran Bay
Elk Island
JACKSON LAKE JUNCTION
Mount Moran 12,605ft
RANGE
SIGNAL MOUNTAIN RD
Moran Junction
MORAN ENTRANCE
BUFFALO VALLEY RD

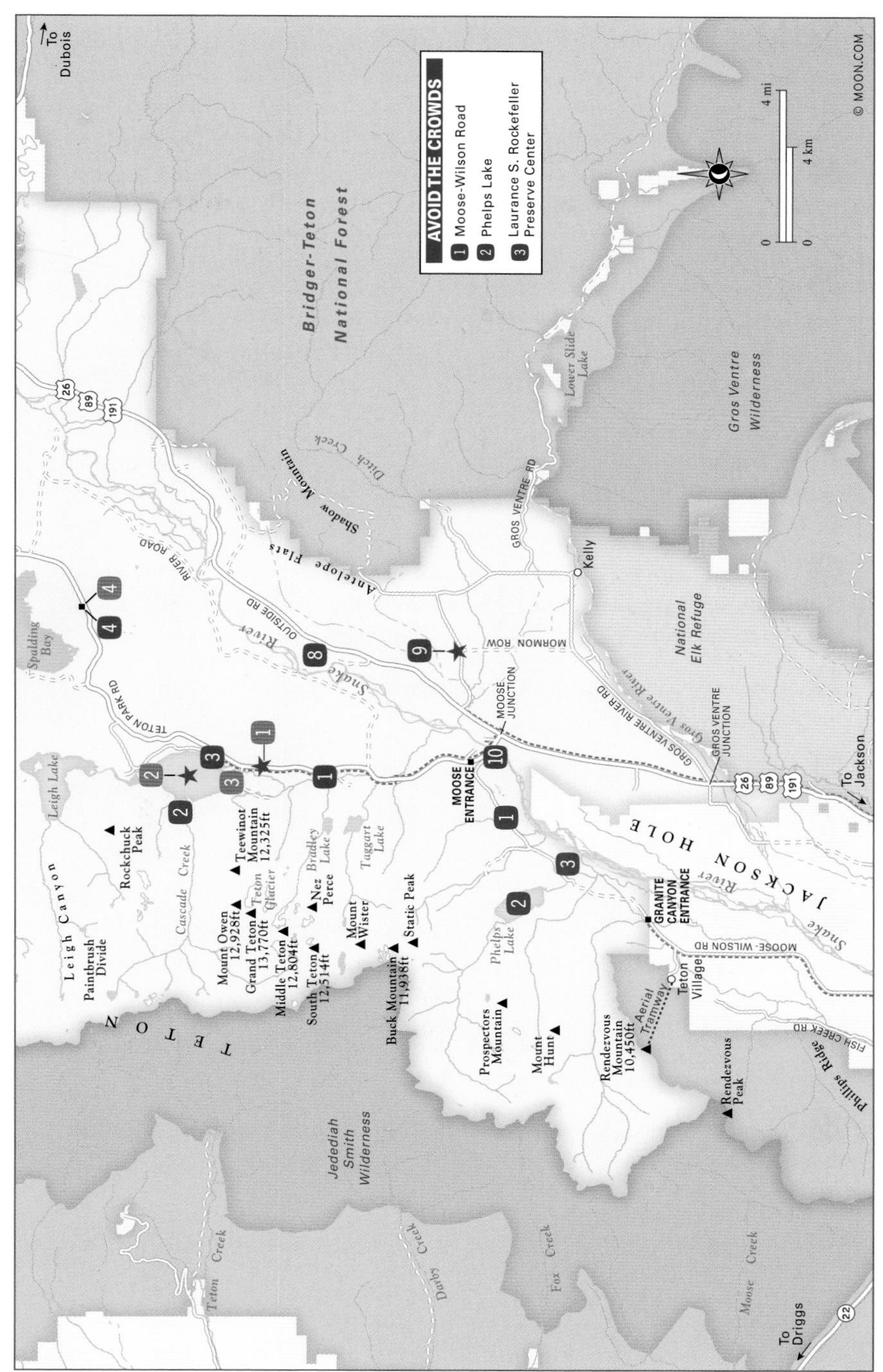
AVOID THE CROWDS
1 Moose-Wilson Road
2 Phelps Lake
3 Laurance S. Rockefeller Preserve Center
To Dubois
Bridger-Teton National Forest
Gros Ventre Wilderness
Lower Slide Lake
Ditch Creek
Shadow Mountain
Antelope Flats
GROS VENTRE RD
Kelly
National Elk Refuge
Gros Ventre River
GROS VENTRE RIVER RD
GROS VENTRE JUNCTION
To Jackson
MORMON ROW
MOOSE JUNCTION
Snake River
OUTSIDE RD
RIVER ROAD
Spalding Bay
TETON PARK RD
Leigh Lake
Leigh Canyon
Paintbrush Divide
Rockchuck Peak
Cascade Creek
Teewinot Mountain 12,325ft
Mount Owen 12,928ft
Grand Teton 13,770ft
Teton Glacier
Middle Teton 12,804ft
South Teton 12,514ft
Nez Perce
Bradley Lake
Taggart Lake
Mount Wister
Buck Mountain 11,938ft
Static Peak
MOOSE ENTRANCE
JACKSON HOLE
Phelps Lake
GRANITE CANYON ENTRANCE
MOOSE-WILSON RD
Teton Village
Aerial Tramway
Rendezvous Mountain 10,450ft
Mount Hunt
Prospectors Mountain
TETON
Jedediah Smith Wilderness
FISH CREEK RD
Phillips Ridge
Rendezvous Peak
Teton Creek
Darby Creek
Fox Creek
Moose Creek
To Driggs
0 4 mi
0 4 km
© MOON.COM

FULL DAY

An early start is necessary to get a parking spot at Jenny Lake. Unfortunately, that means foregoing the Craig Thomas Discovery & Visitor Center, which doesn't open in time. You can add this in at the end of the day, though.

1 Head out on Teton Park Road and make a quick stop at **Teton Glacier Turnout** to nab a photo of Teton Glacier and admire the Grand Teton before aiming for Jenny Lake.

2 Catch an early shuttle boat across Jenny Lake to the west boat dock, where you'll find the trail for **Hidden Falls and Inspiration Point.** The stone stairway climbs to Lower and Upper Inspiration Points for views overlooking blue Jenny Lake and Jackson Hole.

3 Catch the shuttle boat back to the east boat dock. Tour the accessible paved **Discovery Trail** from the boat dock. The path loops out to several overlooks along the shoreline of Jenny Lake before returning to the visitor center area.

4 Back on Teton Park Road, tour the scenic drive at the base of the Tetons north from Jenny Lake and stop at **Mt. Moran Turnout** to see the small glaciers clinging to the peak.

5 Lunch at historic **Jackson Lake Lodge** on the back patio with views of the Tetons.

6 Hop on **horseback** for a one-hour guided trail ride from Jackson Lake Lodge.

7 Head east to **Oxbow Bend.** Scan the water and brush for moose, bears, otters, raptors, and American white pelicans.

8 Make your way south on the Outside Road (US-26/89/191). Past the Teton Point Overlook, turn right to bounce along a short dirt road to **Schwabacher Landing,** a good place for wildlife- and bird-watching.

9 Pick up a final view of the Teton Mountains backdropped behind the historic barns and houses of **Mormon Row.**

10 If you still have energy, stop in the **Craig Thomas Discovery & Visitor Center** (open until 7pm) to learn more about what you saw today.

5

AVOID THE CROWDS

The Laurance S. Rockefeller Preserve Center parking lot is limited to 50 cars. Go early (before 9am) to get a spot. As an alternative, strong hikers can get up high in the Tetons where people are scarce.

1 Go for an early drive on **Moose-Wilson Road** for wildlife-watching, especially for moose around Sawmill Ponds Pullout.

2 Park at Laurance S. Rockefeller Preserve and hike the Lake Creek-Woodland Trail Loop to idyllic **Phelps Lake** near the entrance of Death Canyon. You can make it a short up-and-back loop or add on a circle of the lake.

3 After your hike, tour the **Laurance S. Rockefeller Preserve Center,** which focuses on tactile experiences at the preserve.

More Activities With Fewer Crowds

- If your dream is to get away from the crowds hiking around the low-elevation lakes, skip all the other stops and escape high into the Tetons to tackle the **Paintbrush Divide** loop in one epic day or a three-day backpacking trip.
- **Backpacking Teton Crest Trail**
- **Paddling Jackson Lake's bays**
- **Cross-country skiing and snowshoeing**

3

2

HIGHLIGHTS

★ MORMON ROW

Off Antelope Flats Road

Located in the southeast corner of the park, Mormon Row is a treat for history buffs, photographers, and wildlife fans. The tract was originally a Mormon ranch settlement that started in the 1890s and grew to 27 homesteads. Today, Mormon Row is on the National Register of Historic Places. It retains six clusters of buildings, one ruin, and the famous Moulton barn that appears in the foreground of so many photos of the Grand Teton. Even amateur photographers can capture impressive images of historic buildings backdropped by the Teton Range. Pick up a self-guided tour brochure near the pink house or use the free audio tour on the Grand Teton National Park phone app.

LAURANCE S. ROCKEFELLER PRESERVE CENTER

tel. 307/739-3399; www.nps.gov/grte; 9am-5pm daily early June-late Sept.

The Laurance S. Rockefeller Preserve Center is on a 1,000-acre preserve that was once a ranch owned by the Rockefeller family. The preserve's LEED-certified building contains exhibits that appeal to the senses: visual, tactile, and auditory. Watch high-definition nature videos, view an ultra-large Phelps Lake photograph made from 1-inch nature photos, and listen to natural soundscapes. Rangers lead daily talks and hikes. Kids can check out a backpack for a journaling experience while hiking the preserve's 8 mi (13 km) of trails, including a loop around Phelps Lake. The parking lot is limited to 50

Mormon Row

cars and usually fills up 10am-4pm; plan your visit early in the morning or late in the afternoon and add time for traffic on the Moose-Wilson Road (no RVs or trailers). In May and October, visitors can drive to the center and hike, even when the building is closed. In winter, cross-country skiers and snowshoers tour trails at the preserve.

MENOR'S FERRY HISTORIC DISTRICT

Located on a spur road north of the Moose Entrance Station, Menor's Ferry Historic District preserves buildings from the 1890s. Its location at a narrowing of the Snake River allowed for a ferry to cart people back and forth. A self-guided tour (free audio tours on the Grand Teton National Park phone app) visits the cabins, barns, smokehouse, farm implements, wagons, replica ferry, and **general store** (operated by Grand Teton Association; tel. 307/739-3606; www.grandtetonassociation.org; 10am-4:30pm daily late May-late Sept.). The **Maud Noble Cabin** hosted some of

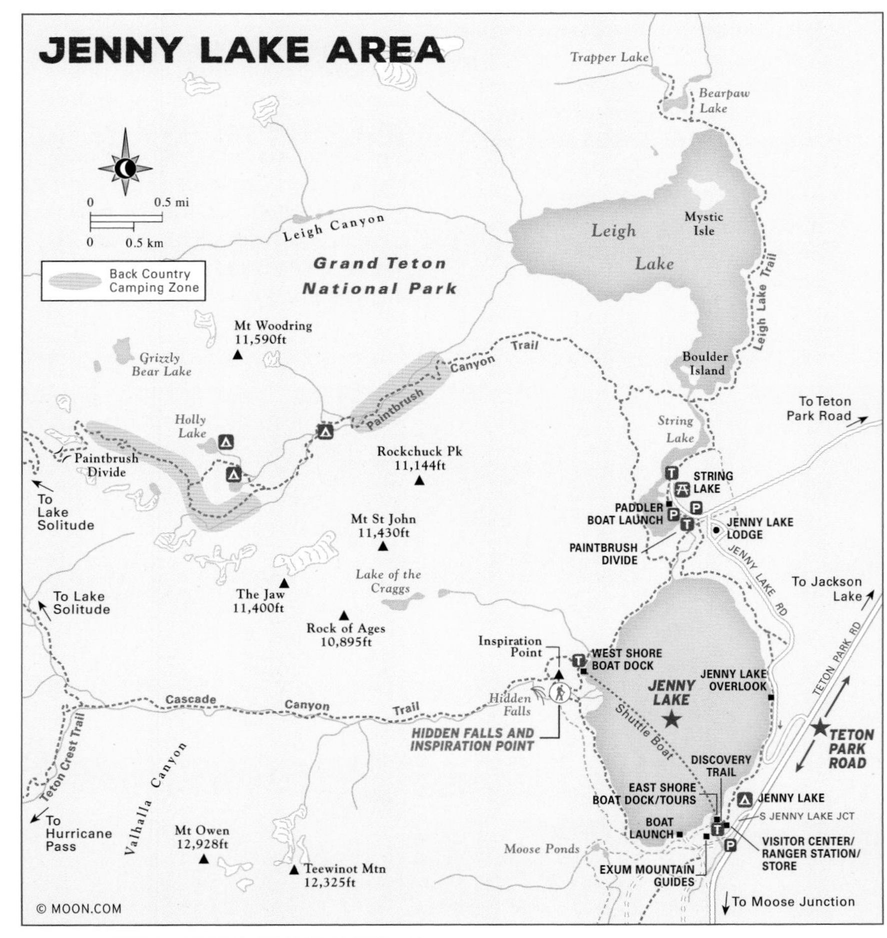

BEST PLACE TO WATCH THE SUNSET

sunset with the Tetons reflecting in the Snake River at Schwabacher Landing

Sunset over the Tetons backlights the jagged mountain range. But sometimes being up close on Teton Park Road doesn't give you the full effect that fits best in a camera. Go to **Schwabacher Landing** off US-26/89/191 to pick up the sky color and peaks reflected in the Snake River. **Oxbow Bend** also works as a substitute if you don't want to drive the dirt access road to Schwabacher Landing. (If you want to see the peaks lit up rather than backlit, go at sunrise.)

the 1923 talks to create Grand Teton National Park.

★ JENNY LAKE

Tucked below the Grand Teton, Jenny Lake is a placid place of beauty. The 2-mi-long (3-km-long), 250-ft-deep (75-m-deep) lake was created behind a moraine in a glacial depression. The lake beckons photographers and artists to capture its grandeur; catch mountain reflections in the morning before afternoon winds crop up. Visitors can lodge or camp and spend days hiking, biking, boating, paddling, fishing, swimming, climbing, backpacking, and wildlife-watching. South Jenny Lake houses a small visitors center, ranger station, store, and campground, and has scenic boat tours.

Jenny Lake Historic District contains a homestead cabin that

Jenny Lake

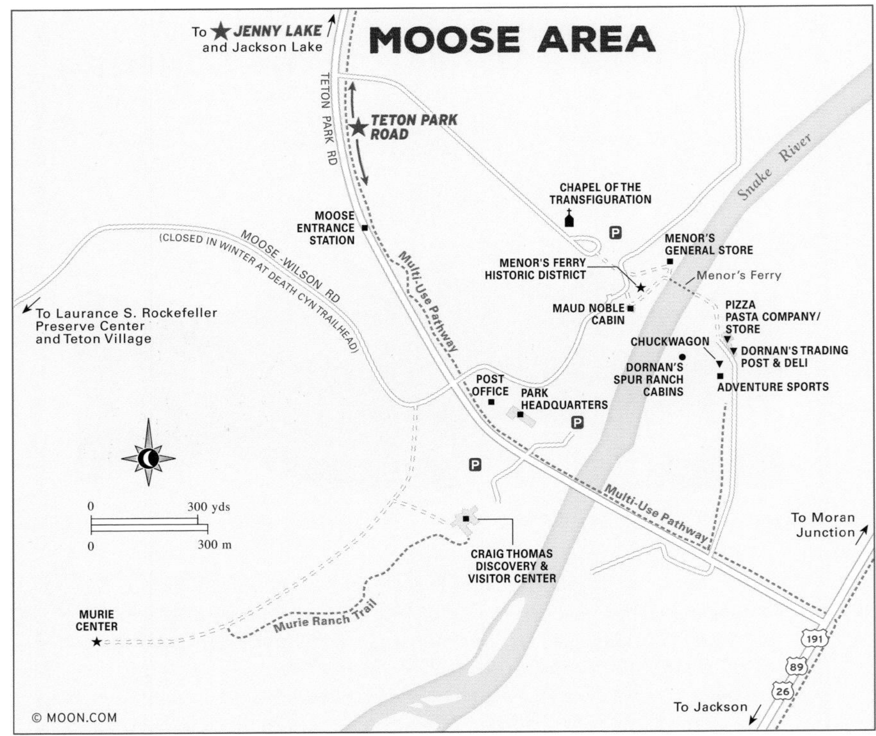

serves as the ranger station. Finished in 2018, the $19 million Jenny Lake Renewal Project rebuilt interpretive plazas, overlooks, and paths to the lake. The plaza near the boat dock orients you to activities and the mountains, and signs provide easy directions. To see the lake backed by the Tetons, take the 0.5-mi (0.8-km) paved, wheelchair-accessible Jenny Lake Overlook path (also called **Discovery Trail**) from the plaza outside the visitors center. It goes to three boulder-rimmed overlooks with seating to absorb views, and several stairways descend to a beach for wading or swimming. The trail also goes to the boat dock for tours, shuttles, and paddling rentals, and to the north a dirt path continues to Jenny Lake Overlook on North Jenny Lake Drive.

Jenny Lake Boating Tour

Depart from dock at South Jenny Lake; tel. 307/734-9227; www.jennylakeboating.com; 11am, 2pm, 5pm daily summer, noon, 2pm spring/fall; $25 adults, $20 seniors, $15 kids

Bring your camera to catch all the views on these one-hour interpretive boat tours. Guides cover tidbits about geology, history, plants, and wildlife during the shoreline loop. Reservations by credit card are highly recommended. Jenny Lake Boating also runs a hiker shuttle with frequent departures across Jenny Lake.

OUTSIDE ROAD

view from Glacier View Turnout

Teton Park Road is also called the Inside Road, and if you want to make a loop from the southern Moose area of the park up to Jackson Lake and back, you can take the two-lane Outside Road (US-26/89/191) for one leg of the trip. Like on Teton Park Road, there are a number of pullouts: At the **Snake River Overlook,** you can see the riffles of the 13th-largest river in the country, and **Teton Point** and **Glacier View Turnouts** offer panoramic mountain views. Watch for bison, elk, moose, and pronghorn on this loop, especially when driving at dusk.

SIGNAL MOUNTAIN

At only 7,720 ft (2,350 m) high, Signal Mountain cowers below the massive Tetons. Formed in part from ash falling from the Yellowstone supervolcano and a glacier leaving it as moraine, Signal Mountain rises alone above the valley of Jackson Hole with the closest peaks 10 mi (16 km) away. The result is big views. Two forested routes climb 800 ft (245 m) to reach the summit. Drive or bike the 5-mi (8-km) paved road (May-Oct.), or hike the 6.8-mi (10.9-km) trail from Signal Mountain Lodge. The summit has two overlooks: **Jackson Point Overlook** on the south with majestic Teton Mountain views, and the **summit overlook** at the top. When driving up, be cautious of bikers enjoying the flying descent. Tiny parking areas do not have room or turnaround space for large RVs and trailers, but you can leave trailers in the base parking lot.

JACKSON LAKE

At 40 square mi (100 square km), Jackson Lake is huge. Its 15-mi (24-km) length runs from the Snake River in the north to Spalding Bay in the south. Fifteen islands inhabit the lake, including Elk Island, the largest. The lake contains nonnative

Oxbow Bend in autumn

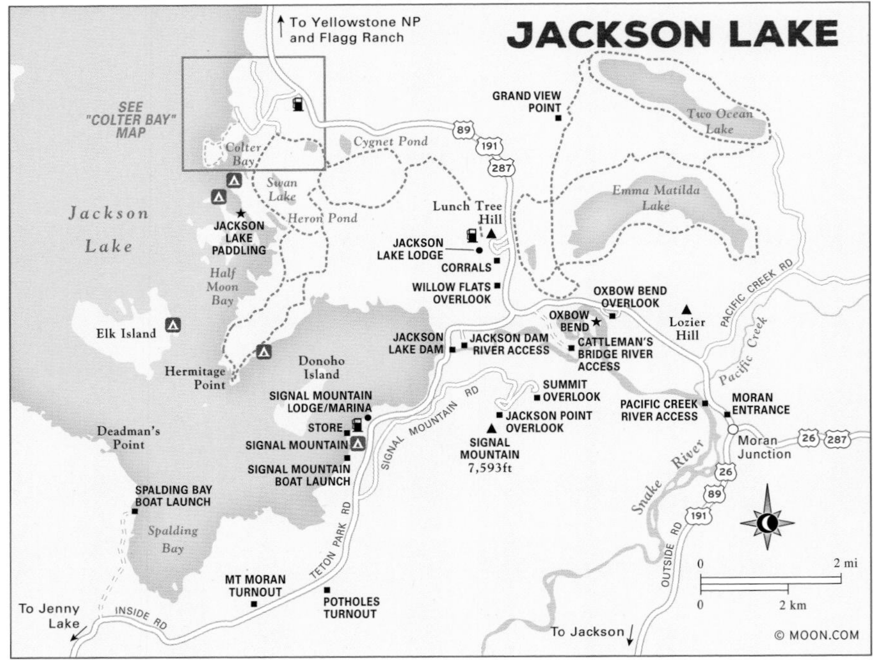

brown and lake trout, but real native prizes are Snake River fine-spotted cutthroat trout and mountain whitefish. **Overlooks** at the head of the lake, Signal Mountain, and Jackson Lake Dam offer good viewpoints. You can explore the lake on a cruise and paddle its islands. Three marinas offer boat launch sites (two rent boats).

Colter Bay

Colter Bay is one of those do-everything places with sights galore. You can settle in for several days without moving the car by staying in a log cabin, tent cabin, RV park, or the campground; then you can picnic, swim, hike, bike, paddle (rentals available), boat, and ride horseback to see the area and enjoy Jackson Lake.

Hiking trails loop peninsulas, passing tiny lakes named for water birds, such as **Cygnet, Swan**, and **Heron.** Bikes can go on the trail to the jetty. Around Colter Bay, Jackson Lake often reflects Mt. Moran and the Teton Mountains at sunrise or sunset.

Stop in the **Colter Bay Visitor Center** (tel. 307/739-3399; 8am-7pm daily early June-early Sept., 8am-5pm daily spring and fall) to see the small collection of Native American artifacts. Ranger programs occur daily, and night sky programs extend the fun to after dark.

Jackson Lake Boat Tour

Grand Teton Lodging Company; tel. 307/543-2811; www.gtlc.com; daily late May-late Sept.; $40-72 adults, $20-44 kids

From the Colter Bay Marina, catch a Jackson Lake boat tour to get out on the water and soak up the lustrous views of Mt. Moran. Scenic daytime cruises (90 min, 10:15am, 1:15pm, and 3:15pm daily) motor out through the

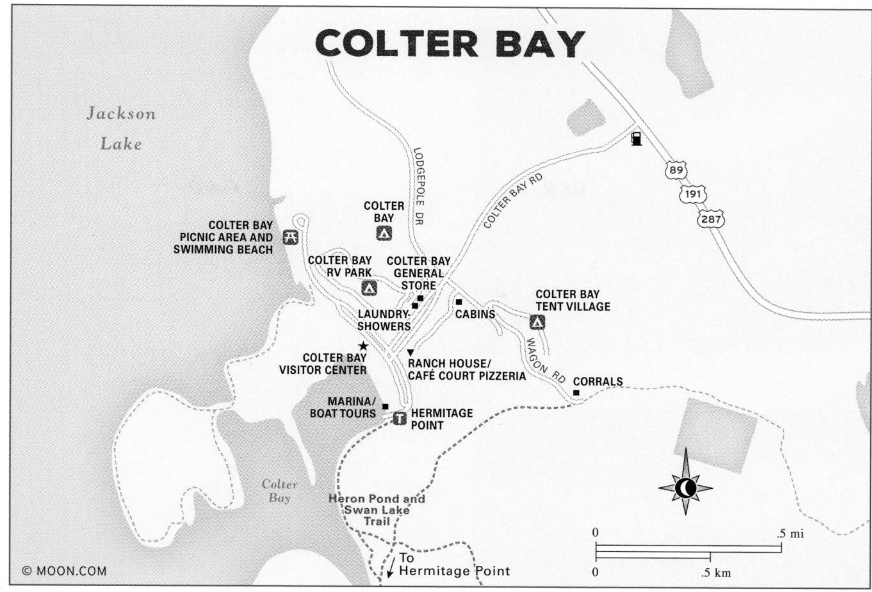

islands on Jackson Lake. June through early September, cruises also combine with an outdoor meal around the campfire on Elk Island for breakfast (7:15am Fri.-Wed. summer, 8am Fri.-Wed. fall), lunch (12:15pm Mon., Wed., Fri., Sat.), and dinner (5:15pm Fri.-Wed.). Reservations are required.

WILDLIFE-WATCHING

Willow Flats Overlook

On US-89/191/287 between the turnoffs to Jackson Lake Lodge and Teton Park Lodge is the large Willow Flats Overlook. Often, you can spot elk or moose from here. Morning also lights up Jackson Lake beyond the willow meadows with a backdrop of the Teton Mountains.

Schwabacher Landing

Here, the Snake River moves at a slow pace, making it serve as an attractant for wildlife and birds. Look for otter, beaver, and moose in the waterway as well as ducks. A worn path trots along the river for exploration. Even if you don't see much wildlife, it offers a spectacular view of the Tetons. North of Moose on US-26/89/191, find the turnoff for Schwabacher Landing between Glacier View and Teton Point Overlooks, and then drive the potholed dirt road (1.2 mi/1.9 km) to its terminus.

Oxbow Bend

Slow-moving convolutions of water through Oxbow Bend yield wildlife habitat and outstanding landscapes for photographers. Located 1 mi (1.6 km) east of **Jackson Lake Junction,** where US-89/191/287 and Teton Park Road meet, Oxbow Bend is one of the best places for wildlife-watching and bird-watching. Bring binoculars or spotting scopes to aid in viewing from the pullout. Look for river otters, beavers, or muskrats in the water, or moose foraging on willows. Squawking and grunting American pelicans add to the cacophony from songbirds, and ospreys and bald eagles hunt for

Chapel of the Transfiguration (top); Antelope Flats (middle); bear crossing Moose-Wilson Road (bottom)

fish. Opt for prime viewing at dawn or dusk, but be cautious of large animals such as bears and moose that might be using the road as a travel corridor.

SCENIC DRIVES

★ TETON PARK ROAD

DRIVING DISTANCE: 20 mi (32 km) one-way
DRIVING TIME: 45 minutes one-way without stops or traffic
START: Craig Thomas Discovery & Visitor Center
END: Jackson Lake Junction

From Jackson Lake Junction in the north to Moose in the south, the Teton Park Road (May-Oct.) gives up-close views of the Teton Mountains. The road (called the Inside Road by locals) **closes in winter** from Signal Mountain Lodge to Taggart Lake Trailhead.

From the Craig Thomas Discovery & Visitor Center in Moose, start by driving north on Teton Park Road. Just past the Moose Entrance Station, turn right to see the **Menor's Ferry Historic District** and the small log **Chapel of the Transfiguration.** Continuing north for 3.7 mi (6 km) leads to the **Teton Glacier Turnout,** where you can look straight up at the small **Teton Glacier.** In about 3 mi (5 km), stop at **South Jenny Lake** to walk from the visitors center to the lake. Continuing north on Teton Park Road, stop at the **Mt. Moran Turnout** to examine the black dike and two small glaciers in its upper cliffs. Watch for wildlife, particularly around sunrise or sunset.

ANTELOPE FLATS

DRIVING DISTANCE: 10 mi (16 km) round-trip
DRIVING TIME: 30 minutes round-trip
START/END: Gros Ventre River Road or Antelope Flats Road turnoff from US-26/89/191

Through a flat, sagebrush plain, a loop on dirt and paved roads tours Antelope Flats, a place of park history, with wildlife-watching especially good around sunrise or dusk. Late-1800s ranches and homesteads left irrigation ditches, old buildings, and barns in **Mormon Row,** where you can take a self-guided tour. The southeast corner of the loop goes through the small burg of **Kelly,** with a population of 130 residents. Access the loop from the Gros Ventre River Road or Antelope Flats Road, both turnoffs from US-26/89/191. In spring, see newborn bison calves and pronghorn fawns, and in fall, watch large herds of elk cross into the National Elk Refuge to the south. Mormon Row and Antelope Flats Roads close November-April, but Gros Ventre River Road stays open year-round.

MOOSE-WILSON ROAD

DRIVING DISTANCE: 8 mi (13 km) one-way
DRIVING TIME: 30 minutes one-way
START: Granite Canyon Entrance
END: Moose Entrance Station

Moose-Wilson Road (mid-May-Oct. no RVs) snuggles into prime wildlife habitat along the southern base of the Tetons between the Granite Canyon and Moose Entrance Stations. Spot moose and birds at **Sawmill Ponds Pullout** and visit the **Laurance S. Rockefeller Preserve Center.** The skinny, shoulder-less paved and gravel road has bumps, potholes, and curves; it shrinks to one lane in many places and requires slow driving. The park has plans to pave it all and add designated pullouts, so check on the status before driving. This road will see construction impacts and closures for the next several years as the north 0.6 mi (1 km) is moved to the junction of Teton Park Road and the turnoff to Menor's Ferry Historic District. On busy days, the congested road sees about 1,000 vehicles, including wildlife-watchers and visitors who want to take a shortcut from Teton Village to Moose. Drive slowly; collisions happen far too often. The park plans to start a queuing system that permits only 200 vehicles at a time on the road on busy days. Go early in the day or late in the evening to avoid long lines.

hiking to Taggart Lake (left); Phelps Lake Overlook (right)

BEST HIKES

PHELPS LAKE

DISTANCE: 3.1-9.9 mi (5-15.9 km) round-trip
DURATION: 2-5 hours round-trip
ELEVATION CHANGE: 350-975 ft (105-295 m)
EFFORT: Easy to moderate
TRAILHEAD: Laurance S. Rockefeller Preserve Center or Death Canyon Trailhead

A maze of trails with well-signed junctions surrounds the low-elevation Phelps Lake in the Laurance S. Rockefeller Preserve, a special area where hiking the trails is more about the experience than reaching destinations. Visiting the preserve's center adds to the hiking experience. Trails circle the lake, which sits at 6,645 ft (2,025 m) at the bottom of Open and Death Canyons. From various viewpoints around the lake, hikers are rewarded with stunning views of the Teton Mountains. The lake provides a year-round destination, although you'll need skis or snowshoes in winter.

Most hikers opt to park at the **Laurance S. Rockefeller Preserve Center,** located off the Moose-Wilson Road 0.6 mi (1 km) south of the Death Canyon turnoff. Arrive before 9am to claim a parking spot in the small 50-car lot that is designed to limit crowds and create a climate of solitude. If it's full, you'll need to hike via the Death Canyon Trailhead. The shortest and easiest route to Phelps Lake is the **Lake Creek-Woodland Trail Loop** (3.1 mi/5 km). The loop tours forests and meadows on both sides of a creek, offering opportunities to watch moose. At the lake, enjoy contemplation from several different constructed rock-slab overlooks. The **Aspen Ridge-Boulder Ridge Loop** (5.8 mi/9.3 km) climbs through large talus fields and aspens that shimmer gold in fall to reach Phelps Lake. The longest hike, the **Phelps Lake Loop** (6.6 mi/10.6 km), climbs via Lake Creek to reach the lake and then loops around the lake for a changing perspective on the Teton Mountains.

For the **Death Canyon Trailhead,** drive three miles south of Moose

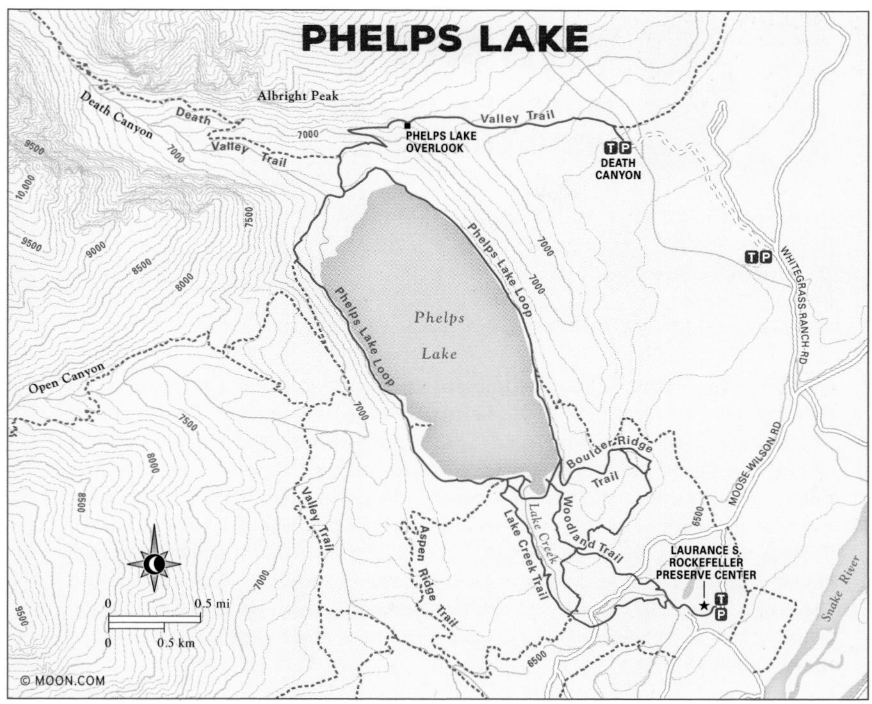

on the Moose-Wilson Road and take signed turnoff right for Death Canyon. Drive 1 mi (1.6 km) to park at the end of the pavement, and walk another 1 mi (1.6 km) on the dirt road to the trailhead. (Driving all the way to the trailhead requires a high-clearance vehicle.) From the Death Canyon Trailhead, climb a fairly steep trail 0.9 mi (1.5 km) through Douglas firs and aspens to **Phelps Lake Overlook,** which takes in the lake plus the Gros Ventre Mountains. You can appreciate the view from here or drop to the lake. To descend to the lake, drop westward down switchbacks to a trail junction and turn left. At the lake, a 4.5-mi (7.2-km) trail loops around the lake. The return to the overlook requires climbing back up. The lake loop tallies 9.9 mi (15.9 km).

TAGGART AND BRADLEY LAKES

DISTANCE: 3-5.9 mi (4.8-9.5 km) round-trip
DURATION: 2-4 hours round-trip
ELEVATION CHANGE: 400-900 ft (120-275 m)
EFFORT: Easy to moderate
TRAILHEAD: Taggart Lake Trailhead off Teton Park Road between Jenny Lake and Moose

Two lower-elevation lakes cower around 7,000 ft (2,100 m) at the base of Avalanche and Garnet Canyons. For a shorter 3-mi (4.8-km) hike, go to Taggart Lake and back. It's scenic, but the longer 5.9-mi (9.5-km) loop adds on Bradley Lake, where you can stare straight up at the Grand Teton. When the lake is glassy, the Grand reflects like a mirror. Get an early start in order to claim a parking spot

TOP HIKE
HIDDEN FALLS AND INSPIRATION POINT

Distance: 2 mi (3.2 km) round-trip
Duration: 2 hours round-trip
Elevation change: 443 ft (135 m)
Effort: Moderate
Trailhead: Jenny Lake Visitor Center

Hidden Falls, a 200-ft (60-m) tumbler in Cascade Canyon, and Inspiration Point, a rocky knoll at 7,257 ft (2,212 m), squeeze between Mt. Teewinot and Mt. St. John. Given the point's perch, the views from the summit live up to its name. You'll look straight down on the blue waters of Jenny Lake, up to the peaks on both sides, and across Jackson Hole to the Gros Ventre Mountains. Hordes of hikers clog this trail, which the $19 million Jenny Lake Renewal Project upgraded with stonework. As of summer 2020, the trail reached Lower Inspiration Point but was closed beyond that to Upper Inspiration Point and Cascade Canyon; check the status before hiking. Hiking time is 2 hours, but you'll need to add an extra hour (or more with long wait lines) for the **boat shuttle.**

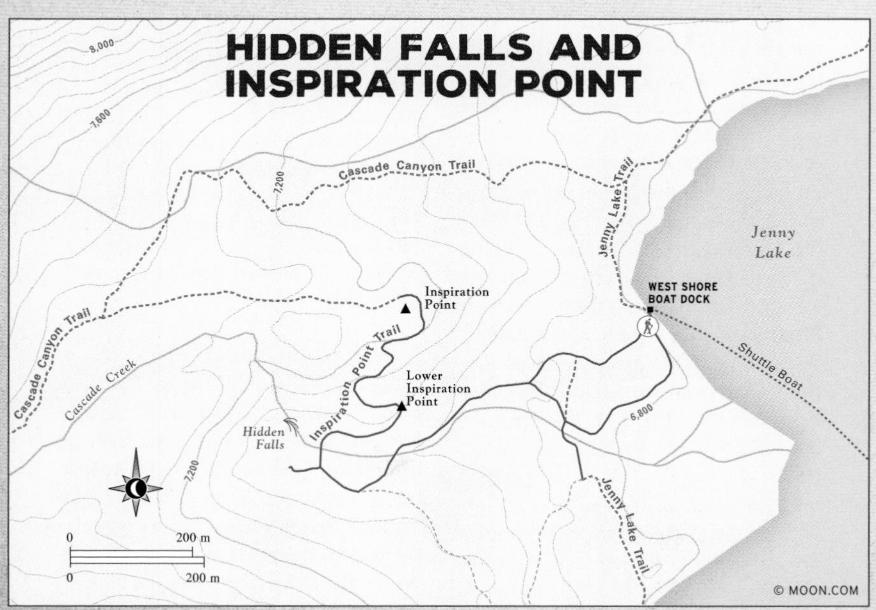

From the **west boat-shuttle dock,** head up the trail to the signed junction. Turn left and the uphill climb starts promptly. At junctions, follow the signs for Hidden Falls as the trail climbs along the north side of frothing Cascade Creek. At a junction for **Hidden Falls,** turn left to ascend Cascade Creek to the bridge crossing to the south side of the creek. Continue to the junction with the Hidden Falls Overlook spur.

To continue to Inspiration Point from the junction with the Hidden Falls spur, cross the two upper **bridges** over Cascade Creek, then climb a sweeping traverse into the rock of **Lower Inspiration Point.** Reaching **Upper Inspiration Point** requires ascending three more switchbacks. The slope can get hot in midsummer; mornings are best for hiking to the point. Enjoy the view before retracing your steps back to the west boat-shuttle dock.

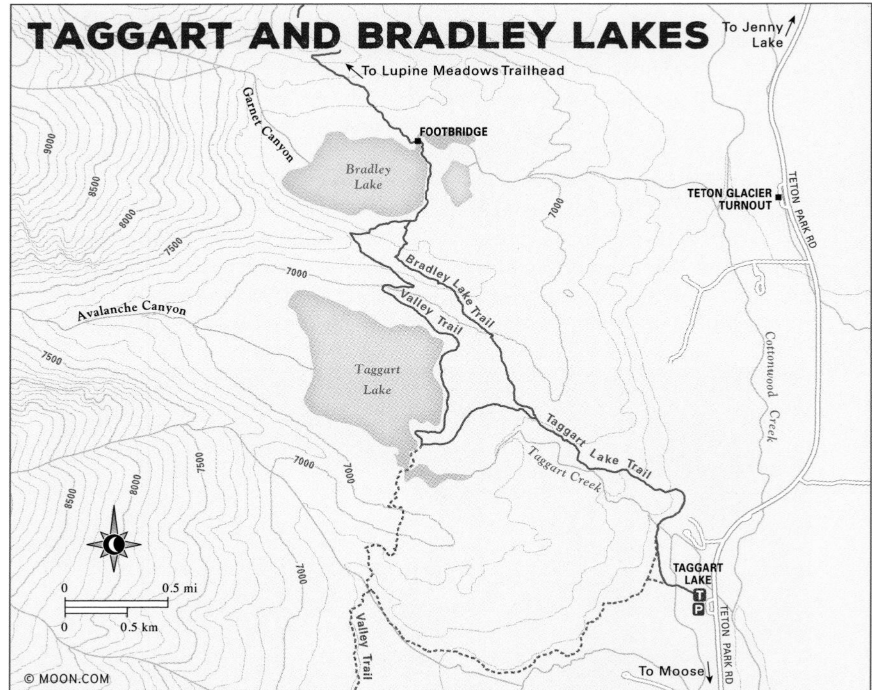

at this popular trailhead. Anglers fish both lakes, and on hot days, both lakes make good swimming holes.

From the trailhead, the trail curves north to cross a tumbling stream before ascending through conifers and meadows growing on glacial moraines to a **signed junction** at 1.1 mi (1.8 km). If you are planning to hike both lakes, you will loop back to this junction. To reach **Taggart,** turn left to hike 0.5 mi (0.8 km) to the lake. Explore the small peninsula to the south for a place to enjoy the water and views.

To continue the loop to **Bradley Lake,** circle north around the shore of Taggart Lake to climb two switchbacks that crest a forested glacial moraine. After dropping to a **signed junction,** turn left to visit Bradley Lake. Beaches flank the east shore, while the north side contains a **footbridge** crossing the outlet. After the lake, retrace your steps back to the last junction and take the fork heading left to climb over the moraine again and complete the loop to the first junction to return to the trailhead.

AMPHITHEATER AND SURPRISE LAKES

DISTANCE: 10.1 mi (16.3 km) round-trip
DURATION: 6 hours round-trip
ELEVATION CHANGE: 2,966 ft (904 m)
EFFORT: Strenuous
TRAILHEAD: Lupine Meadows Trailhead off Teton Park Road south of Jenny Lake

At 9,714 ft (2,961 m), Surprise and Amphitheater Lakes cluster 0.2 mi (0.3 km) apart in a high, narrow subalpine basin on an eastern ridge extending from Grand Teton. Since this out-and-back trail provides access for many technical climbing routes, you may see people loaded with ropes, helmets, and gear on the Garnet Canyon spur. Start early, as the sun-soaked climb can be hot midday.

Begin by hiking 1.7 mi (2.7 km) on a trail that ascends a moraine ridge to the junction with the **Taggart Lake Trail.** At the junction, continue uphill to follow switchbacks that climb steeply on the open, east-facing slope. Views of Jackson Hole get bigger the higher you go; Bradley Lake is below to the south.

After the fourth switchback, a trail cuts left into **Garnet Canyon** for 1.1 mi (1.8 km) until it fizzles out in a boulder field. From there, it offers good views of Middle Teton, the park's third-highest peak. (Adding on this spur increases the total distance by 2.2 mi/3.5 km round-trip.)

Garnet Canyon

To reach the lakes, follow the switchbacks as they climb through a broken forest of whitebark pines and whortleberry. Nearing the lake basin, look up for views of the Grand Teton. At **Surprise Lake,** descend to the shore and enjoy the lake, or circle the lake's east shore to its outlet to overlook Jackson Hole. The main trail passes above the north

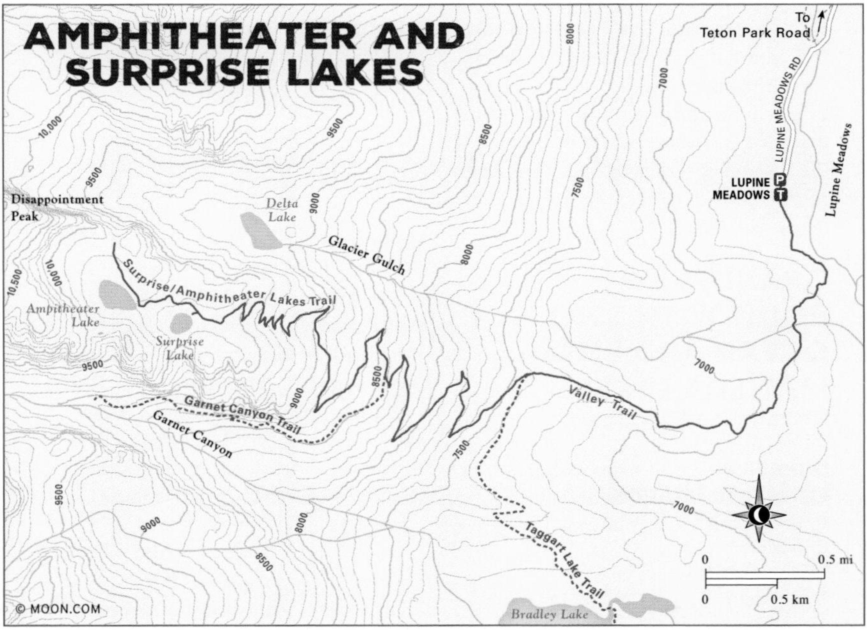

AMPHITHEATER AND SURPRISE LAKES

To Teton Park Road
LUPINE MEADOWS RD
Lupine Meadows
LUPINE MEADOWS
Disappointment Peak
Delta Lake
Glacier Gulch
Surprise/Amphitheater Lakes Trail
Amphitheater Lake
Surprise Lake
Garnet Canyon Trail
Garnet Canyon
Valley Trail
Taggart Lake Trail
Bradley Lake
0 0.5 mi
0 0.5 km

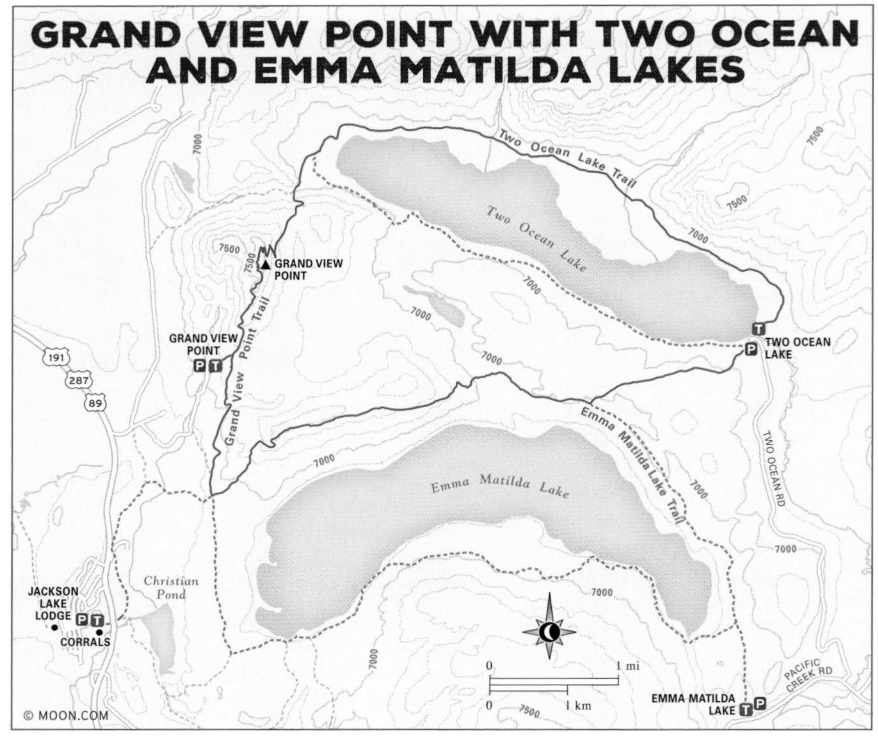

side of Surprise Lake to climb into the small hanging valley housing **Amphitheater Lake,** tucked at the base of Disappointment Peak. After the lake, a rough trail climbs north 0.2 mi (0.3 km) to grab a partial view of the Grand, glacial moraine, and immense cliffs.

GRAND VIEW POINT WITH TWO OCEAN AND EMMA MATILDA LAKES

DISTANCE: 9.7 mi (15.6 km) round-trip
DURATION: 5 hours round-trip
ELEVATION CHANGE: 550-800 ft (170-245 m)
EFFORT: Moderate
TRAILHEAD: Two Ocean Lake Trailhead
DIRECTIONS: From US-89/191/287 1 mi (1.6 km) north of Jackson Lake Junction, take the paved Pacific Creek Road 2 mi (3 km) to a junction with Two Ocean Road. Turn left and drive 2.4 mi (3.9 km) on dirt road to the trailhead at Two Ocean Lake.

Multiple trailheads lead to Grand View Point, an aptly named 7,286-ft (2,221-m) summit with huge panoramic views of Jackson Lake and the Tetons. From the signed Grand View summit, you overlook Two Ocean and Emma Matilda Lakes. West of the summit, a large rocky bluff takes in the jagged peaks of Mt. Moran, Grand Teton, and entire Teton Range.

The **Two Ocean Lake Trail** (6.4 mi/14.2 km round-trip from Two Ocean Lake Trailhead) and **Emma**

Matilda Lake Trail (9.9 mi/15.9 km round-trip from Emma Matilda Lake Trailhead) circumnavigate the respective lakes, but why choose one? You can do a view-filled grand tour of both lakes, and hit Grand View Point along the way.

From the Two Ocean Lake Trailhead, take the **north-shore trail** for the bigger views first. The meadow-lined trail goes 3.4 mi (5.5 km) with a short climb and descent to a **junction** at the head of the lake. From the junction, a steep trail grunts up to **Grand View Point** (1.1 mi/1.8 km). Continue over the point to descend Grand View Point Trail for 1.6 miles (2.6 km), until you reach a four-way junction that turns right to Jackson Lake Lodge, goes straight ahead for the longer and more forested south **Emma Matilda Lake Trail,** or turns left for the north Emma Matilda Lake Trail with better views. After turning left, hike above the north shore of Emma Matilda Lake through loose Douglas fir forest for 2.6 mi (4.2 km) to reach the final junction. Turn left for 1 mi (1.6 km) to return to **Two Ocean Lake Trailhead.**

If you want to do a short hike just to get to **Grand View Point,** the shortest route is a 2.2-mi (3.5-km) out-and-back, with only 550 ft (170 m) of climbing, from the **Grand View Point** parking area to the viewpoint. From the trailhead, hike up a steep 0.2-mi (0.3-km) connector trail to reach the **Grand View Point Trail.** The trail ascends steeply through meadows and forest.

COLTER BAY LAKESHORE

DISTANCE: 2-mi (3-km) loop
DURATION: 1.5 hours
ELEVATION CHANGE: 100 ft (30 m)

Grand View Point (top); Colter Bay Lakeshore Trail (middle); Heron Pond (bottom)

Swan Lake

EFFORT: Easy
TRAILHEAD: Colter Bay Visitor Center

For a short walk with minimum hills and maximum scenery, the Colter Bay Lakeshore Trail provides a double loop that follows the shoreline of the small promontory with multiple inlets. Begin on the paved trail that rims the north shore of the **marina** to tour a breakwater spit. After walking the spit, head west on the trail toward a tiny **isthmus** of rocks that connects two parts of the peninsula. Once across the isthmus, go either way to circle the **1.1-mile (1.8-km) loop.** Side trails reach beaches that yield views across Jackson Lake to the Teton Mountains. Mt. Moran is prominent across the lake from many beaches, which get larger toward the end of the summer. Upon returning to the causeway, follow your original tracks back to the visitors center, or better yet, take the other **spur trail** northeast along the shoreline toward the swimming beach and then return to the visitors center on a trail paralleling the road.

HERON POND AND SWAN LAKE

DISTANCE: 2.6 mi (4.2 km) round-trip
DURATION: 1.5 hours round-trip
ELEVATION CHANGE: 200 ft (60 m)
EFFORT: Easy
TRAILHEAD: Swan, Heron, and Hermitage Point Trailhead at Colter Bay Village

A series of ponds named for birds flanks the hillside east of Colter Bay Village. They have significant growths of yellow pond lilies, leaving little visible water, but they make prime habitat for a variety of wildlife: sandhill cranes, trumpeter swans, ospreys, muskrats, river otters, and great blue herons. You'll pass multiple junctions, all well signed on this forest and meadow trail. A map from the visitors center can help in navigating the junctions. Be ready for mosquitoes. Hikers can also access this loop from Jackson Lake Lodge, which will add on 10 mi (16 km) round-trip.

The trail starts on an **old service road** that curves around the south edge of Colter Bay. After leaving the bay, climb over a loosely forested hill to **Heron Pond,** where the trail follows the northeastern shore to several ultra-scenic viewpoints of Mt. Moran and Rockchuck Peak. At the southeast corner of the pond, turn left at the trail junction to reach **Swan Lake.** After following the shore northward, the trail returns to a junction, where going straight will curve around **Jackson Lake Overlook** back to the trailhead.

BACKPACKING

Grand Teton National Park has immense vertical relief. Most people only go to the low-elevation roads and trails along the base, only a small fraction of the park. But up in the mountains, trails traverse huge shelves thick wildflower meadows, tour below and above stark cliffs, and climb to top-of-the-world passes. Backpacking is the way to get you there.

TETON CREST TRAIL

34-58 mi (55-93 km)

The king of backpacking trips is the Teton Crest Trail, a high-elevation romp demanding major elevation gains and descents. The route crosses Fox Creek Pass, Death Canyon Shelf, Mt. Meek Pass, Alaska Basin, Hurricane Pass, and Paintbrush Divide at 9,600-10,720 ft (2,926-3,267 m). As you traverse the trail northward, the central Tetons dominate the scenery. The **38-mi (61-km) point-to-point** route requires a shuttle between trailheads (Granite Canyon and String Lake), or you can complete the loop by adding on the Valley Trail (20 mi/32 km) to link them on foot. Many crest hikers chop off the 4,000-plus-ft (1,200-plus-m) climb up Granite Canyon by taking the Aerial Tram (fee) at Jackson Hole Mountain Resort to join the Teton Crest Trail 3.8 mi (6.1 km) from Rendezvous Mountain. (Taking the tram reduces total distance to 34 mi/55 km.) For the **58-mi (93-km) point-to-point** trip (5 days), plan to camp at Marian Lake (use Upper Granite as an alternative), Death Canyon Shelf, South Fork Cascade, and Upper Paintbrush. For those adding on the Valley Trail, start and end your trip at Jenny Lake and do the lowland trail first with a night at Bradley Lake in order to finish with the stunning trek through the alpine.

Teton Crest Trail

PAINTBRUSH DIVIDE

19.2 mi (30.9 km)

The Paintbrush Canyon-Cascade Canyon loop (19.2 mi/30.9 km) is a stunning three-day backpacking trip, but for strong hikers, it can also serve as an epic day hike. Outstanding scenery, the high Paintbrush Divide, and Lake Solitude highlight the route. **Camp** one night each at Holly Lake (use Upper Paintbrush zone as alternative) and North Fork Cascade zone.

Spectacular scenery, wildlife, and in-your-face views of the Grand Teton are only a few of its rewards. Crossing through multiple ecosystems, the grueling route climbs Paintbrush Canyon to Holly Lake, then crests the 10,720-ft (3,267-m) Paintbrush Divide to drop to Lake Solitude before connecting with Cascade Canyon for the descent back to the trailhead. Until late July, you may need an ice ax for crossing the divide. For those who only want to explore part of the route, Holly Lake (13 mi/20.9 km, 2,600 ft/800 m elevation gain) and Paintbrush Divide (17 mi/27 km round-trip, 4,350 ft/1,325 m elevation gain) make outstanding destinations in their own right. For hiking the full loop, plan to depart at dawn for maximum daylight.

From the trailhead, follow the path up the east side of **String Lake.** At the junction at **Leigh Lake,** turn left and cross the rocky stream. At the next junction, turn right to circle around the north side of Rockchuck Peak and climb into **Paintbrush Canyon.** The trail goes through conifer forests interrupted by giant talus fields and avalanche paths before switchbacking up through wildflower meadows and boulders to crest into a hanging valley. Listen for the "eeep" of pikas that live around the boulders. At the next trail junction, go right to **Holly Lake** or straight for a more direct route to Paintbrush Divide.

The trail to Holly Lake ascends through broken meadows to reach an idyllic alpine lake that tucks into a tight cirque filled with wildflower meadows and talus slopes. A small

view of the Grand Teton from Paintbrush Divide

point on the southwest shore offers a place to relax and enjoy the scenery. From the lake, an **unmarked path** heads directly up to join the route to **Paintbrush Divide.** The trail climbs steadily 1.7 mi (2.7 km) upward, leaving the small pockets of trees behind and entering alpine scree slopes, where steep snow can linger late into summer. After passing the junction to **Grizzly Bear Lake,** the trail swings north across the slope to switchback steeply under a cliff face and pop out at the summit of Paintbrush Divide. The trail trots along the pass, soaking up views in both directions.

For the full loop to Cascade Canyon, follow the trail as it descends 2.4 mi (3.9 km) of switchbacks to **Lake Solitude**, a larger turquoise lake flanked by wildflower meadows in August. The Grand Teton comes into view to the south. From the lake, the trail heads 2.4 mi (3.9 km) through meadows straight toward the Grand before dropping into the forest to reach the fork in **Cascade Canyon.** From the fork, descend 6.8 mi (10.9 km) and 1,950 ft (595 m) via **Cascade Canyon Trail,** turning north at the base to skirt Jenny Lake back to the String Lake parking lot.

PERMITS

In the popular backpacking areas of the Tetons, some campsites are assigned while others are designated to a backcountry camping zone. All backpackers are required to carry food in a **bear canister** (permit offices have loaners) and have a **backcountry camping permit.** Apply online (www.recreation.gov; apply early Jan.-mid-May; $45/trip) to guarantee your permit in advance. First-come, first-served permits ($35/trip) are available in person 24 hours before departure. Competition for walk-in permits is high in July and August; a line usually forms at the Jenny Lake Ranger Station or Craig Thomas Discovery & Visitor Center one hour before the 8am opening. For more details, read the backcountry camping brochure online (www.nps.gov/grte).

MOUNTAIN CLIMBING

Climbing **Grand Teton** involves 14 mi (22.5 km) of hiking and 6,545 ft (1,995 m) of ascent and descent. Most climbers take an ultra-long day from the valley floor. More than 35 climbing routes lead to the summit, with countless variations, and climbers pioneer new routes almost every year. The most popular and famous route for climbing the Grand is the exposed **Upper Exum Ridge,** considered a classic in mountaineering.

The fastest time for climbing and descending, at 2:53, was set in 2012 by a climbing ranger. Although controversy surrounds the Grand's first ascent, documentation points to a team of four summiting in 1898. A duo reached the top in 1873, although they may have summited The Enclosure instead. Either way, archaeological evidence indicates that Native Americans most likely reached the summit before both groups. Since 1971, ski and snowboard descents have been added to the record books.

GUIDES

EXUM MOUNTAIN GUIDES

South Jenny Lake; tel. 307/733-2297; http://exumguides.com

This company guides climbs and ski mountaineering trips year-round in Grand Teton National Park. Most climbing camps, schools, and guided climbs happen in **summer.** Climbs up Grand Teton, as well as other technical peaks, are offered. In most cases, Exum will supply all the technical climbing gear.

BIKING

MULTI-USE PATHWAY

29 mi (47 km); dawn-dusk, snow-covered in winter

The most popular bike ride is the Multi-Use Pathway, a paved cycling and walking path that parallels the roads between Jenny Lake, Moose, Antelope Flats Road, and Jackson. The mostly level path is perfect for cyclists who don't want to contend with RV traffic and for families with kids. Use caution: Wildlife (including bison) also walks on the trail, and pathways intersect with road crossings. The southern section, from Jackson to Gros Ventre Junction, closes November-April for migrating elk. For a gawk-worthy scenic ride, the **Moose-Jenny Lake Pathway** (7.7 mi/12.4 km) saunters just below the Tetons.

TIPS

Summer offers the best cycling weather, but prepare for potential dousing from afternoon thundershowers and strong winds. If biking paved roads, go in the early morning or late afternoon to avoid peak midday traffic. While cyclists can ride all park roads, shoulders are narrow and giant RVs will zoom by; ride single file for safety. For visibility, wear a helmet and bright colors (most drivers are looking at the peaks or wildlife rather than cyclists).

a family biking through Grand Teton

RENTALS

ADVENTURE SPORTS

12170 Dornan Rd., Moose (on the Multi-Use Pathway); tel. 307/733-3307; https://dornans.com; 9am-6pm daily early May-late Sept.; bike rental $30-75 adults, $22-40 kids

BOATING AND PADDLING

JENNY LAKE

Boating on Jenny Lake is a quiet, idyllic experience, as only motorboats with 10 horsepower or less are permitted, plus any hand-propelled boats. Sailboats, sailboards, waterskiing, and Jet Skis are not allowed. The boat launch is on **Lupine Meadows Road.** After crossing the bridge over Cottonwood Creek, turn right to reach the dirt ramp and small loop for trailer parking.

North of Jenny Lake, **String Lake** connects via a portage to **Leigh Lake.** String Lake has a canoe and kayak launch site in the second parking lot on the left on the **String Lake Picnic Area** road north of Jenny Lake Road.

Rentals

JENNY LAKE BOATING

Jenny Lake boathouse; tel. 307/734-9227; www.jennylakeboating.com; 7am-7pm daily mid-June-mid-Sept., shorter hours in fall; kayak and canoe rental $20/hr, $80/day

ADVENTURE SPORTS

12170 Dornan Rd., Moose; tel. 307/733-3307; https://dornans.com; 9am-6pm daily early May-late Sept.; kayak, canoe, paddleboard rental $22-40/hr, $50-75/day

JACKSON LAKE

Filling a trough scooped out by an ice-age glacier, Jackson Lake is so big it takes multiple days to explore all its nooks and crannies. At full pool, the lake is 15 mi (24 km) long, 7 mi (11 km) wide, and more than 400 ft (120 m) deep. Fifteen islands, several peninsulas, and numerous bays provide places to get away from crowds. To enjoy the solitude of your own beach, go to the **west shore between Steamboat Mountain and Mt. Moran.** By August, the lake level drops, which enlarges beaches.

Motorboats, nonmotorized boats, sailboats, sailboarding, and waterskiing are allowed on Jackson Lake; Jet Skis and motorized personal watercraft are not. Water-skiers and wakeboarders must be out on open water, not in channels or within 500 ft (150 m) of marinas, docks, swimming beaches, and moored boats in bays. While the image of cutting lazy turns in glassy water below the sun-drenched Teton Mountains sounds idyllic, the reality is quite different. Due to chilly water, most water-skiers wear wetsuits or drysuits, and afternoons often see big waves crop up.

Marinas and Launches

If you have a small hand-carried watercraft, you can launch from any beach where you can haul it. Otherwise, Jackson Lake has four boat launches with cement ramps, docks, and trailer parking.

LEEK'S MARINA

tel. 307/543-2831; www.signalmountainlodge.com; daily late May-late Sept.; no rentals

Colter Bay Marina (left); kayakers on Jackson Lake (right)

COLTER BAY MARINA

Grand Teton Lodging Company; tel. 307/543-2811; www.gtlc.com; daily late May-late Sept.; motorboats rentals $48/hr, 2-hr minimum

SIGNAL MOUNTAIN LODGE MARINA

tel. 307/543-2831; www.signalmountainlodge.com; daily mid-May-mid-Sept.; boat rentals $42-145/hr

SPALDING BAY BOAT LAUNCH

Spalding Bay

Spalding Bay Boat Launch has special restrictions for its rocky slope launch without a dock. Only boat trailers with single axles are permitted. A one-day parking permit (available first-come, first-served 24 hours in advance at Colter Bay Visitor Center) is required due to limited space. No overnight parking is allowed.

Best Paddling Bays

Paddlers can find fun cubbyholes to explore on Jackson Lake, with islands and protected bays the best places for touring. Due to big winds that can arise on Jackson Lake, avoid open-water paddles. Placid glassy-lake paddles can mutate fast into whitecaps threatening to swamp boats. Take shoreline routes for safety. The most sheltered paddles are **Signal Mountain Marina** or **Colter Bay Marina.** Between **Colter Bay** and **Half Moon Bay,** a series of channels weaves through multiple islands. To paddle to **Elk Island** from Signal Mountain Marina or boat launch, aim for **Donoho Point** and **Hermitage Point** to break up the open water. To paddle to east-shore locations, use **Spalding Bay boat launch** (permit required) to reach the base of Mt. Moran or launch from **Lizard Creek Campground** (minimal parking) for northwest shore paddling. Jackson Lake has 15 lake-accessed **campsites** (permit required) for overnighting, some on islands.

PERMITS

Two permits are required for boating and most paddling. Boaters must pick up a State of Wyoming **Aquatic Invasive Species (AIS) sticker** (Wyoming Game and Fish; tel. 307/777-4600; https://wgfd.wyo.gov; Wyoming residents $10 motorized,

$5 nonmotorized, nonresidents $30 motorized, $15 nonmotorized) and pass an inspection at the Moran or Moose boat inspection station. Inflatable watercraft smaller than 10 ft (3 m) are exempt. Then, to buy Grand Teton National Park **boat permits** (motorized $40, nonmotorized $12), go to Jenny Lake Ranger Station or any visitors center.

RIVER RAFTING

WILD AND SCENIC SNAKE RIVER

Rafts, kayaks, and canoes can float the Wild and Scenic Snake River below Jackson Lake Dam, which yields wildlife sightings and grand views of the Tetons. Start at **Jackson Lake Dam** or **Cattleman's Bridge Site** to take out at **Pacific Creek** (5 mi/8 km; 2 hours). Only experienced paddlers should put in at Deadman's Bar and take out at Moose Landing (10 mi/16 km; 2 hours), an advanced section with strong currents, waves, logjams, and a maze of braided streams.

Floating the Snake River requires river knowledge and is not for discount store blowup rafts (inner tubes and air mattresses are not allowed). During the winter and early spring (Dec. 15-Apr. 1), the river closes to floating from Jackson Lake Dam to Menor's Ferry.

Guided Raft Trips

Guided floating trips allow you to sit back and enjoy the view—the guide does the rowing. They usually go from Pacific Creek or Deadman's Bar to Moose in the south portion of Grand Teton National Park (mid-May-late Sept.). Departing from **Jackson Lake Lodge** and **Signal Mountain Lodge,** trips usually take up to 4-5 hours, including transportation from the lodge to the river and back; actual float time on the river is about two hours.

JACKSON LAKE LODGE

Grand Teton Lodging Company; tel. 307/543-2811; www.gtlc.com; several trips Mon.-Sat.

SIGNAL MOUNTAIN LODGE

tel. 307/543-2831; www.signalmountainlodge.com; several trips daily

a guided raft trip along Snake River

HORSEBACK RIDING

Grand Teton Lodging Company (tel. 307/543-3100 reservations, tel. 307/543-2811, www.gtlc.com; $48/1 hr, $78/2 hr; reservations recommended) operates three **corrals:** at Colter Bay Village (daily early June-early Sept.), Jackson Lake Lodge (daily late May-early Oct.), and Flagg Ranch (daily June-Aug.). Colter Bay and Jackson Lake Lodge offer one- and two-hour rides, while Flagg Ranch only offers one-hour rides. The two-hour ride from Jackson Lake Lodge is the most scenic, with views of the Tetons and Snake River.

WINTER SPORTS

CROSS-COUNTRY SKIING AND SNOWSHOEING

In winter, some roads in the national park close to vehicles, which means they turn into cross-country ski and snowshoe routes. From the Taggart Lake Trailhead to Signal Mountain Lodge, **Teton Park Road** (14 mi/22.5 km; mid-Dec.-mid-Mar.) becomes a winter ski and snowshoe trail to frozen Jenny Lake.

a ranger leading students on a snowshoe walk

The road is groomed twice a week. Follow protocol on the groomed trail: Snowshoers should walk on the smooth grooming, not the tracks cut for skiing. Find current conditions and grooming reports online at **Jackson Hole Nordic** (https://jhnordic.com).

The closed **Moose-Wilson Road** offers a road tour through a forest, but the road is not groomed. Be ready to break your own trail or follow previous tracks from skiers and snowshoers. From the Granite Canyon Trailhead, you can tour the road north to the Laurance S. Rockefeller Preserve Center (closed in winter) and circle Phelps Lake on trails.

Popular because of winter accessibility and trailhead parking, **Taggart and Bradley Lakes** also make good trail destinations for those who want to get off the roads.

Rentals and Guides

Several companies are licensed to guide winter tours in the national park and instruct avalanche courses. Most trips are scheduled on demand. Consider pairing up with other visitors to reduce rates. You can also rent backcountry skis, cross-country skis, and snowshoes for adults and kids in Jackson and Teton Village.

SNOWSHOE WALKS

tel. 307/739-3399; www.nps.gov/grte; late Dec.-mid-Mar.; free

In winter, rangers guide interpretive snowshoe walks. The two-hour tours meet at the Taggart Lake Trailhead to look for tracks, study snow science, and examine the ecology of winter. Dress in layers, bring water and a pack, and wear snow boots or sturdy hiking boots. Reservations are required starting in early December. Snowshoes are available.

HOLE HIKING EXPERIENCE

tel. 307/690-4453; www.holehike.com

Hole Hiking Experience offers 2- to 6-hour cross-country ski and snowshoe trips.

FOOD

Most restaurants inside the park are first-come, first-served, with the exception of the Mural Room and Poolside Cantina and Barbecue at Jackson Lake Lodge and Colter Bay cookouts. Expect to wait in line for seating, especially during the peak summer season. Dress is casual; however, diners in Jackson Lake Lodge's Mural Room and Signal Mountain Lodge's Peaks Restaurant tend to clean up before meals.

Reservations are required for dinner at Jenny Lake Lodge, the Colter Bay Cookouts, the Mural Room at Jackson Lake Lodge, and dinner at Poolside Cantina and Barbecue.

STANDOUTS

Jenny Lake Lodge

400 Jenny Lake Loop; tel. 307/543-2811; www.gtlc.com; daily June-early Oct.

The dining room at Jenny Lake Lodge is an experience in itself. The log lodge has an intimate restaurant with views of the peaks for a romantic setting. Local and Wyoming food sources are used, and the wine list spans the world. Vegetarian, gluten-free, vegan, organic, all-natural, and low-fat options are available. Breakfast (7:30am-10am; $34) is a gourmet prix fixe menu; you select your starter, egg dish, and sweets. Lunch (11:30am-1:30pm; $12-18) features sandwiches, burgers, salads, and trout and grits. Dinner (6pm-9pm; $98) is a five-course prix fixe affair with menus rotating on a five-night schedule. **Reservations** are recommended for breakfast and lunch and are required for dinner. Lodge guests can make dinner reservations when they book their lodging; nonguests can make reservations beginning March 1. Diners are expected to wear jackets, slacks, and dress attire for dinner.

Jenny Lake Lodge

GRAND TETON NATIONAL PARK FOOD OPTIONS

NAME	LOCATION	TYPE
★ Jenny Lake Lodge	Jenny Lake	prix-fixe restaurant (except at lunch) with dress code
South Jenny Lake General Store	Jenny Lake	grocery
Pizza Pasta Company	Moose	cafeteria-style
Dornan's Chuckwagon	Moose	outdoor sit-down restaurant
Moose Trading Post & Deli	Moose	deli and take-out
Sheffields Restaurant & Bar	Flagg Ranch	sit-down restaurant
Leek's Pizzeria	Leek's Marina	picnic table seating
Café Court Pizzeria	Colter Bay	quick-service and take-out
Ranch House	Colter Bay	sit-down restaurant
Cookouts Boat Cruises	Colter Bay	outdoor dining
Colter Bay General Store	Colter Bay	deli and grocery
★ Mural Room	Jackson Lake Lodge	sit-down restaurant
Blue Heron Lounge	Jackson Lake Lodge	sit-down restaurant
Pioneer Grill	Jackson Lake Lodge	cafeteria-style
Poolside Cantina and Barbecue	Jackson Lake Lodge	outdoor dining
Peaks Restaurant	Signal Mountain Lodge	sit-down restaurant
★ Trapper Grill	Signal Mountain Lodge	sit-down restaurant

FOOD	PRICE	HOURS
upscale local cuisine	splurge (moderate at lunch)	7:30am-10am, 11:30am-1:30pm, 6pm-9pm daily late June-early Oct. (reservations required for dinner)
general goods	budget	8am-7pm daily mid-May-mid-Sept.
casual American and Italian	budget	11:30am-9:30pm daily year-round, shorter winter hours
Western	moderate	7am-11am, noon-3pm, 5pm-9pm daily early June-early Sept.
sandwiches and general goods	budget	9am-5pm daily winter, 8am-8pm daily summer
casual American	moderate	6:30am-10am, 11:30am-2pm, 5:30pm-9:30pm daily June-Sept.
Italian	budget	11am-10pm daily late May-early Sept.
Italian	budget	11am-10pm daily late May-early Sept
Western American	budget	6:30am-10:30am, 11:30am-1:30pm, 5:30pm-9pm daily late May-early Oct.
Western American	splurge	breakfast 7:15am and dinner 5:15pm Fri.-Wed., lunch 12:15pm Mon., Wed., Fri.-Sat. June-mid-Sept. (reservations required)
casual American and general goods	budget	7am-9:30pm daily late May-late Sept.
Western American	splurge	7am-9:30am, 11:30am-1:30pm, (reservations required) 5:30pm-9:30pm daily mid-May-early Oct.
casual American	moderate	11am-midnight daily mid-May-early Oct.
casual American	budget	6am-10:30am, 11am-10pm daily mid-May-early Oct.
casual American; barbecue (dinner)	moderate	11am-4pm, 5:30pm-8pm daily early June-late August (weather permitting)
Western American	moderate	5:30pm-10pm daily mid-May-early Oct.
casual American	budget	7am-10pm daily mid-May-early Oct.

Colter Bay Picnic Area

Mural Room at Jackson Lake Lodge

101 Jackson Lake Lodge Rd.; tel. 307/543-2811; www.gtlc.com; daily mid-May-early Oct.

Dining in the Mural Room is an experience for the panoramic views of the Tetons outside and the murals depicting western Native American and Wyoming trapper life inside. Dinner reservations are imperative for a window seat. For breakfast (7am-9:30am daily; $10-20), partake of the buffet or order from the menu. The buffet's Belgian waffle iron puts a moose imprint on the waffle; pastries, bread, and cinnamon rolls are baked on-site. Lunch (11:30am-1:30pm daily; $12-22) serves elk chili, organic greens, sandwiches, and entrées of trout and duck. For dinner (5:30pm-9:30pm daily; $18-48), appetizers, soups, and salads lead into main courses of prime rib, elk rib eye, bison, trout, and salmon.

Trapper Grill

Signal Mountain Lodge, 1 Inner Park Rd.; tel. 307/543-2831; www.signalmountainlodge.com; 7am-10pm daily mid-May-early Oct., hours shorten in fall

With indoor dining or outdoor deck seating, Trapper Grill has large menus with choices for families and hungry hikers. Breakfast (7am-11am; $10-15) serves eggs Benedict, skillets, and omelets. Lunch and dinner menus ($10-20) have soups, salads, sandwiches, burgers, and Tex-Mex entrées such as trout tacos. Giant nachos are a post-hiking favorite. You can also order from the menus in Deadman's Bar, where the views are more limited.

BEST PICNIC SPOTS

Lakeview

Located on US-89/191/287 between Lizard Creek Campground and Leek's Marina

Lakeview is popular due to its water and mountain views, plus Jackson Lake access for water play. The rough parking lot fits only small RVs. The picnic area has tables and a vault toilet.

Colter Bay

Located in Colter Bay on Jackson Lake at the end of Colter Bay Road

Swim in Jackson Lake while gaping at an outstanding view of the Teton Mountains at this picnic area. Buoys mark the swimming area and keep boats out. The large picnic area has tables, some fire rings with grills (bring your own wood), and flush toilets.

String Lake

Access via North Jenny Lake Road off Teton Park Road

String Lake is a paddling and swimming favorite due to protection from big winds and shallower water that is slightly warmer than most other lakes. Bring kayaks, canoes, paddleboards, and floaties. The large picnic area in the trees has tables, flush toilets, and fire rings with grills (bring your own firewood).

GRAND TETON NATIONAL PARK CAMPGROUNDS		
NAME	**LOCATION**	**SEASON**
★ **Jenny Lake Campground**	Jenny Lake	early May-late Sept.
Gros Ventre	Kelly	early May-early Oct.
Headwaters Campground & RV Park	John D. Rockefeller, Jr. Memorial Parkway	mid-May-Sept.
Grassy Lake Road	John D. Rockefeller, Jr. Memorial Parkway	June-Sept.
Lizard Creek	Lizard Creek on Jackson Lake	early June-early Sept.
★ **Colter Bay RV Park**	Colter Bay on Jackson Lake	mid-May-early Oct.
★ **Colter Bay Campground**	Colter Bay on Jackson Lake	late May-Sept.
★ **Signal Mountain Campground**	Signal Mountain on Jackson Lake	mid-May-mid-Oct.

CAMPING

Most campgrounds inside Grand Teton National Park include picnic tables, fire rings, bear boxes for food storage, and drinking water. Shared hiker and biker campsites cost $12 per person. ADA sites are available. Some campgrounds have flush toilets.

Reservations

Only Colter Bay RV Park and Headwaters Campground take reservations. **Make reservations** starting 366 days

SITES AND AMENITIES	RV LIMIT	PRICE	RESERVATIONS
49 tent-only sites; vault toilets; vehicle size limit: 8 ft (2.4 m) wide/14 ft (4.3 m) long	n/a	$32	no
350 RV and tent sites; flush toilets; dump station; 10 accessible sites available	45 ft/14 m	$33 ($64 with electrical hookups)	large groups only
175 sites; flush toilets	60 ft/18 m	$42 tents, $85 RVs with hookups	RV sites only
14 primitive sites in 8 locations; vault toilets; no drinking water	20 ft/6m with high clearance	free	no
43 drive-in sites; 17 walk-in tent sites; flush toilets	30 ft/9 m	$34	no
112 pull-through RV-only sites; laundry; showers; dump stations	45 ft/14 m	$86-91 RV-only sites	yes
350 tent and RV sites; 9 walk-in tent sites; 11 group sites; 13 accessible sites; flush toilets; laundry; showers; dump stations	45 ft/14 m	$36 ($64 accessible sites with electricity)	group sites only
81 tent and RV sites; 4 tent-only sites; flush toilets	30 ft/9 m	$36 ($58 with electricity)	no

in advance. All other campgrounds are first-come, first-served.

Tips

Colter Bay RV Park is one of the first campgrounds to book out because of its location and availability of full hookups. For first-come, first-serve campgrounds, plan to arrive in the morning to get a spot . . . and very early morning for Jenny Lake. You are better off keeping a campsite for the duration of your stay rather than packing up and trying to go to another campground.

STANDOUTS

Jenny Lake Campground

early May-late Sept.; $32

The most-coveted campground in the park, Jenny Lake Campground has front-row seating with exceptional scenery right below the Teton Mountains. You can park the car and hike for days. Trails lead to Hidden Falls, Inspiration Point, Leigh Lake, Cascade Canyon, and Paintbrush Canyon, plus peaks for climbing. Jenny Lake also has scenic cruises, kayak and canoe rentals, fishing, paddling, and the paved Multi-Use Pathway running south to Moose.

In a hilly, loose pine forest with big boulders, the campground has 49 **tent-only** campsites, including several walk-in sites. RVs, pop-ups, trailers, truck campers, and generators are prohibited, and vehicles must be smaller than 8 ft (2.4 m) wide and 14 ft (4.3 m) long. Each site allows a maximum of two tents, one vehicle or two motorcycles, and six people. Bathroom facilities are vault toilets. Locate the campground by turning from Teton Park Road into South Jenny Lake and veering right. The campground fills by early morning, but you may need to start trolling for a site around 7am.

Colter Bay RV Park and Campgrounds

Colter Bay Village; tel. 307/543-3100; www.gtlc.com

Located at Jackson Lake in a lodgepole forest, the Colter Bay Campgrounds are part of Colter Bay Village, which houses a visitors center, amphitheater for evening naturalist programs, general store, two restaurants, coin-op laundry and showers, gas, disposal stations (fee), hiking trails, boat launch, swimming beach, and a marina with motorboat, canoe, and kayak rentals.

Behind the store, the **RV park** (mid-May-early Oct.; $86-91) has 112 pull-through and back-in campsites with hookups for water, sewer, and electricity. RV campsites often book up in January; you can make

cooking over the fire at Colter Bay Campground

reservations 366 days in advance. No tents or fires are permitted in the RV park, but you can use your own gas or charcoal grill. RV length, including rigs and trailers, is limited to 45 ft (14 m), and sites are stacked close together.

The large tent and RV **campground** (late May-Sept.; $36, first-come, first-served) contains 350 sites without hookups, 9 walk-in tent sites, 11 group sites, and 13 ADA campsites with electricity ($64), which often fill up before noon. Some loops are generator-free zones. Sites are assigned at the staffed check-in station. If you arrive after the station closes, a whiteboard lists available sites. Reservations are available for group campsites only. **Winter camping** (Dec.-mid-Apr.; $5) is in the plowed parking lot at Colter Bay.

Signal Mountain Campground

1 Inner Park Rd.; tel. 307/543-2831; www.signalmountainlodge.com; mid-May-mid-Oct., $36, first-come, first-served

The Signal Mountain Lodge complex houses a restaurant, convenience store, gas station, boat launch, and marina with guided fishing and rentals of canoes, kayaks, and motorboats. On a bluff overlooking Jackson Lake, Signal Mountain Campground commands one of the best panoramic views of the Teton Mountains. The campground loops around a hillside, where some of the sites yield million-dollar views. There are 81 sites for tents or RVs, 4 tent-only campsites, and 24 sites with electricity ($58). A mix of fir and spruce trees provides some shade, but most small campsites are sunny midday. Low brush and trees create partial privacy. The narrow campground road and parking pads can pose challenges for RV drivers unskilled in squeezing into tight spots; RVs are limited to 30 ft (9 m). Loop 3 is generator-free. Due to its popularity, this campground fills sometimes by late morning.

LODGING

In general, inside-park lodging is rustic with minimal amenities. Televisions, air-conditioning, mini-fridges, microwaves, and wireless Internet are often not available. All the in-park lodges are seasonal, open late spring into fall.

Reservations

Lodging inside the south end of Grand Teton National Park is limited to a few cabin complexes, ranches, and campgrounds. These fill fast, especially in midsummer. **Advance reservations are a must.**

Grand Teton Lodging Company (tel. 307/543-3100; www.gtlc.com) operates three lodging complexes at **Flagg Ranch, Colter Bay Village,** and **Jackson Lake Lodge.** Make reservations starting 366 days in advance, especially for Jackson Lake Lodge. For guests, complimentary shuttles run between Jackson Lake Lodge, Colter Bay Village, South Jenny Lake, and the town of Jackson.

Tips

Reservations go fast, so the earlier you can plan the better. View rooms at Jackson Lake Lodge and on the lakefront at Signal Mountain Lodge

GRAND TETON NATIONAL PARK LODGING

NAME	LOCATION	SEASON
★ Jenny Lake Lodge	Jenny Lake	June-early Oct.
AAC Climber's Ranch	Jenny Lake	early June-mid-Sept.
Dornan's Spur Ranch Cabins	Moose	May-Oct., Dec.-Mar.
Headwaters Lodge & Cabins	Flagg Ranch	June-late Sept.
Colter Bay Cabins	Colter Bay	late May-late Sept.
Colter Bay Tent Village	Colter Bay	late May-early Sept.
★ Jackson Lake Lodge	Jackson Lake	mid-May-early Oct.
★ Signal Mountain Lodge	Signal Mountain	mid-May-mid-Oct.

get snapped up when reservations open. Last-minute reservations can be available, but you may not have much choice for room styles or dates.

STANDOUTS

Jenny Lake Lodge

400 Jenny Lake Loop; tel. 307/543-3100; www.gtlc.com; June-early Oct.; $555-1,230

Secluded in the woods at North Jenny Lake, Jenny Lake Lodge offers a slice of old-style rustic luxury and is the highest-priced lodging inside Grand Teton National Park. The 37 log cabins, built in 1920, have been revamped to an upscale historical feel with modern amenities (Wi-Fi, refrigerator) but still have old-fashioned rockers on porches for soaking up views. Visitors often mistakenly assume the lodge sits right on the lake; it does not. But from many of the cabin decks or windows, the tops of the Tetons poke up above the tall pines. The complex includes a dining room that specializes in gourmet and multi-course meals. Hiking trails depart from the lodge, and South Jenny Lake offers scenic cruises, kayak and canoe rentals, a visitors center, stores, and the Multi-Use Pathway for bicycling. The lodge has cruiser-style bicycles and horseback riding for guests. Breakfast, lunch, and activities are included in the Signature Stay Package.

Lodging is in **three types of log cabins:** freestanding cabins, duplex cabins that share a common porch, and cabin suites. All the cabins have western furnishings, private bathrooms, wireless Internet, handmade quilts, and down comforters. Freestanding cabins have a king or two

OPTIONS	PRICE
cabins	cabins starting at $555
shared dorm-style bunk rooms (no bedding or other linens provided)	bunks $22 for members, $33 for nonmembers
cabins	cabins starting at $125
motel rooms, camper cabins (no electricity, bedding, or other linens)	rooms starting at $245; camper cabins $78
motel rooms, cabins	**rooms starting at $200**
tent cabins (bedding provided for a fee)	tent cabins $80
hotel rooms, motel rooms in cottages, suites	rooms and cottages starting at $346
hotel and motel rooms, cabins	rooms starting $230

queens. Duplex cabins have a queen and a twin bed. Suites have one bedroom with a king or two queens and a sitting room with a sofa bed and wood-burning stove. One suite has a jetted tub.

Jackson Lake Lodge

101 Jackson Lake Lodge Rd.; mid-May-early Oct.; $346-476 rooms and cottages, $771-871 suites

The crown of Grand Teton National Park lodging, Jackson Lake Lodge is

view from the patio of Jackson Lake Lodge

STAYING AT A GUEST RANCH

entrance to historic Triangle X Ranch

Several guest ranches line **US-26/89/191** between Moose and Moran Junction. Some are inholdings—private properties inside the national park. From these ranches, the views of the Teton Mountains provide an exquisite backdrop for horseback riding, which is one of the main reasons to stay at a ranch. Rates are all-inclusive with lodging, meals, and horseback riding. Bring long pants and sturdy shoes for riding. The ranches are also home to elk, pronghorn, bison, bears, and wolves.

Triangle X Ranch

2 Triangle X Ranch Rd.; tel. 307/733-2183; http://trianglex.com; mid-May-mid-Oct. and late Dec.-mid-Mar.

The Triangle X Ranch is a dude ranch operated for five generations by the Turner family. Lodging is in one-, two-, or three-bedroom log cabins with private bathrooms. Early June-late August is peak season for the ranch, when seven-night stays, Sunday to Sunday, are the program ($1,996-2,850 pp weekly). Outside of peak season, four-night stays are available (mid-May-early June and Sept.-Oct., $285-319 pp per day). Winter season ($150 pp per night) has cross-country skiing and snowshoeing (no horseback riding).

Moose Head Ranch

21255 N. US-89; tel. 307/733-3141; www.mooseheadranch.com; early June-mid-Aug.; $450-800 pp per night

Moose Head Ranch is a 1925 family-run homestead and dude ranch on an inholding. Log cabins for guests surround the main lodge, where gourmet breakfasts and lunches are served buffet-style and dinner dresses up fish and game entrées. Sunday nights have cookouts. The ranch has fly-fishing and swimming ponds.

porch of Jenny Lake Lodge

a National Historic Landmark built in 1955 with a dining room, lounge, lobby, and patio commanding a panoramic view of the Tetons. The modern international architecture features 60-ft-tall (20-m-tall) lobby windows to soak up the view. Many visitors assume the lodge sits on the shore of Jackson Lake, but it sits about 1.5 mi (2.4 km) from the water, and the closest access to lake activities is Colter Bay Marina. The lodge overlooks Willow Flats, which allows for unobstructed views of the mountains and sometimes moose- and elk-watching. The property includes several restaurants, a lounge, gift shops, Native American artifacts, and horse corrals. Behind the lodge parking lot as an afterthought to the property, the 25-yard, heated outdoor swimming pool (late May-Aug.) has a snack cabana and kiddie pool. Concierges aid in setting up fly-fishing, river floats, park tour trips, and horseback rides. Hiking trails are right out the door.

Jackson Lake Lodge has 385 rooms spread throughout the property; all have private baths and Wi-Fi. Rooms come with or without views of the Teton Mountains and Jackson Lake; non-view rooms look out on conifers or buildings. Rooms are in three locations: the main lodge, separate two-story lodges, or cottages. On the third floor of the main lodge, rooms have two queens. Those facing the Tetons do not have balconies. Separate from the main lodge, three two-story buildings have rooms facing the Tetons with patios or balconies. In the forest, cottages are actually motel rooms in single-story buildings. Rooms have a king, two queens, or two doubles. Mountain View Suite cottages add on an indoor sitting area to soak up the scenery. Some rooms have mini-fridges, and some require a two- or three-night minimum.

Signal Mountain Lodge

1 Inner Park Rd.; tel. 307/543-2831; www.signalmountainlodge.com; mid-May-mid-Oct.; $230-440

Signal Mountain Lodge has million-dollar views of Jackson Lake, Mt. Moran, and the Teton Mountains. Because it overlooks the lake, the lodge is so popular that it **takes reservations 16 months out.** The complex has two restaurants, a bar, marina, motorboat rentals, canoe and kayak rentals, laundry and showers, gift shops, campground, camp store, and wireless Internet. Guided fishing trips and white-water rafting are available. From the lodge, you can drive, mountain bike, or hike to the top of Signal Mountain.

The lodge has a variety of different room options with or without views. Rooms have various combinations of king, queens, doubles, twins, and sofa beds. Some of the units have extra amenities, such as gas fireplaces, jetted tubs, microwaves, mini-fridges, and sitting areas. Older rustic log cabins can sleep 2-6 people. Motel-style rooms can sleep 2-4 people. Premier Western Rooms have wood furnishings, granite and slate bathrooms, and air-conditioning. Lakefront units have kitchenettes, balconies or shared patios, and views of Jackson Lake and the Tetons. If you want to stay overlooking the water, these lakefront units are the only option in the park—hence their appeal.

INFORMATION AND SERVICES

Services in Grand Teton National Park can be found at Moose, Jenny Lake, Jackson Lake Lodge, and Colter Bay. Near the Moose Entrance, **Moose** is where the Craig Thomas Discovery & Visitor Center is located; a post office, general store, gas, and other services are nearby. On the south end of **Jenny Lake,** there's a visitor center, interpretive plazas, campground, and a boat dock for tours, shuttles, and paddling rentals. **Jackson Lake Lodge** has visitor services, gas, horseback riding, and trailheads. **Colter Bay Village** at Jackson Lake is one of those do-everything places with a visitors center, gas, cabins, RV park, campground, and boat rentals. **Flagg Ranch** has a lodge, campground, store, gas, information center, and visitor services.

Entrance Stations

Moose Entrance

year-round; $35 vehicle, $30 motorcycles, $20 hike-in/bike-in/ski-in

The Moose Entrance Station sits on Teton Park Road on the west side of the Snake River.

Granite Canyon Entrance

year-round; $35 vehicle, $30 motorcycles, $20 hike-in/bike-in/ski-in

The Granite Canyon Entrance Station (no RVs or trailers) sits just north of Teton Village on the Moose-Wilson Road. In winter, the road is only open for cars for about a half mi (0.8 km) for ski and snowshoe trailhead access.

Moran Entrance

year-round; $35 vehicle, $30 motorcycles, $20 hike-in/bike-in/ski-in

Moran Entrance, just west of Moran Junction, is open year-round and provides access to North Grand Teton along with the connecting US-26/89/191/287. The Moran Entrance is 29 mi (47 km) southeast of Yellowstone's South Entrance and 30 mi (48 km) north of Jackson, Wyoming. If you are arriving from Yellowstone National Park, John D. Rockefeller, Jr. Memorial Parkway and Grand Teton National Park have no entrance stations—but you will go through another entrance station to get back into certain sections of the park if you go out the Moran station or the Moose station.

Visitors Centers

Craig Thomas Discovery & Visitor Center

tel. 307/739-3399; www.nps.gov/grte; 8am-7pm daily Apr.-Oct., shorter hours spring and fall

The Craig Thomas Discovery & Visitor Center, called the Moose Visitor Center by locals, has large windows that take advantage of the Teton Mountains. Constructed with a combination of public and private funding, the $22 million building has exhibits on the natural history of the park and mountaineering, large bronze wildlife sculptures, a 30-ft (98-m) climbing wall, in-floor videos, kids' exhibits, and a topographic map with laser technology that shows wildlife migration and glacier progression. The theater also shows a documentary on the park, and Native American crafts are displayed on select days. The information desk has maps, schedules of ranger programs and hikes, current weather data from park monitors, and permits for backcountry camping and boating. A large **Grand Teton Association bookstore** (tel. 307/739-3606; www.grandtetonassociation.org) sells field guides and books on wildlife, human history, and geology.

Jenny Lake Visitor Center

tel. 307/739-3392; www.nps.gov/grte; 8am-7pm daily mid-May-late Sept., shorter hours spring and fall

The small Jenny Lake Visitor Center is at South Jenny Lake. Stop to pick up activity schedules, ranger program information, and maps. The center has a relief map of the park and a few geology exhibits. A small bookstore run by **Grand Teton**

Association (tel. 307/739-3606; www.grandtetonassociation.org) sells field guides and books on natural history, human history, and geology. Also located in the complex is the **Jenny Lake Ranger Station** (tel. 307/739-3343; 8am-5pm daily early June-early Sept.), which contains climbing displays. Go to the ranger station for backcountry camping and boating permits, along with information on mountain climbing routes and conditions.

Colter Bay Visitor Center

tel. 307/739-3399; 8am-7pm daily mid-May-early Oct., 8am-5pm daily spring and fall

Located in Colter Bay Village at the marina, the Colter Bay Visitor Center has maps and information on hiking, boating, weather, backcountry permits, and activities. An auditorium shows documentaries on Grand Teton National Park during the day. In summer, you can participate in interpretive programs, see craft demonstrations, and go on tours of the tiny **Indian Arts Museum,** which features intricate beadwork, clothing, jewelry, tools, and weapons among 46 other restored pieces of the 1,416-piece David T. Vernon collection. A **Grand Teton Association store** (tel. 307/739-3606; www.grandtetonassociation.org) carries books on wildlife, wildflowers, hiking, history, geology, and natural history.

TRANSPORTATION

Getting There and Around

From Yellowstone National Park

US-89/191/287 is open year-round between Yellowstone National Park and Grand Teton National Park. Between the two parks, the road crosses John D. Rockefeller, Jr. Memorial Parkway (8-mi/13-km, 15 min.). From the signed north entrance to Grand Teton, which has no entrance station, the highway runs 16 mi (26 km) and 35 minutes past Colter Bay Village and Jackson Lake Lodge to Jackson Lake Junction, the north turnoff for Teton Park Road.

From Jackson, Wyoming

Open year-round, US 26/89/191 runs 13 mi (21 km), about 25 minutes, north to Moose Junction. Turn left to go to the Moose Entrance Station, visitors center, Teton Park Road, and the Moose-Wilson Road.

From Teton Village, Wyoming

Use the Granite Canyon Entrance to drive the narrow, slow Moose-Wilson Road (7 mi/11 km, 30 min., open mid-May-Oct.) to connect with Teton Park Road and Moose.

Teton Park Road

With spectacular views, Teton Park Road (also known as the Inside Road) hugs the base of the Teton Mountains for 20 mi (32 km) between Moose Junction and

Jackson Lake Junction, passing the Jenny Lake and Signal Mountain visitor services areas en route. It is fully open for vehicles May-October but closes between Signal Mountain Lodge and Taggart Lake Trailhead November-April.

Road Conditions

Two-lane paved roads are the norm in Grand Teton National Park. Speed limits range 25-55 mph (40-89 kph) in the park, but the highway speed limits drop to 45 mph (72 kph) after dark to protect bison, bears, wolves, and other wildlife. Secondary roads, such as Antelope Flats Road and Mormon Row, are dirt. Due to limited snow-free seasons, construction happens in summer; you may encounter waits of 15-30 minutes in these zones (specific construction sites are listed online).

In winter, US-26/89/191 and US 89/191/287 are plowed. But snowstorms can cause whiteouts, and roads can be icy. Check conditions for park roads (tel. 307/739-3682).

Parking

During July and August, parking lots at trailheads pack out. Spaces fill up early at the **Jenny Lake** parking lots at South Jenny Lake, String Lake Trailhead, and Lupine Meadows Trailhead. Arrive early (before 9am) to claim a spot.

The Laurance S. Rockefeller Preserve Center limits parking to 50 cars. Plan to be there before 9am.

Shuttles

Shuttles in Grand Teton are minimal, but for guests of Grand Teton Lodging Company (www.gtlc.com), complimentary shuttles run between Jackson Lake Lodge, Colter Bay Village, South Jenny Lake, and the town of Jackson.

Jenny Lake Boat Shuttle for Hikers

Jenny Lake Boating (tel. 307/734-9227; www.jennylakeboating.com; 7am-7pm daily early June-early Sept., 10am-4pm daily mid-May-early June and mid-late Sept.; round-trip $18 adults, $15 seniors, $10 kids, one way $10 adults, $8 kids) runs shuttles across Jenny Lake from the east boat dock near the visitors center to the west boat dock at the base of Mt. Teewinot. Shuttles run every 10-15 minutes throughout the day. The last boat leaves the dock at the posted closing time. Reservations are not required. The shuttle chops off mileage for many hiking destinations: Hidden Falls, Inspiration Point, Cascade Canyon, and Lake Solitude.

Gas

In summer, gas stations operate at Flagg Ranch, Colter Bay Village, Jackson Lake Lodge, Signal Mountain Lodge, Moran, and Moose. At Moran and Moose, gas is available year-round.

Castle Geyser

GEOLOGIC WONDERS

WHY DOES YELLOWSTONE NATIONAL PARK ATTRACT MORE than 4 million visitors a year? It is one of the few places on earth where people can watch volcanic outbursts. Instead of eyeing only explosive aftermath, visitors can gape at the action with erupting geysers, bubbling mud pots, fuming vents, and steaming hot pools. All the action is due to Yellowstone's hot spot, a place where the molten magma rises near to the earth's surface. Here are a few of the geologic features on view in Yellowstone, and where to see them.

Clepsydra Geyser (top); Great Fountain Geyser (middle); Riverside Geyser (bottom)

GEYSERS

Perhaps Yellowstone's most famous features, geysers blow super-hot water into the air. These eruptions are all about clogged plumbing. Similar to hot springs, geysers have underground pipes that let boiling water bubble up to the surface. But contrary to free-flowing hot springs, geyser pipes constrict, producing a backup of water and bubbles. When the pressure becomes too great, the explosion occurs.

More than half the earth's active geysers are in Yellowstone. Some erupt nonstop, while others blow on schedule, intermittently, or after long hiatuses of years. Yellowstone's active geysers produce two eruption patterns: **Cone geysers** shoot water into the air in a narrow stream, and **fountain geysers** spray water in multiple directions, usually from a pool.

Old Faithful Visitor Education Center and the **NPS Yellowstone National Park app** predict eruptions for Old Faithful and other geysers. You can also find predictions and past eruptions for many geysers in the park through **Geyser Times** (https://geysertimes.org).

Where To See Them

CONE GEYSERS

- Old Faithful Geyser (page 95)
- Riverside Geyser (page 98)
- Clepsydra Geyser (page 93)
- Steamboat Geyser (page 102)

FOUNTAIN GEYSERS

- Grand Geyser (page 98)
- Great Fountain Geyser (page 94)

Old Faithful is less crowded in winter.

Firehole Lake (top left); Sapphire Pool in Biscuit Basin (top right); Mud Volcano (bottom left); Abyss Pool at West Thumb Geyser Basin (bottom right)

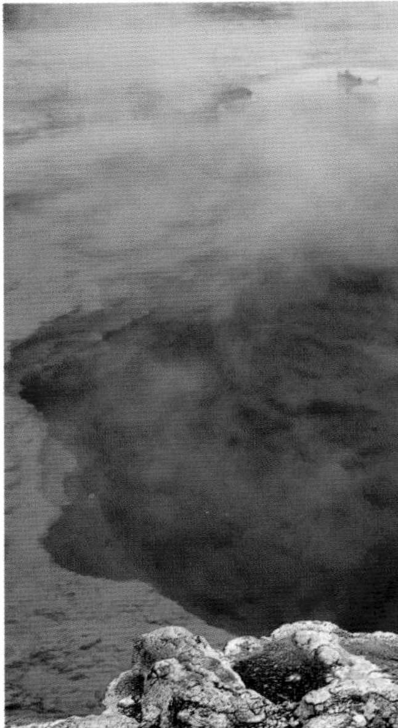

HOT SPRINGS

Hot springs are created from underground channels just like geysers. But their larger channels don't clog up with steam bubbles, and cooler water is exchanged back down. Those factors prevent eruptions. At 199°F (93°C), most hot springs don't exceed the boiling point.

Yellowstone's hot springs exhibit **vibrant colors** from two sources: Blues (the hottest on the color spectrum) come from the refraction of sunlight on the water, and other colors often fringing the pools are from **thermophiles,** or heat-loving life forms.

Where To See Them

- Firehole Lake (page 94)
- Grand Prismatic Spring (page 95)
- Morning Glory Pool (page 98)
- Sapphire Pool (page 100)
- Abyss Pool (page 140)

MUD POTS

Mud pots form in depressions when hot water saturates clay-like sediments. Below the mud pot, as steam pushes upward into the saturated sediments, gaseous bubbles surface to pop and gurgle. Mud pots often have hydrogen sulfide gases that produce a rotten egg smell. **Minerals** tint mud pots different colors, like the pink and gray of Fountain Paint Pot.

Where To See Them

- Mud Volcano (page 139)
- Fountain Paint Pot (page 93)
- Artists Paintpots (page 101)

Morning Glory Pool in the Upper Geyser Basin

Castle Geyser (top); Fountain Paint Pot (middle); Roaring Mountain (bottom)

FUMAROLES

Fumaroles are holes or vents in the ground, but instead of filling with hot water, they convert the small amount of water into super-hot steam. At Norris Hot Springs, Black Growler has reached 300°F (149°C). Often the steam creates noise, such as roars, hisses, or whistles, as it rushes through the vent.

Where To See Them

- Roaring Mountain (page 62)
- Black Growler (page 103)

VOLCANIC SCULPTURES

Hydrothermal activity creates fantastical sculptures. But some sculptures come from different components.

Sinter Cones

Within the caldera, the landscape is built on rhyolite, formed from thick, liquid flows of the Lava Creek eruption 640,000 years ago. Beige-colored minerals and silica solidified in the rhyolite. Many of the fountains and cones in the geyser basins are created from water gushing up through the rhyolite and bringing silica with it to cling as building-block crystals on the sculptures.

WHERE TO SEE THEM

- Castle Geyser (page 98)
- Grotto Geyser (page 98)
- Giant Geyser (page 98)
- Lone Star Geyser (page 112)
- White Dome Geyser (page 94)
- Liberty Cap (page 60)

Black Growler at Norris Geyser Basin

Travertine Terraces

The terraces at Mammoth Hot Springs are unique. They are made from calcium carbonate that comes from limestone underground. As the water comes to the surface, it brings calcium carbonate with it to spill out over the terraces. That's what creates the smooth-sculpted features that look more like frozen water.

WHERE TO SEE THEM

- Palette Spring (page 60)
- Canary Spring (page 60)

PETRIFIED TREES

A series of volcanic eruptions 40-50 million years ago petrified trees in Yellowstone. They were ancient redwoods, some up to 4 ft (1 m) in diameter and 40 ft (12 m) tall. They were swept along in lahars, flows of volcanic debris. Silica in the debris soaked into the living trees, petrifying them into rock. While redwoods no longer populate the park, their presence in petrified form indicates that Yellowstone once had a wetter, more tropical climate.

Where To See Them

- Petrified Tree (page 62)

BOBBY SOCKS TREES

Lodgepole pines that populate the Yellowstone caldera today grow well in the sand-like sediments. But shifting thermal areas affect forests, killing the trees. Dead tree trunks stand erect in pools of hot water. Because many of the dead lodgepoles turn white around the base of their trunk after soaking up silica in the water, they have garnered the name "bobby socks trees."

Where To See Them

- Opalescent Pool (page 101)

bobby socks trees (top); Lone Star Geyser (bottom left); Canary Spring in winter (bottom right)

Grotto and Rocket Geysers in Upper Geyser Basin

SAFETY AROUND HYDROTHERMALS

Geyser basins can be dangerous places. It's up to you to keep yourself safe while experiencing the wonders of Yellowstone.

Can I soak in the hot springs at Yellowstone?
No. Water seething from the ground is scalding hot, often near boiling. Some water is acidic, which adds a further hazard. In addition, some thermally heated waters contain micro-organisms that can lead to fatal diseases.

Why do we have to stay on boardwalks?
The ground in geyser basins frequently changes as water channels move locations underground and shift hot spots. Even though boardwalks must be moved from time to time to accommodate the changing hot spots, boardwalks are the safest route through a geyser basin. Just keep an eye on the edges to avoid falling off. Boardwalks also keep you off the surface crusts which are thin and fragile. Many of those crusts, which can break with the weight of a human, hide scalding water below.

Do I need to worry about the air in hydrothermal areas?
Some geyser basins emit toxic gases, and some people may experience more of a reaction to them. Leave a geyser basin immediately if you feel sick.

Red Spouter at Fountain Paint Pot

grizzly bear cub

WILDLIFE-WATCHING

THE GREATER YELLOWSTONE ECOSYSTEM, WHICH INCLUDES Yellowstone and Grand Teton National Parks and surrounding areas, houses one of the greatest concentrations of mammals in the Lower 48 states of the United States. Bring binoculars so you can maintain a safe distance while observing wildlife.

BISON

Bison have rebounded from the small herd of 23 that remained in Yellowstone in the late 1800s. Today, the parks have some of the largest bison herds in the world: The Yellowstone herds numbered around 4,500-5,500. Of all the potential wildlife to see, you are most likely to spot bison, and perhaps get caught in a bison jam as the large bovines walk onto roadways.

bison in Antelope Flats (top); bison calf (bottom)

Although these 1,000-2,000-pound (450-900-kg) animals seem docile, they can run up to 40 mph (64 kph)—more than three times faster than humans—and jump 6-ft (2-m) fences. Identify females by narrower heads and thinner curved horns that are often asymmetrical. Bison cluster in smaller herds in winter, with about 20 members as opposed to 200 or more in summer. Because the bison feed mostly on grasses, geyser basins provide a refuge, as heat from geothermal activity keeps the snow thin or melted with patches of dry grasses. Bison also migrate in winter to lower elevations outside the park, where food is more readily attainable. Herds winter in the Lamar, Hayden, and Firehole River Valleys. How can these weighty ungulates walk through deep snow? Herds walk in winter on groomed roads to avoid sinking in deep snow, and when they do travel in deep snow, they walk single file, allowing the bison in front to break trail.

You can see bison in the park year-round. Seasonal herd migrations occur **April-June** and **October-November,** when bison use the roads to travel between summer and winter habitats. **May** offers a chance to see newborn calves, nicknamed "red dogs" for their rust-colored fur. Keep your distance from bison: **Stay at least 25 yards away.** All too frequently people suffer injuries from getting too close.

Where to See Them

- Lamar Valley (page 63)
- Hayden Valley (page 139)
- Antelope Flats (page 193)

GRIZZLY BEARS

In the 1800s, more than 100,000 grizzly bears roamed grasslands and foothills in the Lower 48, but loss of habitat and predator extermination programs whittled their numbers down to a handful of small populations in the Northern Rockies. In the 1970s, the isolated region's 136 grizzlies were listed as threatened on the Endangered Species List. With a recovery plan in place, biologists managed the rebound of grizzlies and today, more than 700 grizzlies populate the Greater Yellowstone Ecosystem.

Grizzlies stand 3-4 ft (1 m) tall on all fours and weigh in at 300-600 pounds (140-270 kg). Despite their weight, they are fast runners: In 3 seconds, a grizzly can cover 180 ft (55 m). In profile, the grizzly has one notable feature: a hump on its shoulders. The solid muscle mass provides the grizzly's forelegs with power for digging and running. In comparison to black bears, which are also present in the parks, grizzly ears look too small for their heads. You can recognize grizzly paw prints by looking out for 4-inch-long (10-cm-long) claws with pads in a relatively straight line.

Omnivores and opportunistic feeders, these bears will eat anything, but contrary to popular opinion, humans are not on their menu of favorite foods. In Yellowstone, seasonal trail and backcountry campsite closures protect feeding zones, particularly where sows take cubs in spring. Sometimes, the Moose-Wilson Road in Grand Teton closes for bears feeding on berries.

Safety

With a few precautions, you can eliminate bear scares. At all times, stay 100 yards (the length of a football field) away from bears.

- **Make noise.** To avoid surprising a bear, use your voice—sing loudly, hoot, or holler—and clap your hands. Bears tend to recognize human sounds as ones to avoid; they'll usually

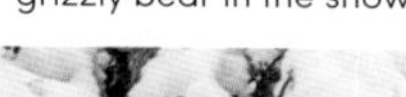

grizzly bear in the snow

bison herd in Lamar Valley

grizzly bear on Moose-Wilson Road (top left); gray wolf (top right); sandhill crane flying over Lamar Valley (bottom left); bull moose fight (bottom right)

wander off if they hear people approaching. Make loud noise in thick brushy areas, around blind corners, near babbling streams, and against the wind.

- **Hike with other people and in broad daylight.** Avoid hiking alone and in the early morning, late evening, or at night. Keep children near. Very few bear attacks happen to groups of four or more.
- **Respect trail closures.** Trail and backcountry campsite closures are usually in heavy bear feeding areas. Staying out of these areas guarantees hikers a safer experience.
- **Avoid bear feeding areas.** If you stumble across an animal carcass, leave the area immediately and notify a ranger. Toward summer's end, be cautious around huckleberry patches.
- **Never approach a bear.** Head swaying, teeth clacking, laid-back ears, a lowered head, and huffing or woofing are signs of agitation: Clear out slowly.
- **If you do surprise a bear, back away.** Contrary to all inclinations, do not run. Instead, back away slowly, talking quietly and turning sideways or bending your knees to appear smaller and nonthreatening. Avoid direct eye contact. Leave your pack on; it can protect you if the bear attacks.
- **Use pepper spray or play dead.** If you surprise a bear that attacks in defense, aim pepper spray at the bear's eyes. Protect yourself and your vulnerable parts by assuming a fetal

The elk rut takes place in late September.

position on the ground with your hands around the back of your neck. Play dead. Move again only when you are sure the bear has vacated the area.

- **If a bear stalks you as food, or attacks at night, fight back.** Bears rarely stalk humans as prey. If one does, use any means at hand, such as pepper spray, shouting, sticks, or rocks, to tell the bear you are not an easy food source. Try to escape up something, like a building or a tree.

Where to See Them (From a Distance)

- Dunraven Pass (page 143)
- Lamar Valley (page 63)
- Absaroka Mountains (page 65)
- Moose-Wilson Road (page 193)

WOLVES

Gray wolves were placed on the Endangered Species List in the 1970s, but they have seen a recovery in population. Today, about 500 wolves populate the Greater Yellowstone Ecosystem with 10 packs that use Yellowstone National Park.

Wolf rules are strict. Packs of 5-10 animals form hierarchies led by the alpha male and female, the only breeders. Packs inhabit fairly large ranges of 100-300 square miles. After the alpha female gives birth to the pups, the other adults in the pack aid in caring for the young. Ninety percent of wolves' winter diet consists of elk—each wolf eats about 22 elk per year. Because of their dependence on elk, they often follow the herds.

Wolves are active year-round, with mating usually occurring in February. Wolf pups, born in **April,** weigh 1 pound (0.5 kg) and are blind. Maintain a distance of 100 yards (the length of a football field) away from wolves.

Where to See Them

- Lamar Valley (page 63)
- Swan Lake Flat (page 61)
- Hayden Valley (page 139)

ELK

What's all the bugling about? The park's most numerous large mammal puts on a stately show—during fall when elk breed, bulls bugle to attract cows into their harems. A bugle starts with a bellow that rises into a squeal and finishes with grunts. The bugle also shows the bull's prowess to other bulls, a statement that he's ready to fight for the harem and a warning for other bulls to steer clear. Elk also produce the largest antlers of the ungulates. Elk calving happens in **late spring** (Apr.-May), and their spring and fall migrations are some of the biggest migrations in North America. Maintain a distance of 25 yards away from elk.

Where to See Them

- Madison River (page 93)
- Mammoth Hot Springs Terraces (page 59)
- Antelope Flats (page 193)
- Willow Flats Overlook (page 191)

MOOSE

Moose are huge. A bull moose can weigh up to 1,000 pounds (450 kg); their shoulders are often taller than a human, and their antlers span 5 ft (1.5 m) from tip to tip. Usually seen alone, moose often hang around wetlands: ponds, marshes, streams, and lakes. With a diet that is 60 percent water and 40 percent plants, moose feed mostly on willows and aquatic greenery, eating up to 50 pounds of food per day in the summer but only 12 pounds per day in winter. Gangly moose calves are born in late May–June. During the fall rut, both bulls and cows make noises in search of mates, but only bulls will fight each other with their antlers for dominance. Bulls shed their antlers in winter and grow new ones starting each spring. You can recognize cows by their lack of antlers. Maintain a distance of 25 yards away from moose.

Where to See Them

- Pelican Creek (page 137)
- Soda Butte Creek (page 65)
- Moose-Wilson Road (page 193)
- Oxbow Bend (page 191)

BIGHORN SHEEP

Of all the ungulates, native bighorn sheep face the greatest risk. Once widely scattered across most western mountain ranges, the sheep today live in isolated pockets. The

elk cow grooming her calf (top); bull moose (middle); herd of bighorn sheep (bottom)

Tetons now contain less than 50, half as many as a decade ago. In the Greater Yellowstone Ecosystem, bighorns pick up disease from domestic sheep, which can decimate wild herds. A disease outbreak in 2009-2010 reduced populations by 50 percent. Fragmented habitat threatens the sheep's future.

Bighorn sheep opt to winter in lower elevations of the northern valleys of the Gardner, Lamar, and Yellowstone Rivers. November-April, they feed on dry grasses exposed in the thin snowpack of windblown slopes. In mating season, **November-December,** bighorn rams butt horns in fights of dominance, often injuring each other with scars or horn damage. **June** is the month to spot ewes with newborn lambs. Maintain a distance of 25 yards away from bighorn sheep.

Where to See Them

- Absaroka Mountains (page 65)
- Lamar Valley (page 63)
- North Entrance Road (page 64)

PRONGHORN ANTELOPE

As the second-fastest animal in the world, pronghorn can run 50 mph (80 kph) for 5-6 miles. These ungulates have reddish to tawny backs, white underbellies, and a patterned face topped by horns on both bucks and does, although only the bucks have a small prong on their horns. More than 500 pronghorns populate Yellowstone, and 300-400 pronghorns live in the valley in Grand Teton. **Spring** brings the chance to see pronghorn fawns, and the annual **spring** and **fall** pronghorn migrations in the Greater Yellowstone Ecosystem are among the world's remaining long-distance migrations. Look for these agile runners in grasslands where they find abundant food. Maintain a distance of 25 yards away from pronghorns.

Where to See Them

- Lamar Valley (page 63)
- Northeast Entrance Road (page 64)
- Antelope Flats (page 193)

PIKAS

In subalpine country, choruses of eeks, screams, and squeaks bounce through rockfalls. The noisemakers

pronghorn antelope (top); pika in talus slopes (bottom left); harlequin duck at LeHardy Rapids (bottom right)

are pikas, which look like tail-less guinea pigs and live around talus boulders surrounded by meadows. In summer, they collect greenery into hay piles under rocks to dry. Since they do not hibernate, they feed on the hay piles in winter and can even feed on their own scat to survive. These members of the rabbit family are threatened by warming climates; their short round ears do not dissipate heat well.

Where to See Them

- Terrace Mountain Hoodoos (page 65)
- Holly Lake (page 204)

BIRDS

The Greater Yellowstone Ecosystem has almost 300 species of birds: songbirds, waterfowl, shorebirds, and raptors. About 150 species nest in Yellowstone National Park.

bald eagle

Songbirds show up in spring, and the trees liven with their songs during breeding and nesting season. By August, the forests quiet as many begin migrating south. Mountain chickadees, gray jays, red-breasted nuthatches, and American dippers are year-round residents.

Waterfowl and Shorebirds

Waterfowl and shorebirds are common due to the region's big lakes, wetlands, and rivers. Visitors can see American pelicans, sandhill cranes, great blue herons, and a variety of ducks and geese. The trumpeter swan is among the rarest. The swan is North America's largest bird, with a wingspan of 8 feet (2 m).

WHERE TO SEE THEM

- Lamar Valley: Sandhill cranes (page 63)
- LeHardy Rapids: Harlequin ducks (page 142)
- Hayden Valley: Trumpeter swans (page 139)

Raptors

Nineteen species of raptors nest in the Greater Yellowstone Ecosystem. These include golden eagles, bald eagles, ospreys, peregrine falcons, and owls. The park service monitors nests, keeping tabs on 21 bald eagle nests in Yellowstone. Recoveries of bald eagles and peregrine falcons have removed them from the Endangered Species List.

WHERE TO SEE THEM

- Heron Pond and Swan Lake: Osprey (page 202)
- Oxbow Bend: Bald eagles (page 191)

SAFETY AROUND WILDLIFE

While there are no guarantees of spotting wildlife, huge broad meadows in the parks make it easy to see animals. You may spy bison, elk, moose, deer, pronghorn, wolves, raptors, mountain lions, or bears. Remember that wildlife is just that—*wild*. Though bison, elk, or even bears may appear tame, they are not. Gorings are too common. Here are a few hints to remain safe.

- **Do not approach wildlife.** Although our inclinations tell us to scoot in for a closer look, crowding wildlife puts you at risk and endangers the animal, often scaring it off. Stay at least **100 yards/meters away** (the length of a football field) from bears and wolves. For all other wildlife, stay at least **25 yards/meters away**. Both parks have volunteer wildlife brigades to help visitors along roadways and geyser basins maintain their distance.
- **Do not feed any animal.** Feeding can amp up their aggression. Because human food is not part of their natural diet, they may suffer at foraging on their own. If you see a carcass on a trail, move away and report it to park rangers. No doubt an animal is nearby protecting it.
- **Store food properly.** Follow instructions for food storage. They are designed to protect you and wildlife. Bears, wolves, and coyotes may become more aggressive when acquiring food, and ravens can strew food and garbage, making it more available to other wildlife. Your actions may affect the next camper staying at your campsite.
- **Be aware of behavior.** Let the animal's or bird's behavior guide your behavior. If the animal appears twitchy or nervous, or points eyes and ears directly at you, back off: You're too close. If you behave like a predator stalking an animal, the creature will assume you are one.
- **Pull over if you want to watch wildlife from a road.** If you see wildlife along a road, use pullouts or broad shoulders to drive completely off the road. Do not block the middle of the road. Use the car as a blind to watch wildlife, and keep pets inside. If you see a bear, you're better off just driving by slowly (bear jams tend to condition the bruin to become accustomed to vehicles). Watch for cars, as visitors can be injured by inattentive drivers whenever a bear jam occurs.
- **Make noise.** Make noise when hiking to avoid bears and mountain lions. Hike with others, and keep kids close.
- **Do not run.** If you stumble upon a bear or a mountain lion, above all, do not run. Be calm, and group together to appear bigger. Back away slowly. If attacked, fight back with everything: rocks, sticks, or kicking.

Artist Point at Grand Canyon of the Yellowstone

GETTING THERE

Yellowstone and Grand Teton National Parks are far from metropolitan cities and have little in the way of public transportation infrastructure from the large regional towns of Bozeman and Billings, Montana, and Jackson, Wyoming. You will most likely need a car to see the parks. All driving times given below are for dry roads in summer.

AIR

Yellowstone Airport (West Yellowstone)

WYS; 721 Airport Rd., West Yellowstone, MT; 406/646-7631, www.yellowstoneairport.org
SEASON: early May-mid Oct.
DRIVING TIME TO YELLOWSTONE: 5 minutes to West Entrance

Bozeman Airport (Yellowstone International)

BZN; 850 Gallatin Field Rd., Belgrade, MT; tel. 406/388-8321; www.bozemanairport.com
SEASON: year-round
DRIVING TIME TO YELLOWSTONE: 1.5 hours to North Entrance (open year-round); 2 hours to West Yellowstone Entrance (open mid-Apr.-early Nov.)

Yellowstone Regional Airport (Cody, Wyoming)

COD; 2101 Roger Sedam Dr., Cody, WY; tel. 307/587-5096; http://flyyra.com
SEASON: May-Oct.
DRIVING TIME TO YELLOWSTONE: 75-minute drive to the East Entrance (open late May-Oct.)

Jackson Hole Airport

JAC; 1250 E. Airport Rd., Jackson; tel. 307/733-7682; www. jacksonholeairport.com
SEASON: year-round
DRIVING TIME TO YELLOWSTONE: 90 minutes to South Entrance (open mid-May-early Nov.)
DRIVING TIME TO GRAND TETON: none; the airport is located inside the park on roads open year-round

FAST FACTS

YELLOWSTONE

- **Inaugurated:** 1872
- **Visitation in 2019:** 4,020,287
- **Area:** 3,472 sq mi (8,991 sq km)

GRAND TETON

- **Inaugurated:** 1929 for original park, 1950 when Jackson Hole National Monument was added to park
- **Visitation in 2019:** 3,405,614
- **Area:** 484 sq mi (1,255 sq km)

Billings Logan International Airport

BIL; 1901 Terminal Circle, Billings, MT; tel. 406/247-8609; www. flybillings.com
SEASON: late May-mid-Oct.
DRIVING TIME TO YELLOWSTONE: 3 hours over the ultra-scenic Beartooth Highway to the Northeast Entrance (open late May-mid-Oct.)

Idaho Falls Regional Airport

IDA; 2140 N Skyline Dr, Idaho Falls, ID; 208/612-8221; www.idahofallsidaho.gov/181/Airport
SEASON: year-round
DRIVING TIME TO YELLOWSTONE: 1.75 hours to entrance at West Yellowstone (open mid-Apr.-early Nov.)
DRIVING TIME TO GRAND TETON: 2.25 hours to Moose entrance (open year-round)

Salt Lake City International Airport

SLC; 776 N. Terminal Dr.; tel. 801/575-2400; www.slcairport.com
SEASON: year-round

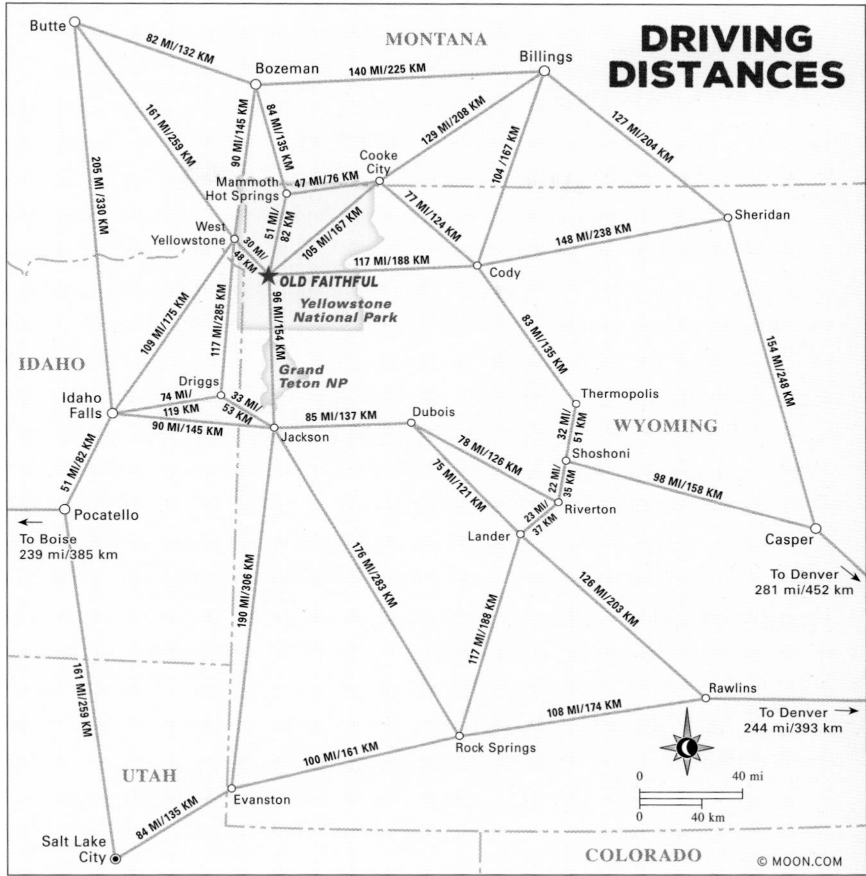

DRIVING TIME TO YELLOWSTONE: about 4.5 hours to West Yellowstone Entrance (open mid-Apr.-early Nov.)

DRIVING TIME TO GRAND TETON: 5 hours to Moose Entrance (open year-round)

CAR

Getting to Yellowstone and Grand Teton requires navigating wild country where gas stations are few and far between; sometimes 75 mi (120 km) apart. Schedule gas fill-ups at major towns. Winter blizzards and icy roads can turn a two-hour drive into a four-hour nightmare. To get current road conditions, including weather and construction zones, call 511 or consult state highway agency websites:

- **Montana:** www.mdt.mt.gov/travinfo
- **Wyoming:** www.wyoroad.info
- **Idaho:** https://lb.511.idaho.gov/idlb

Driving Times

Driving to the Yellowstone region from surrounding metropolitan areas can take 5 hours or more. All times given below are for dry roads in summer.

- **Salt Lake City, Utah:** 5 hours
- **Boise, Idaho:** 6 hours
- **Denver, Colorado:** 8 hours

- **Calgary, Alberta:** 9 hours
- **Seattle, Washington:** 11 hours
- **Minneapolis, Minnesota:** 14.5 hours

BUS

Greyhound (tel. 800/231-2222; www.greyhound.com) stops in Bozeman and Billings in Montana and Cody, Wyoming, but does not travel into Yellowstone. **Karst Stage** (tel. 406/556-3540; karststage.com) operates buses from the Bozeman airport to West Yellowstone or Gardiner, MT, and Mammoth Hot Springs. **Salt Lake Express** (tel. 208/656- 8824; www.saltlakeexpress.com) runs buses between Salt Lake City, Idaho Falls Airport, West Yellowstone, Jackson Hole Airport, and Jackson.

Once you arrive at the parks via bus, you may need to take a tour to see the sights. Neither park has an internal bus system.

PARK ENTRY

For each park, the **entrance fee** is $35 per vehicle ($30 motorcycles; $20 pedestrians, cyclists, skiers) and is good for 7 days. Other fee options include the **Annual Park Pass** ($70) for Yellowstone or Grand Teton, and the **Interagency Annual Pass** ($80), which is good for all national parks and federal fee areas. U.S. fourth graders, those with disabilities, and military personnel can get free interagency passes, and seniors can buy lifetime interagency passes ($80). You can buy your entrance pass in advance online at www.yourpassnow.com.

GETTING AROUND

DRIVING

Yellowstone and Grand Teton National Parks have two-lane roads that are easy to drive. However, several factors escalate concerns.

Wildlife

Wildlife uses the roads: Bison back up traffic as they walk down the yellow line, and traffic jams clog the road when bears feed nearby. Deer, elk, and coyote run out in front of cars, and they are especially difficult to see around dawn or dusk. Watch for wildlife at all times: Both Yellowstone and Grand Teton see more than 100 animal deaths each year due to vehicles. If you encounter wildlife while driving, give them room: Stay 25 yards/meters from most wildlife, and 100 yards/meters from wolves and bears. Stay in your car, especially if animals come near. Drive slowly, and avoid honking at them. Just enjoy the show. You may be able to inch by them if they seem calm. Bison may look docile, but one kick can dent your vehicle.

Junctions

Yellowstone has four-way junctions that clog with cars. With each lane dividing into several lanes at stop signs (no lights control traffic flow), first-time visitors can find the crowded junctions intimidating, especially with lines of RVs and cars covering up the directional markers painted on the lanes. To turn right, get into the right lanes. To go straight or turn left, stay in the middle or left lane. When you reach the front of the line, use the rule of yielding to the right.

Speeds and Driving Times

Due to wildlife, traffic, weather, and maximum speed limits of 35-45 mph (56-72 kph) in Yellowstone and 35-55 mph (56-89 kph) in Grand Teton, national park miles take longer to cover than the same miles at home. Adding to the time, road construction happens every summer. Long winters force road repairs and reconstruction to take place in the same season as high visitation. Look online to see where construction is planned and how it may affect your travel.

Road Closures

Although roads may close temporarily in summer for various reasons, especially construction, the National Park Service aims to keep all roads open May-early November. Some roads can open mid-April. Winter road closure for wheeled vehicles is November to mid-April. Check online for construction closures.

Weather

Due to high elevation, snow can show up every month of the year, even in summer. Sudden snowstorms, whiteouts, or fog can reduce visibility and slicken road surfaces. Adjust your speed accordingly.

TRAVELING BY RV

Traveling Yellowstone and Grand Teton by RV is a fun way to go. Most roads are easy to drive, although they can be narrow, curvy, and shoulder-less.

Campground Limits

Most of the campgrounds inside Yellowstone and Grand Teton do not have hookups, but, a few do. In Yellowstone, Fishing Bridge RV Park has hookups. Headwaters Campground & RV Park on John D. Rockefeller, Jr. Memorial Parkway and Colter Bay RV Park in Grand Teton have hookups. Outside of the parks, you'll find private campgrounds with hookups in Gardiner, West Yellowstone, and near Jackson Hole.

Many park campgrounds have campsites that fit limited RV lengths. Check on these when making reservations. More options are available for RVs 30 ft (9 m) or less rather than larger RVs.

Road Concerns

Unfortunately, RVs are not permitted everywhere. In Yellowstone, RVs, buses, and trailers have limited spots in some parking lots. They also are not allowed on Upper Terrace, Blacktail Plateau, and Firehole Lake Drives. In Grand Teton, the Moose-Wilson Road is closed to RVs, including trailers, due to the narrow, curvy road. Trailers are also not permitted on Signal Mountain Road, but there is a parking lot to drop them at the bottom of the road.

In Yellowstone, Grand Loop Road in one section requires caution for RV drivers: For 19 mi (31 km), the road between Tower Fall and Dunraven Pass is steep, curvy, narrow, and along cliffs.

NEARBY TOWNS

If not staying in one of the parks, the towns of West Yellowstone, Montana, and Jackson, Wyoming, offer the most options for food and lodging nearby.

NEAR NORTH YELLOWSTONE

Gardiner, Montana

Located 5 mi (8 km) north of Mammoth Hot Springs, the town of Gardiner borders the park's North Entrance and makes a good base, with rafting, fly-fishing, restaurants, bars, and shops.

FOOD

Due to limited dining inside the park, many people drive 15 minutes from Mammoth to Gardiner for dinner. Most restaurants shorten their hours or days in winter, so call ahead to confirm when they are open. Summer visitors pay a 3 percent resort tax added to meals.

LODGING

Gardiner bustles in summer with tourists. Most of Gardiner's lodging properties, including several national chain motels, rim the highway through town on the north side of the bridge crossing the Yellowstone River. Find a full listing of Gardiner lodging options online (www.visitgardinermt.com), including vacation home rentals. Rates are highest June-September, then lower in fall, winter, and spring. For summer or winter holiday lodging, make reservations 6-9 months in advance.

INFORMATION

The **Gardiner Chamber of Commerce** (216 Park St.; tel. 406/848-7971; www.visitgardinermt.com; 9am-5pm Mon.-Fri., 1pm-4pm Sat.-Sun.) maintains an information center. It is a good place to get information on Gardiner, the nearby Custer Gallatin National Forest and Absaroka-Beartooth Wilderness, as well as recreation, lodging, and dining. (It is also one of the few places to find public restrooms in Gardiner.)

Silver Gate and Cooke City, Montana

The tiny mountain outposts of Silver Gate and Cooke City flank the park's Northeast Entrance and anchor the Beartooth Highway. Because the towns sit at 7,500 ft (2,300 m) in elevation, the altitude may bother some people, causing labored breathing or fitful sleeping. Basic no-frills motels line the main drag of US-212 in Cooke City, and there are only a few options for food. Be aware that no cell service is available, and Internet is limited.

The **Cooke City Chamber of Commerce** (206 W. Main St.; tel. 406/838-2495; www.cookecitychamber.org; 9am-5pm daily summer, Mon.-Fri. winter) runs a tiny visitors center with current conditions on the Beartooth Highway, Internet connection, local outfitters and guides, and information on the nearby Custer Gallatin and Shoshone National Forests. The chamber website also offers complete lodging listings, including vacation homes.

NEAR OLD FAITHFUL

West Yellowstone, Montana

With the park entrance on its eastern edge, West Yellowstone is the largest tourist town on Yellowstone's boundary. Part of the town retains its mom-and-pop souvenir shops, which crowd in summer with scads of visitors. In winter, it serves as a cross-country ski, snowmobile, and snowcoach tour headquarters for touring the park.

FOOD

For a small town, West Yellowstone packs in nearly 40 restaurants, with mainstays being pizza, burger, and barbecue joints. It is also a tourist town that sees huge crowds in summer, so expect lines at restaurants. About half the restaurants close in winter; those that stay open shorten hours in the off-season, and some take a few weeks off in early spring and early December. Many restaurants sell to-go lunches.

CAMPING

Campers requiring **RV hookups** should head to West Yellowstone where private campgrounds have flush toilets, showers, potable water, wireless Internet, dump stations, and hookups; most also have laundries. Summer is crowded; reservations are a must.

LODGING

West Yellowstone houses a mix of circa 1950 mom-and-pop motels interspersed with three-story modern hotels. More than 50 lodging properties cram into the town and sprawl throughout surrounding ranchland. Due to limited lodging at Old Faithful, many visitors choose to stay in West Yellowstone, as the drive between the two places is only 30 mi (48 km).

Some motels are open year-round, while others are summer season only. Reservations are recommended 6-12 months in advance for summer, when the town packs out. Summer sees the highest prices, with rates $100-200 higher than winter, spring, and fall.

INFORMATION

Inside the **West Yellowstone Visitor Information Center** (30 Yellowstone Ave.; tel. 307/344-7381; www.nps.gov/yell; 8am-8pm daily late May-Sept., 8am-4pm weekdays Oct.-early Nov. and late Apr.-late May, 8am-5pm weekdays early Nov.-late Apr.) is the **West Yellowstone Chamber of Commerce** (tel. 406/646-7701; www.destinationyellowstone.com) and a National Park Service desk. In addition to information, the service desk issues backcountry permits (8am-4:30pm daily June-Aug.). Restrooms are available.

NEAR GRAND TETON

Jackson, Wyoming

The town of Jackson, located at the south end of Jackson Hole valley, anchors the southern portal for exploring Grand Teton and Yellowstone National Parks. From its antler arches in the Jackson Town Square to the iconic Million Dollar Cowboy Bar, the town melds the Old

West with modern places to stay and dine year-round.

FOOD

Jackson is packed with restaurants open year-round; some shorten hours or days in spring, fall, and winter. Expect meal prices to be spendy due to Jackson's resort-town status. Some resort restaurants north of town have gorgeous Teton Mountain views from their dining rooms, but the fun dining is at independent restaurants in town. Make reservations for dinner or you may have a wait.

CAMPING

With the exception of an RV park in the town of Jackson, a few private campgrounds scatter around Jackson Hole. They have sites with full hookups (water, sewer, electric), flush toilets, showers, drinking water, laundries, camp stores, and wireless Internet.

LODGING

Staying in downtown Jackson offers a compact town where you can walk from lodging to restaurants, shopping, activities, and nightlife. To the west of town is a strip with motels that are beyond walking distance for many, but you can hop on the START bus to downtown. Count on more amenities than in the national parks: Air-conditioning, wireless Internet, minifridges, and televisions are common. Prices for familiar chains will be inflated due to the resort nature of the town.

INFORMATION

Located a half mile north of the Jackson Town Square at the southeast corner of the National Elk Refuge, the **Jackson Hole and Greater Yellowstone Visitor Center** (532 N. Cache St.; tel. 307/733-3316; www.jacksonholechamber.com, 8am-7pm daily summer, 9am-5pm daily winter) has interpretive displays on the National Elk Refuge (www.fws.gov) and information for visitors. The interagency center also represents **Grand Teton National Park** (www.nps.gov/grte), **Bridger-Teton National Forest** (www.fs.usda.gov/btnf), and **Jackson Chamber of Commerce** (www.jacksonholechamber.com). Information is available on camping, lodging, wildlife-watching, activities, events, and road conditions for all four agencies. You can pick up maps and permits; the center also rents bear canisters and panniers.

Teton Village, Wyoming

One mile south of the Granite Canyon entrance to Grand Teton National Park, **Jackson Hole Mountain Resort** is a full-service ski and summer resort. Its tram whisks sightseers to the top of the Tetons for spectacular views of Jackson Hole, the Grand Teton, and hiking. Teton Village sprawls around the base of the resort's lifts.

FOOD

Teton Village contains plentiful dining options and bars. Some are located slopeside in hotels; others are independent. You can eat waffles at the top of the tram or dine on gourmet steaks in upscale restaurants.

LODGING

While one hostel attracts budget travelers, the lure of Teton Village for many visitors is the plentiful upscale and luxury lodging. Hotels, lodges, and residences are available, and the nighttime ambiance is quieter than in Jackson.

INFORMATION

Jackson Hole Mountain Resort (www.jacksonhole.com) offers skiing and snowboarding in winter, and hiking, mountain biking, and sightseeing in summer.

FARTHER AFIELD

Big Sky, Montana

Driving time to Yellowstone: about 1 hour to West Entrance (open mid-April-early Nov.)

Located 47 mi (76 km) north of Yellowstone's West Entrance, Big Sky is a huge, bustling, upscale resort centered around a ski area and summer recreation. Lone Peak dominates the view from the golf course to the resort. Summer and winter bring on the crowds, rocketing the population from 2,500 to 10,000. Due to the proximity to Yellowstone, some visitors prefer staying at Big Sky rather than the closer West Yellowstone simply because of the ambience, luxury accommodations, and breathing room. Big Sky draws the rich and famous with lodges, vacation homes, and shopping hubs sprawled across several miles. Big Sky links to Yellowstone via US-191 south with year-round access.

FOOD

Big Sky is an upscale resort community where you can expect dining prices to be higher than elsewhere. In summer and winter, make reservations for dinner or you may have a long wait. Cookouts are another dining option. Reservations are required for cookouts. Most events do not serve alcohol; ask if they permit BYOB. Big Sky also has several markets for groceries, deli foods, meats, fruits, veggies, beer, wine, and baked goods.

LODGING

Big Sky is an upscale resort community with more than 3,000 rooms, condos, townhomes, and vacation homes with modern conveniences such as wireless Internet. It has accommodations across the spectrum, from family hotels to ultra-pricey luxury vacation homes, but lacks chain hotels. Several property management companies rent condos, townhomes, and vacation homes. **Big Sky Resort** (tel. 800/548-4486, https://bigskyresort.com) has slopeside hotels and condos on the flanks of Lone Peak. **Big Sky Luxury Rentals** (tel. 406/668-3956; https://vacationbigsky.com) has luxury vacation homes. **Big Sky Vacation Rentals** (tel. 888/915-2787; www.bookbigsky.com) has vacation homes across price ranges.

INFORMATION

At the junction of US-191 and Lone Mountain Trail, the **Big Sky and Greater Yellowstone Visitor Information Center** (55 Lone Mountain Trail; tel. 406/996-3000; https://visitbigskymt.com; 8:30am-5:30pm daily summer, 8:30am-5:30pm Mon.-Fri. winter) is a place to get oriented before driving up through Big Sky. Operated by the Big Sky Chamber of Commerce, the center has brochures, maps, and information for Big Sky and Yellowstone.

Red Lodge, Montana

Driving time to Yellowstone: about 2 hours to Northeast Entrance (late May-mid-Oct.)

Red Lodge, Montana, serves as the eastern springboard for the scenic Beartooth Highway to Yellowstone's Northeast Entrance, 68 mi (109 km) away. Due to snow burying the road in winter, Yellowstone is only accessible from Red Lodge late May-mid-October, when plowing opens the Beartooth Highway to the park's Northeast Entrance. Downtown shop, hotel, and restaurant fronts retain the look of the Old West with two-story brick facades, but they cater to tourists rather than horses.

FOOD

Many of the Red Lodge restaurants cluster in the historic downtown area. Hours shorten in spring, winter, and fall.

LODGING

Red Lodge has a few chain motels, but mostly independent hotels that are open year-round. Summer sees the most visitors and the highest prices. Reservations are highly recommended for July and August. Hunting season in fall and the winter ski season also bring in the visitors. Spring usually has the lowest rates.

INFORMATION

The **Red Lodge Visitor Center** (701 N. Broadway Ave.; tel. 406/446-1718;

www.redlodge.com; hours vary) is a small information center run by the Red Lodge Chamber of Commerce. Guides and maps on Red Lodge and Beartooth Highway; Yellowstone National Park information; and a self-guided historical tour are available. The building has restrooms indoors and picnic tables.

Cody, Wyoming

Driving time to Yellowstone: 75 minutes to the East Entrance (May-Oct.)

Cody, Wyoming, offers a Wild West base of operations for Yellowstone's East Entrance. It houses the extensive Buffalo Bill Museums as well as nightly rodeos and twangy western music. Seasonal Buffalo Bill Scenic Byway (US-14/16/20) connects Cody to the East Entrance of Yellowstone on a route that climbs through the spires and crags of Shoshone Canyon and the Absaroka Mountains. But the route is only viable May-Oct., due to snow-buried roads in winter.

Many visitors prefer using Cody as an airline gateway for Yellowstone. Though limited, flights can be cheaper than those into Jackson Hole.

FOOD

In Cody, most restaurants are open year-round but reduce their hours in fall, winter, and spring. In summer, make reservations for dinner or you may be waiting in line.

LODGING

Cody has several moderate hotel chains, plus a few of the budget variety, although budget rates in summer may be higher than average. Summer is high season in Cody, when hotels pack out and prices are highest. To guarantee your choice of lodging, make reservations six months in advance. For a full list of hotels and lodges, check the **Park County Travel Council** website (www.yellowstonecountry.org); for vacation rentals, contact **Cody Lodging Company** (tel. 307/587-6000; www.codylodgingcompany.com).

INFORMATION

The **Cody Country Visitor Center** (836 Sheridan Ave.; tel. 307/587-2777; www.codychamber.org; 8am-7pm daily late May-late Sept., 8am-5pm Mon.-Fri. late Sept.-late May) has information, maps, brochures, and road conditions. The center also sells tickets to most summer events and attractions.

RECREATION

HIKING

Miles of hiking trails tour the Greater Yellowstone Ecosystem. Yellowstone National Park has 900 mi (1,450 km) of trails; Grand Teton National Park has 200 mi (320 km) of trails. A section of the 3,100-mi (5,000 km) **Continental Divide Trail** goes northward through Yellowstone.

Yellowstone has two types of trails: traditional dirt trails and boardwalk trails. The short boardwalk trails are designed for protecting visitors and sensitive features in high-traffic geothermal areas. In geothermal areas without boardwalks, stick to the trail to avoid scalding by boiling water. Grand Teton trails are traditional dirt trails, with the exception of the paved Multi-Use Pathway.

In both parks, bridges do not span all streams. You may need to ford creeks. In June, melting snow can raise water levels, making hiking poles helpful for stream crossings. Streams tend to be at their highest levels in the afternoon and lowest levels in the morning. Consult visitors centers on trail conditions before you go.

Most hiking trails are open to horse travel. If you meet up with horses while hiking, step off the trail on the downhill side, if possible, to let them pass. Trail etiquette dictates that uphill hikers have the right of way; downhill hikers should step aside to let them pass, unless the uphill hikers opt to take a breather to rest. When planning hikes, consider the higher altitude. You may hike less distance or more slowly than at lower elevations. Many trailhead parking lots pack out midsummer; plan for early starts to claim a parking space. Most trails ban mountain bikes or e-bikes in the parks, with the exception of paved pathways and trails that specifically allow them.

Hiking with kids can be either a nightmare or a hoot. To make it more fun, take water and snacks along to prevent hunger and thirst from zapping their energy. Take extra layers to keep kids warm if the weather turns. Help them connect with the environment while hiking by asking them about what they see and why things are the way they are. If you make hiking a fun experience for them, they'll want to do it again.

Trail Signs

The national parks have good trail signage. Some signs are just directional pointers with destination names. Others have multiple destinations with distances. Distances, when included, are listed in miles with only a few adding distances in kilometers. Geyser basin trailheads have large maps of thermal features and boardwalks posted, and Upper Geyser Basin adds "you are here" signs at every junction. Trail closures for seasonal bear management are permanently signed with the closure dates.

Bears

TRAIL AND CAMPSITE CLOSURES

With a high density of grizzly and black bears in the Greater Yellowstone Ecosystem, Yellowstone National Park has implemented Bear Management Areas to prevent human-bear conflicts. During certain seasons of high bear use in these areas, the park service closes trails or does not permit off-trail hiking. Backcountry campsites close, too. Some trails require hiking with four or more people or during daylight hours only. These restrictions affect day hiker trails, paddle destinations on Yellowstone Lake, and backpacker routes.

Most of the Bear Management Areas are located around Yellowstone Lake, Hayden Valley, Pelican Valley, Tower-Roosevelt, the Firehole River geyser basin areas, and northwest Yellowstone. All restrictions are seasonal, but the seasons vary depending on the region. Lists of Bear Management Areas, seasonal dates of impacts, and a map of the regions are in the *Backcountry Trip Planner* (www.nps.gov/yell) or in visitors centers or permit centers. Grand Teton National Park and Jackson Hole also have annual seasonal closures (www.nps.gov/grte), such as Hermitage Point and Willow Flats in early summer.

SAFETY

Human noise on the trail in the form of talking, singing, hooting, and hollering can prevent bear encounters. You may feel silly at first, but everyone does it.

Most hikers carry pepper spray with a capsicum derivative to deter bear attacks. Unlike insect repellents, do not use bear sprays on your body, in tents, or on gear; spray it directly into a bear's face, aiming for the eyes and nose. Wind and rain may reduce its effectiveness. Small purse-size pepper sprays are too small to deter bears; buy or rent an eight-ounce can. Practice how to use it, but still make noise on the trail.

See the *Wildlife-Watching* chapter for more tips.

Weather Concerns

Weather in Yellowstone and Grand Teton is unpredictable. Warm summer days can disintegrate into rainy squalls or snowstorms. Afternoons see hefty wind gusts, bringing with them showers, thunder, and lightning. If lightning approaches, descend from peak tops, high ridges, and open meadows into forest for more protection. Hikers should plan on early starts in order to descend in elevation by the time afternoon storms hit. Pack layers and always take rain gear, even when the weather looks like a blue-sky day.

In winter, when snow buries trails, hikers travel by snowshoes or cross-country skis. Most trails are not marked with tree tags or other route-finding devices; navigation skills are required. Some trails also cross avalanche zones: Take beacons, probes, and shovels. Know how to use them and assess snow stability. Be aware of travel etiquette: On roads where snow-coaches and snowmobiles travel, skiers and snowshoers should travel facing oncoming traffic to allow vehicles to pass. With skier-set tracks, snowshoers should blaze their own trails.

Guides

Yellowstone licenses companies to guide hikes and backpacking trips; Grand Teton permits no guided hiking. Lists of approved concessionaires for Yellowstone are available online (www.nps.gov/yell). National Park Service naturalists guide free day hikes in both parks. Consult the park newspapers for schedules and locations.

Blisters

Incorrect socks and ill-fitting shoes cause most blisters. Cotton socks absorb water from the feet while you're hiking and hold onto it, providing a surface for friction. Synthetic or wool-blend socks wick water away from the skin. To prevent blisters, recognize "hot spots" or rubs, applying moleskin, blister pads, or New-Skin to sensitive areas. In a pinch, slap duct tape on trouble spots. Once a blister occurs, apply blister bandages or Second Skin, a product developed for burns that cools blisters and cushions them. Cover Second Skin with moleskin to absorb future rubbing, and secure it in place.

BACKPACKING

Yellowstone and Grand Teton National Parks have backcountry campsites that offer solitude, scenery, and unique experiences. Trip-planning brochures detail campsite locations, regulations, permits, and safety concerns. Only Yellowstone permits concessionaires to guide backpacking trips.

Permits

Both national parks require permits for backcountry camping. A percentage of backcountry campsites may be reserved in advance; others are available as walk-in permits a day or two in advance. Both parks also have a *Backcountry Trip Planner* (www.nps.gov/yell or www.nps.gov/grte) that details campsites, regulations, annual bear closures, mileages, and routes.

In Yellowstone, advance reservations can be made starting January 1 ($25, submit form available online). Permits are also available first-come, first-served 48 hours before departure ($3/person/night, $15/party max, kids 8 and under free) at nine ranger stations or visitors centers in the park.

In Grand Teton, backcountry camping permits are available in advance online (www.recreation.gov; apply early Jan.-mid-May; $45/trip). Walk-in permits ($35/trip) are available first-come, first-served in person 24 hours before departure. Competition for walk-in permits is high in July and August; a waiting line usually forms at the Jenny Lake Ranger Station one hour before opening at 8am. Permits are also available at the Craig Thomas Discovery & Visitor Center in Moose. You may need an ice ax into early August for steep snowfields on the Teton Crest.

Food Storage

Proper food storage while backpacking is essential in bear country. In Yellowstone, bear boxes are provided at a few backcountry campsites for storing food. In other places, hang food from bars or poles. Pack along a 35-ft (11 m) rope and stuff sack to hang food. In Grand Teton, bear canisters are required for storing food. Permit offices have loaners, and rental gear shops in surrounding towns have them, too.

BOATING AND PADDLING

Before hauling a boat to either national park, read up on the requirements and regulations for motorized boats and

DARK SKIES

As of late 2020, neither Yellowstone nor Grand Teton were certified as International Dark sky parks, but they were working toward that goal. On the scale that measures light pollution, they both rank high in minimal artificial light. That leaves plenty of places to absorb the Milky Way and starscapes. Bring binoculars or a telescope plus a night sky map to enjoy the experience even more. Warm layers for cooler nighttime temperatures and camp chairs aid in making the experience comfortable.

SKYWATCHING SPOTS

When you arrive at one of these skywatching spots, turn off your headlights immediately to avoid disturbing the experience of others. Your eyes will take about 30 minutes to adjust fully to the darkness. Do not use white-light headlamps as they will disrupt the adjustment of your eyes; use red lights or cover white lights with red cellophane.

Lamar Valley

This huge, high-elevation valley in North Yellowstone has many pullouts perfect for stargazing. Choose those farthest away from the few lights around Lamar Valley Ranch.

Firehole Lake Drive

Take advantage of pullouts on Firehole Lake Drive in Yellowstone to watch the night sky. On warmer nights with less steam, features such as Firehole Lake or the pools around Great Fountain Geyser can add to photography fun.

Lake Butte Overlook

A short spur off the East Entrance Road in Yellowstone goes to an overlook of Yellowstone Lake. For safety, plan to arrive before dark to assess the hillside for a spot for viewing.

Mormon Row and Antelope Flats

In Grand Teton, pullouts afford views of the stars with a silhouette of the Teton Mountains. Choose pullouts out of sight of the small village of Kelly.

hand-propelled watercraft including paddleboards, rubber rafts, and angler float tubes (www.nps.gov/yell or www.nps.gov/grte). Jet Skis and motorized personal watercraft are not permitted in either park. At minimum, you will need an AIS inspection and boating permit. You may also need a fishing license and overnight boat camping permit. Be aware that winds can crop up fast, creating large waves on Yellowstone Lake and Jackson Lake.

All boats must pass an **Aquatic Invasive Species (AIS) inspection.** It's free in Yellowstone at ranger stations near the lakes, but Grand Teton charges

STARS OVER YELLOWSTONE PROGRAMS

Rangers lead free nighttime **stargazing programs** at several locations. Check the park newspaper or online (www.,nps.gov/yell) for hours and dates, as they vary throughout the summer due to changing twilight times and dates for moonless nights. In Northern Yellowstone, stargazing programs take place at **Forces of the Range.** Closest to Old Faithful, **Madison Campground Amphitheater parking lot** hosts tours of the night sky. Periodically, additional programs offer telescope viewing to see star clusters, planets, and nebulae.

ASTRONOMY NIGHTS IN GRAND TETON

Grand Teton rangers host free astronomy programs at **Colter Bay Visitor Center** and its neighboring amphitheater. Find schedules for these programs in the park newspaper, online (www.nps.gov/grte), or at visitors centers.

the Milky Way above Roosevelt Arch at the North Entrance to Yellowstone

a fee ($5-15 nonmotorized, $10-30 motorized) at inspection stations near park entrances.

Also, both parks require **boating permits,** available from visitors centers, marinas, or ranger stations near lakes. In Yellowstone, boating permits cost $7-10 for nonmotorized watercraft and $10-20 for motorized boats. In Grand Teton, they cost $12 for nonmotorized and $40 for motorized.

Yellowstone

Motorized boats are only allowed on **Yellowstone Lake** and **Lewis Lake.** Yellowstone Lake has two marinas for launching, and Lewis Lake has one boat launch. Boat rentals and charters for fishing and sightseeing are only available at Bridge Bay Marina (tel. 307/344-7311; www.yellowstonenationalparklodges.com). **No kayak, canoe, or paddleboard rentals are available inside Yellowstone National Park.** Bring your own or rent in Jackson Hole. No park waters allow parasailing, wakeboarding, waterskiing, boats longer than 40 ft (12 m), or river rafting.

Grand Teton

Boating on **Jenny Lake** is a quiet, idyllic experience, as only motorboats with 10 horsepower or less are permitted, plus any hand-propelled watercraft (but no sailboats, sailboards, or waterskiing). Rent canoes and kayaks at the tour boat dock from **Jenny Lake Boating** (tel. 307/734-9227; https://jennylakeboating.com).

Motorboats, nonmotorized boats, sailboats, sailboarding, and waterskiing are allowed on **Jackson Lake.** You can launch from Colter Bay Marina, Signal Mountain boat launch, or Leeks Marina. Rent motorboats, canoes, and kayaks at **Colter Bay Marina** (tel. 307/543-3100; www.gtlc.com) or canoes and kayaks at **Signal Mountain Lodge Marina** (tel. 307/543-2831; www.signalmountainlodge.com). Both marinas also have fishing charters.

WINTER SPORTS

Yellowstone and Grand Teton offer outstanding cross-country skiing and snowshoeing in winter. Select snow-buried roads in both parks are groomed for skiing with tracks set in some locations. On these groomed trails, snowshoers should stay off the parallel skier tracks. Plenty of trails also offer routes for winter fun. With skier-set tracks, snowshoers should blaze their own trails. On Yellowstone roads, where snowcoaches and snowmobiles travel, skiers and snowshoers should stick on the right side to give vehicles room to pass. Winter trail maps are available online (www.nps.gov/yell or www.nps.gov/grte) and at visitors centers. Some guided trips are available from park lodges in Yellowstone or in Jackson.

In Yellowstone, **guided snowmobile tours** depart mostly from Flagg Ranch and West Yellowstone. To snowmobile on your own, you'll need a permit acquired in the annual **lottery** (www.recreation.gov; early Sept.-early Oct.). If you bring your own snowmobile, it must be an approved BAT (Best Available Technology) snowmobile; otherwise, rentals are available in West Yellowstone.

PARK TOURS

A variety of bus tours, wildlife-watching, tours, and boat tours, as well as snowcoach and snowmobile tours in winter, are available in the parks. Visit the parks' **websites** (www.nps.gov/yell or www.nps.gov/grte) to find lists of all companies licensed to operate in the parks.

Yellowstone lodge operator **Xanterra** (tel. 307/344-7311; www.yellowstonenationalparklodges.com) operates wildlife-watching, geyser basin, and winter snowcoach tours in Yellowstone. Similarly, **Grand Teton Lodging Company** (tel. 307/543-2811; www.gtlc.com) offers tours in Grand Teton. Both require reservations.

STANDOUTS

YELLOWSTONE FOREVER INSTITUTE

tel. 406/848-2400; www.yellowstone.org

With expert instructors, Yellowstone Forever trips focus on wildlife-watching, bird-watching, hiking, cross-country skiing, snowshoeing, sightseeing, and natural history exploration. The institute runs single-day and multiday field seminars, learning programs, private tours, and programs for kids, youth, teens, college students, and families.

TETON SCIENCE SCHOOL

tel. 307/733-1313; www.tetonscience.org

With three campuses, two in Grand Teton National Park and one in Jackson, the Teton Science School runs programs in Grand Teton and Yellowstone. They offer wildlife-watching trips, summer camps, and programs for kids, teens, adults, and families. Programs can be half day, full day, or multiday. Some programs add hiking, cross-country skiing, or snowshoeing.

RANGER PROGRAMS

Rangers present free programs in both parks. These in 20- to 45-minute presentations are a terrific way to learn about wildlife, history, safety, and geology. Find program schedules and topics in the park newspaper, at visitors centers, on campground bulletin boards, in park hotels, and online.

YELLOWSTONE

Daytime and evening programs cover volcanic activity, wildlife, history, and astronomy. Photography, art, and social media programs also run periodically. Find schedules online (www.nps.gov/yell). Most programs run May-September, with a few extending into fall. Winter has select programs at two locations.

Ranger Talks

Ranger talks are usually scheduled regularly at visitor centers.

- **Albright Visitor Center:** North Yellowstone; summer, winter
- **Old Faithful Visitor Education Center:** summer, winter; evening programs run in both seasons
- **Madison Information Center:** Old Faithful and Geyser Basins; summer
- **Canyon Visitor Education Center:** Canyon and Lake Country; summer, including evening programs
- **Fishing Bridge Visitor Center:** Canyon and Lake Country; summer, including evening programs
- **Grant Visitor Center:** Canyon and Lake Country; summer, including evening programs in the neighboring amphitheater

Campground Amphitheater Programs

Rangers also lead evening programs at the following in-park campground amphitheaters on summer evenings.

NORTH YELLOWSTONE

- Mammoth Campground, including periodic stargazing programs on moonless nights

OLD FAITHFUL AND THE GEYSER BASINS

- Madison Campground
- Norris Campground

CANYON AND LAKE COUNTRY

- Bridge Bay Campground

Guided Walks and Hikes

National Park Service rangers lead free guided hikes during the summer.

NORTH YELLOWSTONE

Guided hikes tour the **Mammoth Hot Springs Terraces.** Learn about the natural history of the travertine terraces at the hot springs. Check in at the Albright Visitor Center for a current schedule and location of where to meet.

OLD FAITHFUL AND GEYSER BASINS

Around Old Faithful, walks usually meet at **Old Faithful Visitor Education Center** or at an appointed feature in the **Upper Geyser Basin.** Guided walks also go to **Mystic Falls** and around **Norris Geyser Basin.** In **winter,** rangers lead snowshoe hikes in the Old Faithful area and West Yellowstone. Reservations are required for some hikes (tel. 307/344-2750 or in person at the visitors center).

CANYON AND LAKE COUNTRY

Naturalist rangers lead walks and hikes in Canyon, West Thumb, and Fishing Bridge. Some walks to popular locations such as **Storm Point, Yellowstone Lake Overlook,** and Canyon rim trails run daily, while others are offered weekly.

Kid-Friendly Programs

Drop into any visitors center to pick up the Yellowstone **Junior Ranger activity guides** ($3, or downloadable free from www.nps.gov/yell under "Learn About the Park"). Kids complete the activities in the booklets that come in three age-specific versions to capture a breadth of interests. In winter kids can check out a "Junior Ranger snowpack" to help complete the activities in the Yellowstone winter booklet. Afterward, stop in at a visitors center to show the completed work to a ranger, get sworn in as a Junior Ranger, and receive a Yellowstone badge.

Yellowstone also gears free summer **ranger programs** toward kids. Outside visitors centers, **Wildlife Olympics** (noon-3pm Mon. Old Faithful, Wed. Canyon, Fri. Mammoth) lets kids compare their physical abilities to animals. Drop in for any amount of time.

GRAND TETON

Check for current program schedules, topics, and locations online (www.nps.gov/grte). Most happen only early June through early September.

Ranger Talks

Informative free National Park Service programs take place during the day in summer at the following visitor centers.

- **Colter Bay Visitor Center** (including evening programs in the adjacent amphitheater or indoor auditorium)
- **Craig Thomas Discovery & Visitor Center**
- **Jenny Lake Visitor Center**
- **Laurance S. Rockefeller Preserve**

Campground Programs

- **Gros Ventre Campground Amphitheater** has twilight programs.

Guided Walks and Hikes

Grand Teton National Park does not permit guided hikes led by concessionaires, but naturalist rangers lead short hikes (2-3 hr, 2-4 mi/3-6 km). Pick up tokens first thing in the morning at Jenny Lake Visitor Center to join the guided hike to **Hidden Falls and Inspiration Point;** in September, the guided hike switches to Moose Ponds, but no reservations are needed. Reservations are required for the guided hike to **Phelps Lake** at the Laurance S. Rockefeller Preserve Center (tel. 307/739-3654). In September, meet a ranger to hike to **Taggart Lake.**

In summer, rangers lead naturalist hikes daily to **Swan Lake.** The free hikes meet at 1pm at the flagpole in front of the Colter Bay Visitor Center for the 3-mi (4.8-km) walk. Plan about three hours with lots of stops to learn about wildlife, wetland communities, and flora.

Kid-Friendly Programs

Available in visitor centers, the Grand Teton **Junior Ranger activity guide** ($3, or downloadable free at www.nps.gov/grte under "Learn About the Park") gives kids activities to learn about the park. Then, they stop in at a visitors center to share their work with a ranger, get sworn in as a Junior Ranger, and receive the Grand Teton badge.

ACCESSIBILITY

Yellowstone and Grand Teton National Parks detail accessibility in **brochures** available at visitors centers (large print available). To prepare ahead of time, **online information** is available under "Plan Your Trip" (www.nps.gov/yell or www.nps.gov/grte). The NPS

Yellowstone National Park phone app and NPS Grand Teton National Park phone app include audio tours, services, and accessible locations. Download the apps before you leave home.

Both parks have TDD (Yellowstone tel. 307/344-2386, Grand Teton tel. 307/739-3301) and ADA facilities, although they are not ubiquitous. All lodging facilities have a few rooms or cabins that are accessible. Inquire about these through the individual concessionaires that run the lodging properties. Most campgrounds have a few wheelchair-accessible sites and restrooms. These are listed in the accessibility brochures and online for both parks and also under the individual campground descriptions online.

TRAILS

Yellowstone and Grand Teton have some paved and hard-surface trails that are wheelchair-accessible. While some of the boardwalk trails at the geothermal areas in Yellowstone are wheelchair-accessible, a handful of boardwalks have steps at some point. Find the accessible boardwalks listed in the accessibility brochures, online, and in the apps. In Grand Teton, the paved **Multi-Use Pathway** has flat portions that are wheelchair-friendly, and the **Discovery Trail at Jenny Lake** goes to lakefront overlooks before curving down to the water level.

Both parks also offer some interpretive activities that are accessible. Locate these in the seasonal park newspapers. While pet dogs are not permitted on backcountry trails, service dogs are allowed, although due to bears, they are discouraged. With service dogs, be safe by sticking to well-traveled trails during midday.

PASSES

Blind or permanently disabled U.S. citizens and permanent residents can get a free lifetime National Parks and Federal Recreational Lands **Access Pass** (https://store.usgs.gov/pass/access.html). The pass admits the pass holder plus three other adults in the same vehicle; children under age 16 are free. Pass holders also get 50 percent discounts on federally run tours and campgrounds. Passes are available in person at entrance stations (proof of medical disability or eligibility for receiving federal benefits is required).

TRAVELING WITH PETS

LIMITATIONS

Pets are allowed in the national parks, but only in limited areas: campgrounds, parking lots, and roadsides. They are not allowed on trails, boardwalks, beaches, in the backcountry, or on the Multi-Use Pathway in Grand Teton. Preventing conflicts with wildlife is the main reason. To hike with your pooch, go to surrounding national forests.

CAMPGROUNDS AND LODGING

While outside a vehicle or in a campground, pets must be caged or on a leash 6 ft (2 m) or shorter. Be kind enough to avoid leaving them unattended in a car anywhere. Be considerate of wildlife and other visitors by keeping your pet under control and disposing of waste in garbage cans.

Inside Yellowstone, several of the cabin complexes permit pets for a fee ($25). Check for additional restrictions when you make reservations. In general, lodging in Grand Teton does not permit pets, but many outside-park locales in Jackson do.

HEALTH AND SAFETY

EMERGENCY SERVICES

Ranger stations can provide assistance during emergencies. There are also a few medical clinics within and near the parks. All hospitals are outside the parks.

Medical Clinics

- **Mammoth Clinic:** Mammoth Village, North Yellowstone; tel. 307/344-7965; year-round

CORONAVIRUS IN YELLOWSTONE & GRAND TETON

At the time of writing in November 2020, Yellowstone and Grand Teton have entered their usual winter closures for roads, lodges, and most services after a summer of evolving concerns over COVID-19. During summer 2020, the National Park Service recommended masks in both parks; however, the main Yellowstone concessionaire Xanterra required face masks to be worn indoors and at some outdoor locales. Teton County, which includes Grand Teton National Park, mandated masks indoors and in outdoor lines or congested areas.

While park lodges and campgrounds were open for summer 2020, most restaurants were not. Some eateries converted to takeout. Some activities continued, such as horseback rides, boat tours, and sightseeing tours, but all ranger programs in both parks were cancelled for the season. For winter 2020, Mammoth Hot Springs Hotel remained open, with snowcoaches servicing Old Faithful on day trips only; Old Faithful Snow Lodge was closed.

Now more than ever, Moon encourages its readers to be courteous and ethical in their travel. We ask travelers to be respectful to residents, and mindful of the evolving situation in their chosen destination when planning their trip.

BEFORE YOU GO

Check local websites (listed below) for **local restrictions** and the **overall health status** of the destination. If you're traveling to or from an area that is currently a COVID-19 hotspot, please reconsider your trip to protect the national park rangers and concessionaire staff.

If possible, take a **coronavirus test** with enough time to receive your results before your departure.

If you plan to fly, check with your airline and the state and county health authorities for **updated travel requirements.**

Check the websites for the parks, as well as concessionaires you wish to patronize, to confirm that they're open, and to learn about any specific visitation requirements, such as limited occupancy, activity restrictions, or reduced services.

Pack **hand sanitizer, a thermometer,** and plenty of **face masks.** Packing snacks, a large refillable water jug, and a cooler will help you handle reduced services in the parks.

Assess the risk of entering crowded spaces and joining tours.

Expect general disruptions. Activities may be postponed or cancelled, and some tours and venues may require reservations, enforce lower capacity limits, be operating during different hours than the ones listed, or be closed entirely.

RESOURCES

State Public Health Information

- **Wyoming:** https://health.wyo.gov/publichealth/infectious-disease-epidemiology-unit/disease/novel-coronavirus
- **Montana:** https://dphhs.mt.gov/publichealth
- **Idaho:** https://coronavirus.idaho.gov

County Public Health Information

- **Wyoming:** www.parkcounty.us/CoronaVirus.html, www.tetoncountywy.gov/2061/COVID-19, www.fremontcountywy.org/government/departments/public_health/covid-19.php
- **Montana:** https://park-county-coronavirus-response-parkcounty.hub.arcgis.com, www.healthygallatin.org/coronavirus-covid-19
- **Idaho:** www.co.fremont.id.us

National Park Service

- **Yellowstone National Park:** www.nps.gov/yell
- **Grand Teton National Park:** www.nps.gov/grte

Concessionaire (Lodgings, Restaurants, Tours)

- **Yellowstone:** www.yellowstonenationalparklodges.com
- **Grand Teton:** www.gtlc.com, www.signalmountainlodge.com

- **Old Faithful Clinic:** Old Faithful Ranger Station, tel. 307/545-7325; year-round
- **West Yellowstone Clinic:** 11 S. Electric St., West Yellowstone; tel. 406/646-9441; http://chphealthmt.org; year-round
- **Lake Clinic:** Lake Village, Canyon and Lake Country; tel. 307/242-7241; mid-May-mid-Sept.
- **Grand Teton Medical Clinic:** Jackson Lake Lodge, Grand Teton National Park; tel. 307/543-2514, after hours tel. 307/733-8002; http://grandtetonmedicalclinic.com; mid-May-early Oct.

Hospitals

The nearest hospitals are in Livingston and Bozeman, Montana, to the north; Cody, Wyoming, to the east (inaccessible in winter); and Jackson, Wyoming, to the south.

- **Livingston HealthCare Hospital:** 320 Alpenglow Ln., Livingston, MT; tel. 406/222-3541, www.livingstonhealthcare.org
- **Bozeman Deaconess Hospital:** 915 Highland Blvd., Bozeman, MT; tel. 406/585-5000; www.bozemandeaconess.org
- **West Park Hospital:** 707 Sheridan Ave., Cody, WY; tel. 307/527-7501; www.westparkhospital.org
- **St. John's Medical Center:** 625 E. Broadway, Jackson; tel. 307/733-3636; www.tetonhospital.org

LAND AND WATER HAZARDS

Drowning from falling into swift or scalding water is one of the top causes of death in the Greater Yellowstone Ecosystem. Be extremely cautious around lakes, fast-moving streams, and waterfalls. Rivers can be swift, frigid, clogged with submerged obstacles, unforgiving, and sometimes lethal. A second cause of injuries and death is falling while climbing off-trail on steep, cliffy terrain.

Hydrothermal Dangers

It's really cool to see geysers and mud pots, but they are dangerous in several ways. Boiling geothermal waters have scalded people stupid enough to think of them as hot tubs. They've even caused death. Breakable crusts surrounding features can hide boiling waters. Some thermals contain infectious parasites that can be fatal or emit toxic gases. To protect yourself, **stay on boardwalks and trails.** If gases make you feel sick, leave the area.

Winter Dangers

While **ice** often looks solid to step on, it harbors unseen caverns beneath. Buried crevasses (large vertical cracks) are difficult to see, and snow bridges can collapse as a person crosses. **Steep-angled snowfields** also pose a danger from falling. Use an ice ax and caution, or stay off them. If you want to slide on the snow for fun, slide only where you have a safe run out away from rocks and trees.

Diseases

Inhaling dust from deer mice droppings can lead to **hantavirus** infections, with accompanying flu-like symptoms. Avoid burrows and woodpiles thick with rodents. Store all food in rodent-proof containers. If you contract the virus, get immediate medical attention.

Lakes and streams can carry parasites like ***Giardia lamblia.*** If ingested, they cause cramping, nausea, and severe diarrhea for up to six weeks. Avoid giardia by boiling water (for one minute, plus one minute for each 1,000 ft/300 m of elevation above sea level) or using a 1-micron filter. Bleach also works (add two drops per quart and wait 30 minutes). Tap water in campgrounds, hotels, and picnic areas has been treated.

Bugs can carry diseases such as **West Nile virus** and **Rocky Mountain spotted fever**. Protect yourself by wearing long sleeves and pants, plus using insect repellent in spring and summer when mosquitoes and ticks are common. If you are bitten by a tick, remove it, disinfect the bite, and see a doctor if lesions or a rash appears.

PERSONAL SAFETY

Due to the high elevation and arid climate, **dehydration,** which often manifests first as a headache, can come on quickly. While in the Greater Yellowstone Ecosystem and especially while hiking, drink lots of water. Carry enough water to consume more than you normally would. With children, monitor their fluid intake.

Some visitors from sea level feel lightheadedness, headaches, or shortness of breath at the **high altitudes** of Yellowstone and Grand Teton. To acclimatize, slow down the pace of hiking and drink lots of fluids. If symptoms spike, descend in elevation as soon as possible. Altitude also increases UV radiation exposure. To prevent **sunburn,** use a strong sunscreen and wear sunglasses and a hat.

Insidious and subtle, **hypothermia** sneaks up on exhausted and physically unprepared hikers. The body's inner core loses heat, reducing mental and physical functions. Watch for uncontrolled shivering, incoherence, poor judgment, fumbling, mumbling, and slurred speech. Avoid becoming hypothermic by staying dry. Don rain gear and warm, moisture-wicking layers, rather than cottons that won't dry and fail to retain heat. Get hypothermic hikers into dry clothing and shelter. Give warm, nonalcoholic and non-caffeinated liquids. If the victim cannot regain body heat, strip and use skin-to-skin contact with another person in a sleeping bag.

RESOURCES

YELLOWSTONE NATIONAL PARK

Yellowstone National Park
www.nps.gov/yell
Official National Park Service website for the park.

Yellowstone Forever
www.yellowstone.org
Home of Yellowstone fundraising, educational institute, and bookstores throughout the park (online sales available).

Trail Guides Yellowstone
www.trailguidesyellowstone.com
A Yellowstone National Park concessionaire that guides hiking and backpacking trips, but also offers detailed trail descriptions with photos on their website.

GRAND TETON NATIONAL PARK

Grand Teton National Park
www.nps.gov/grte
Official National Park Service website for the park.

Grand Teton Association
www.grandtetonpark.org
Helps support the park and runs the visitor center bookstores and online sales.

Teton Science School
www.tetonscience.org
Educational programs for Grand Teton, Yellowstone, and Jackson Hole.

Teton Hiking Trails
www.tetonhikingtrails.com
Detailed information on hiking trails in Grand Teton National Park.

TRAVEL

Idaho Department of Commerce
https://visitidaho.org

Montana Office of Tourism
www.visitmt.com

Wyoming Travel and Tourism
www.travelwyoming.org

INDEX

K

L

M

LIST OF MAPS

PHOTO CREDITS

Page 1 © Jkraft5 | Dreamstime.com; page 8 © Becky Lomax (top), © Sergioboccardo | Dreamstime.com (middle), © NPS/Jacob W. Frank (bottom); page 9 © Becky Lomax (top), © NPS/Neal Herbert (middle); © Becky Lomax (bottom); page 10 © Becky Lomax; page 12 © Becky Lomax; page 14 © NPS/ Neal Herbert; page 15 © Becky Lomax; page 16 © Sainaniritu | Dreamstime.com (top), © Smontgom65 | Dreamstime.com (bottom); page 17 © NPS/Jacob W. Frank (top); © Paulbradyphoto | Dreamstime.com (bottom); page 18 © Lorcel | Dreamstime.com; page 20 © Becky Lomax (top), © NPS/Jacob W. Frank (bottom); page 21 © Rmbarricarte | Dreamstime.com; page 22 © Wirepec | Dreamstime. com; page 23 © Becky Lomax; page 24 © Jovannig | Dreamstime.com; page 25 © Becky Lomax; page 26 © NPS/Neal Herbert (left), © NPS/Neal Herbert (right); page 28 © Miamilady | Dreamstime.com; page 30 © Becky Lomax (top), © Mechuralukas | Dreamstime.com (bottom); page 31 © NPS/Diane Renkin; page 32 © Swdesertlover | Dreamstime.com (left), © Rmguinther | Dreamstime. com (right); page 34 © NPS/Jim Peaco (top), © Becky Lomax (bottom); page 35 © Becky Lomax; page 36 © NPS/Tobiason; page 39 © NPS/Jacob W. Frank (top), © NPS/Jacob W. Frank (left), © Becky Lomax (right); page 41 © Becky Lomax; page 42 © NPS/Jacob W. Frank; page 44 © Becky Lomax; page 45 © NPS/ Diane Renkin; page 46 © Becky Lomax; page 47 Peanutroaster | Dreamstime. com; page 48 © Crbellette | Dreamstime.com; page 52 © NPS/Neal Herbert; page 53 © NPS/Jacob W. Frank (top), NPS/Neal Herbert (middle), © Becky Lomax (bottom); page 55 © Pjworldtour | Dreamstime.com (left), © Becky Lomax (right); page 57 © Kingtrac | Dreamstime.com (left), RIRFStock | Dreamstime.com (right), © Becky Lomax (bottom); page 58 © NPS/Jim Peaco (left), © Becky Lomax (right); page 59 © Becky Lomax; page 61 © NPS/Diane Renkin; page 62 © Delstudio | Dreamstime.com; page 63 © Tamifreed | Dreamstime.com; page 64 © Tloventures | Dreamstime.com; page 65 © Becky Lomax; page 66 © Larson755 | Dreamstime. com; page 67 © Becky Lomax (top), © Swisshippo | Dreamstime.com (middle), © Kellyvandellen | Dreamstime.com (bottom); page 69 © Sergioboccardo | Dreamstime.com; page 70 © NPS/Jacob W. Frank; page 75 © NPS/Jacob W. Frank (left), © Becky Lomax (right); page 78 © NPS; page 84 © Becky Lomax; page 87 © Luckyphotographer | Dreamstime.com (top), © NPS/Jim Peaco (middle), Sergioboccardo | Dreamstime.com (bottom); page 89 © Becky Lomax (left), © Becky Lomax (right); page 91 © Becky Lomax (left), © NPS/Jacob W. Frank (right), © Becky Lomax (bottom); page 92 © NPS/Jacob W. Frank (left), Henryturner | Dreamstime.com (right); page 95 © NPS/Jacob W. Frank (top), NPS/ Jacob W. Frank (left), Jaahnlieb | Dreamstime.com (right); page 96 © NPS/Jacob W. Frank (top), © NPS/Neal Herbert (middle), © Luckyphotographer | Dreamstime. com (bottom); page 98 © NPS/Jacob W. Frank (top), © NPS/Jim Peaco (middle), © NPS/Jacob W. Frank (bottom); page 99 © Jkraft5 | Dreamstime.com; page 100 © Haveseen | Dreamstime.com (left), © Minyun9260 | Dreamstime.com (right); page 101 © Becky Lomax (left), © NPS/Jacob W. Frank (right); page 104 © Becky Lomax (top), © NPS/Diane Renkin (middle), © NPS/Jacob W. Frank (bottom); page 106 © Becky Lomax (left), © NPS/Jim Peaco (right); page 107 © NPS (left), © Becky Lomax (right); page 108 © Becky Lomax; page 111 © NPS/Neal Herbert; page 113 © NPS/Jacob W. Frank (left), © Becky Lomax (right); page 115 © NPS/ Jim Peaco; page 117 © Becky Lomax; page 119 © NPS; page 121 © Becky Lomax; page 122 © NPS/Jacob W. Frank; page 124 © Ronniechua | Dreamstime.com; page 127 © NPS/Diane Renkin; page 129 © Becky Lomax (top) © Wallentine |

States & Provinces

Regions & Getaways

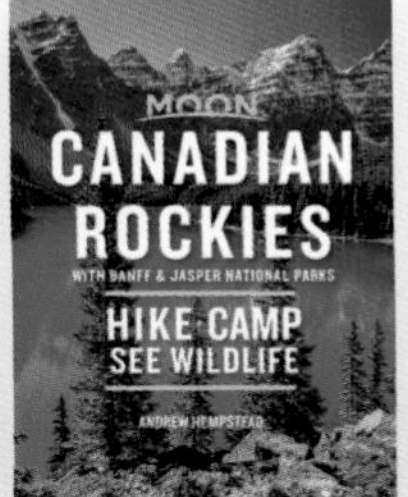

Cities

Road Trips

Moon has you covered, PNW!

MOON.COM | @MOONGUIDES

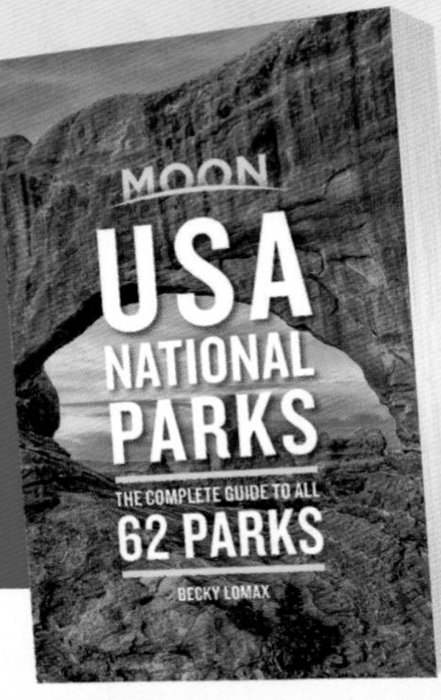
MOON
USA
NATIONAL
PARKS
THE COMPLETE GUIDE TO ALL
62 PARKS
BECKY LOMAX

MOON
ACADIA
NATIONAL PARK
HILARY NANGLE

MOON
ARCHES &
CANYONLANDS
NATIONAL PARKS

MOON
BANFF
NATIONAL
PARK
HIKE·CAMP
SEE WILDLIFE
ANDREW HEMPSTEAD

MOON
DEATH VALLEY
NATIONAL PARK
JENNA BLOUGH

MOON
GLACIER
NATIONAL PARK
HIKING · CAMPING
LAKES & PEAKS
BECKY LOMAX

MOON
GRAND
CANYON
HIKE·CAMP
RAFT THE
COLORADO RIVER
TIM HULL

MOON
MOUNT RUSHMORE
& THE BLACK HILLS
Including the Badlands

MOON
ROCKY
MOUNTAIN
NATIONAL PARK
HIKE·CAMP
SEE WILDLIFE
ERIN ENGLISH

MOON
SEQUOIA &
KINGS CANYON
HIKING·CAMPING
WATERFALLS & BIG TREES
LEIGH BERNACCHI

ROAD TRIP GUIDES FROM MOON

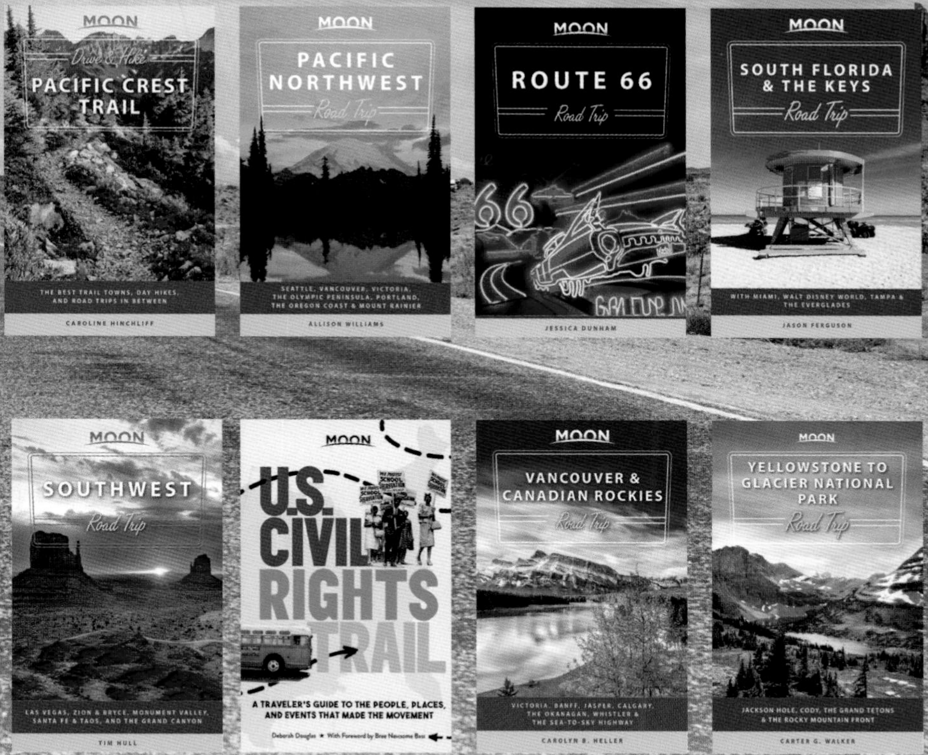

MOON
Drive & Hike
PACIFIC CREST TRAIL
THE BEST TRAIL TOWNS, DAY HIKES, AND ROAD TRIPS IN BETWEEN
CAROLINE HINCHLIFF

MOON
PACIFIC NORTHWEST
Road Trip
SEATTLE, VANCOUVER, VICTORIA, THE OLYMPIC PENINSULA, PORTLAND, THE OREGON COAST & MOUNT RAINIER
ALLISON WILLIAMS

MOON
ROUTE 66
Road Trip
JESSICA DUNHAM

MOON
SOUTH FLORIDA & THE KEYS
Road Trip
WITH MIAMI, WALT DISNEY WORLD, TAMPA & THE EVERGLADES
JASON FERGUSON

MOON
SOUTHWEST
Road Trip
LAS VEGAS, ZION & BRYCE, MONUMENT VALLEY, SANTA FE & TAOS, AND THE GRAND CANYON
TIM HULL

MOON
U.S. CIVIL RIGHTS TRAIL
A TRAVELER'S GUIDE TO THE PEOPLE, PLACES, AND EVENTS THAT MADE THE MOVEMENT
Deborah Douglas ★ With Foreword by Bree Newsome Bass

MOON
VANCOUVER & CANADIAN ROCKIES
Road Trip
VICTORIA, BANFF, JASPER, CALGARY, THE OKANAGAN, WHISTLER & THE SEA-TO-SKY HIGHWAY
CAROLYN B. HELLER

MOON
YELLOWSTONE TO GLACIER NATIONAL PARK
Road Trip
JACKSON HOLE, CODY, THE GRAND TETONS & THE ROCKY MOUNTAIN FRONT
CARTER G. WALKER

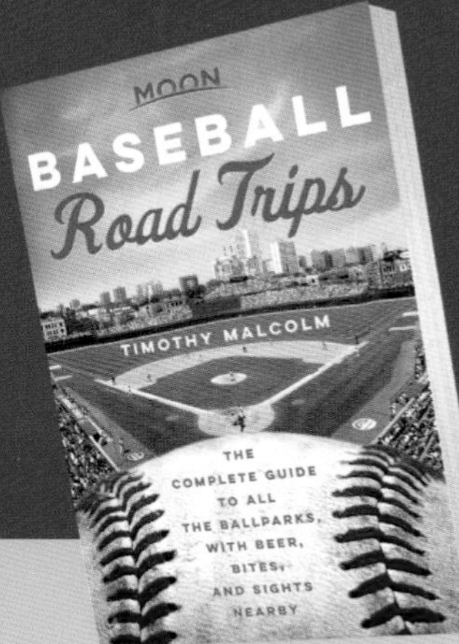

Moon Baseball Road Trips

The Complete Guide to All the Ballparks, with Beer, Bites, and Sights Nearby

Sunshine, hot dogs, friends, and the excitement of the game: Baseball is called America's pastime for a reason. Experience the best of the MLB cities and stadiums with strategic advice from road tripper and former baseball writer Timothy Malcolm.

MAP SYMBOLS

Highway	City/Town	Parking Area	Small Park
Primary Road	State Capital	Trailhead	Mountain Peak
Secondary Road	National Capital	Bike Trailhead	Unique Natural Feature
Unpaved Road	Top 3 Sight	Camping	Unique Hydro Feature
Trail	Top Hike	Picnic Area	Waterfall
Paved Trail	Highlight/Sight	Mass Transit	Ski Area
Pedestrian Walkway	Accommodation	Airport	Glacier
Ferry	Restaurant/Bar	Airfield	
Railroad	Other Site	Place of Worship	

CONVERSION TABLES

°C = (°F - 32) / 1.8
°F = (°C x 1.8) + 32
1 inch = 2.54 centimeters (cm)
1 foot = 0.304 meters (m)
1 yard = 0.914 meters
1 mile = 1.6093 kilometers (km)
1 km = 0.6214 miles
1 fathom = 1.8288 m
1 chain = 20.1168 m
1 furlong = 201.168 m
1 acre = 0.4047 hectares
1 sq km = 100 hectares
1 sq mile = 2.59 square km
1 ounce = 28.35 grams
1 pound = 0.4536 kilograms
1 short ton = 0.90718 metric ton
1 short ton = 2,000 pounds
1 long ton = 1.016 metric tons
1 long ton = 2,240 pounds
1 metric ton = 1,000 kilograms
1 quart = 0.94635 liters
1 US gallon = 3.7854 liters
1 Imperial gallon = 4.5459 liters
1 nautical mile = 1.852 km

MOON BEST OF YELLOWSTONE & GRAND TETON
Avalon Travel
Hachette Book Group
1700 Fourth Street
Berkeley, CA 94710, USA
www.moon.com

Editor: Grace Fujimoto
Copy Editor: Hannah Brezack
Production and Graphics Coordinator: Darren Alessi
Cover Design: Marcie Lawrence
Interior Design: Tabitha Lahr
Moon Logo: Tim McGrath
Map Editor: Kat Bennett
Cartographer: John Culp
Proofreader: Nikki Ioakimedes

ISBN-13: 978-1-64049-530-2

Printing History
1st Edition — May 2021
5 4 3 2 1

Front cover photo: © Adam Jones/Getty Images
Back cover photos: bison in Lamar Valley © Pierre Jean Durieu | Dreamstime.com (top); Mount Moran © Sooksan Kasiansin | Dreamstime.com (middle); Punch Bowl © Mirekdeml | Dreamstime.com (bottom)

Printed in China by RR Donnelley